Microsoft® Windows® SharePoint® Services Step by Step

Olga Londer

Todd Bleeker

Penelope Coventry

James Edelen

PUBLISHED BY
Microsoft Press
A Division of Microsoft Corporation
One Microsoft Way
Redmond, Washington 98052-6399

Library of Congress Control Number 2004116598

Printed and bound in the United States of America.

5 6 7 8 9   QWT   9 8 7 6

Distributed in Canada by H.B. Fenn and Company Ltd.

A CIP catalogue record for this book is available from the British Library.

Microsoft Press books are available through booksellers and distributors worldwide. For further information about international editions, contact your local Microsoft Corporation office or contact Microsoft Press International directly at fax (425) 936-7329. Visit our Web site at www.microsoft.com/ learning/. Send comments to *mspinput@microsoft.com*.

Microsoft, Active Desktop, ActiveX, BizTalk, FrontPage, InfoPath, IntelliSense, JScript, Microsoft Press, MS-DOS, MSN, OneNote, Outlook, PowerPoint, SharePoint, Visual Studio, Windows, the Windows logo, Windows NT, and Windows Server are either registered trademarks or trademarks of Microsoft Corporation in the United States and/or other countries.

The example companies, organizations, products, domain names, e-mail addresses, logos, people, places, and events depicted herein are fictitious. No association with any real company, organization, product, domain name, e-mail address, logo, person, place, or event is intended or should be inferred.

Acquisitions Editors: Hilary Long and Juliana Aldous Atkinson
Project Editor: Sandra Haynes
Technical Editor: Robert Lyon
Editorial and Production: Online Training Solutions, Inc.

Body Part No. X10-96111

Contents

What do you think of this book?
We want to hear from you!
Microsoft is interested in hearing your feedback about this publication so we can continually improve our books and learning resources for you. To participate in a brief online survey, please visit: *www.microsoft.com/learning/booksurvey/*

Contents

Contents

Getting Help

Every effort has been made to ensure the accuracy of this book and the contents of its CD-ROM. If you run into problems, please contact the appropriate source for help and assistance.

Getting Help with This Book and Its CD-ROM

If your question or issue concerns the content of this book or its companion CD-ROM, please first search the online Microsoft Press Knowledge Base, which provides support information for known errors in or corrections to this book, at the following Web site:

www.microsoft.com/learning/support/

If you do not find your answer in the online Knowledge Base, send your comments or questions to Microsoft Learning Technical Support at:

mspinput@microsoft.com

Getting Help with Microsoft Windows SharePoint Services or Microsoft Windows Server 2003

If your question is about Microsoft Windows SharePoint Services or Microsoft Windows Server 2003, and not about the content of this Microsoft Press book, please search the Microsoft Help and Support Center or the Microsoft Knowledge Base at:

support.microsoft.com

In the United States, Microsoft software product support issues not covered by the Microsoft Knowledge Base are addressed by Microsoft Product Support Services. The Microsoft software support options available from Microsoft Product Support Services are listed at:

support.microsoft.com

Outside the United States, for support information specific to your location, please refer to the Worldwide Support menu on the Microsoft Help and Support Web site for the site specific to your country:

support.microsoft.com

Using the Book's CD-ROM

The CD-ROM inside the back cover of this book contains practice files you'll use as you work through the exercises in this book. The CD-ROM also contains site templates that you might use if you choose to do exercises independently. By using practice files and site templates, you won't waste time creating your own samples files and sites—instead, you can jump right in and concentrate on learning how to get the most of your Microsoft Windows SharePoint Services implementation.

The CD-ROM also includes two supplemental chapters that provide valuable information. "Using Windows SharePoint Services with InfoPath 2003" (UsingInfoPath.pdf) covers how to create a form library from InfoPath 2003, modify an existing form library, fill out a form, and edit an existing form. "Finding Information on the SharePoint Site" (FindingInformation.pdf) explores Microsoft Windows SharePoint Services search at three levels: searching an entire site, searching a specific list or document library, and searching multiple document libraries simultaneously. Be sure to explore the contents of these supplemental PDFs.

Finally, the CD-ROM also includes an electronic version of the book in PDF format and the Microsoft Office System Reference Pack to help you get the most out of your SharePoint experience.

Minimum System Requirements

Client Computer

To use this book, your client computer should meet the following requirements:

- **Operating System**   Although you can use any Microsoft operating system, Microsoft Windows XP Professional Edition is recommended.

- **Software**   Microsoft Internet Explorer 5.01 SP1 or later; Internet Explorer 5.5 or later is recommended.

  Microsoft Office Word 2003, Microsoft Office Excel 2003, Microsoft Office Access 2003, Microsoft Office Outlook 2003, and Microsoft Office InfoPath 2003.

Server Computer

To use this book, you must have access to a server running Windows SharePoint Services. The server computer should meet the following requirements:

- **Operating System**   Microsoft Windows Server 2003

- **Software**   Microsoft Windows SharePoint Services 2.0

Note　The CD-ROM for this book does not contain the Windows Server 2003 operating system or the Windows SharePoint Services software. You must have access to a working Windows SharePoint Services site before using this book. Microsoft Windows SharePoint Services 2.0 can be downloaded from Microsoft's Web site for no cost.

Installing the Practice Files

You must install the practice files on your hard disk before you can use them in the chapters' exercises. Follow these steps to prepare the CD's files for your use:

Important　Installing the practice files requires the privileges of a local system administrator.

1　Insert the CD-ROM into the CD-ROM drive of your computer.

An End User License Agreement should appear automatically.

Important　If the End User License Agreement does not appear, open a window for your CD-ROM drive, and then double-click the StartCD executable file.

After you accept the End User License Agreement, a menu screen appears.

2　Click **Install Practice Files**.

3　Follow the on-screen instructions to install the practice files to *My Documents \Microsoft Press\SharePoint Services SBS*.

Using the Practice Files

Each exercise is preceded by text that lists the files needed for that exercise. The text also explains any preparation you need to take before you start working through the exercise, as shown here:

USE the Plants_Price.xls document in the practice file folder for this chapter. This practice file is located in the *My Documents\Microsoft Press\SharePoint Services SBS\Chapter 11* folder.

Wherever possible, we start each chapter with a standard Windows SharePoint Services team site. It doesn't mean that if you follow all exercises in all chapters in sequence, you have to start with a new team site for every chapter—you can use the same site throughout the whole book.

However, if you choose to do exercises independently and not in sequence, be aware that there are exercises in some chapters that depend on other exercises performed earlier in the book. If this is the case, we will tell you where the prerequisite exercise is located in the book, so that you can complete the prerequisite exercises, as shown below:

BE SURE TO complete the "Adding Documents" exercise in Chapter 5 on page XXX.

Alternatively, if you have sufficient rights, you can create new starting sites for chapters by using the site template STP files that are provided on the CD-ROM for those chapters that have dependencies on exercises earlier in the book. The site template will have the prerequisite exercises already completed for you. This option is for advanced users who might not want to do a prerequisite exercise in another chapter. For exercises that require a prerequisite exercise to be completed, we will tell you the name and location of the STP site template, as shown below:

Alternatively, you can create a practice site for this chapter based on site template Chapter 6 Starter.stp in the practice file folder for this chapter. The practice file folder is located in the *My Documents \Microsoft Press\SharePoint Services SBS\Chapter 06* folder. See "Using the Book's CD-ROM" on page vii for instructions on how to create a practice site.

If you choose to use the provided site template STP files, please refer to "(*Optional*) Using the STP Site Templates" later in this section for instructions on how to create a practice site.

The following table lists the practice files and optional site templates, if the chapter or supplemental material requires them.

Folder	Chapter	Practice Files and STP Files
Chapter 01	Introduction to Windows SharePoint Services	No practice files
Chapter 02	Navigating a SharePoint Site	No practice files
Chapter 03	Creating and Managing Sites	No practice files
Chapter 04	Working with Lists	No practice files
Chapter 05	Creating and Managing Libraries	NeedlepointHolly.doc pjcov.JPG Purchase Order Template.xsn WaterOak.doc
Chapter 06	Working with Library Settings	Chapter 6 Starter.stp
Chapter 07	Working with Document Workspaces	Chapter 7 Starter.stp
Chapter 08	Working with Meeting Workspaces	Chapter 8 Starter.stp
Chapter 09	Working with Surveys and Discussion Boards	GardenSurvey.xls
Chapter 10	Using Windows SharePoint Services with Outlook 2003	Chapter 10 Starter.stp
Chapter 11	Using Windows SharePoint Services with Excel 2003 and Access 2003	GardenCo.mdb Plants_Price.xls Sales_Figures.xls
Chapter 12	Working with Web Parts	Chapter 12 Starter.stp

Folder	Chapter	Practice Files and STP Files
Supplemental Material	Using Windows SharePoint Services with InfoPath 2003 (UsingInfoPath.pdf)	Purchase Orders Template.xsn
Supplemental Material	Finding Information on the SharePoint Site (FindingInformation.pdf)	Finding Information Starter.stp

Uninstalling the Practice Files

After you finish working through this book, you can uninstall the practice files by following these steps:

1 In Control Panel, open **Add or Remove Programs**.

2 In the list of installed programs, click **Microsoft Windows SharePoint Services Step by Step**, and then click the **Remove** button.

3 Click **Yes** when the confirmation dialog box appears.

(*Optional*) Using the STP Site Templates

To create a practice site for a chapter based on a site template STP file provided on the CD-ROM, perform the following steps:

BE SURE TO verify that you have sufficient rights to upload a site template to a top-level site and to create a site in the site collection. If in doubt, see the Appendix on page 260.

OPEN the top-level SharePoint site to which you'd like to upload the site template STP file. If prompted, type your user name and password, and then click OK.

1 On the top link bar, click **Site Settings** to display the **Site Settings** page.

2 In the **Administration** section, click **Go to Site Administration** to display the **Site Administration** page.

3 In the **Site Collection Galleries** section, click **Manage site template gallery** to display the **Site Template Gallery** page.

> **Note** If you see a Go to Top-level Site Administration link in the Site Collection Administration section at the bottom of the page, you are not on the top-level site administration page. A site template can only be uploaded to the site template gallery on a top-level site. To display the Site Administration page for the top-level site, click Go to Top-level Site Administration and then repeat the previous step.

4 Click **Upload Template** to display the **Site Template Gallery: Upload Template** page.

5 Click the **Browse** button to display the **Choose File** dialog box.

6 Navigate to *My Documents\Microsoft Press\SharePoint Services SBS\Chapter XX* (where *XX* is the chapter number), click the STP file that you want to use to create the new site, and then click the **Open** button.

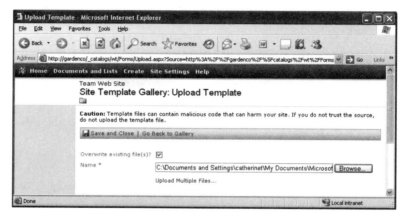

7 Click **Save and Close** to complete the upload and redisplay the **Site Template Gallery** page.

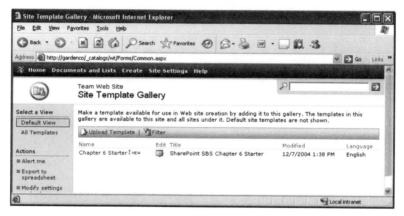

You can now create a new child site based upon the uploaded template.

8 Open the SharePoint site that you'd like to create the new practice site within.

9 On the top link bar, click **Site Settings** to display the **Site Settings** page.

10 In the **Administration** section, click **Manage sites and workspaces** to display the **Sites and Workspaces** page.

11 Click **Create** to display the **New SharePoint Site** page.

12 In the **Title** text box, type a logical name for the new site; you could simply provide the chapter number, for example Chapter06.

13 Optionally, in the **Description** text box, type a description, for example SharePoint SBS Chapter 6 Practice Site.

14 In the **URL name** text box, repeat the same name as you typed into the **Title** text box.

15 In the **Permissions** section, leave the default **Use same permissions as parent site** option selected.

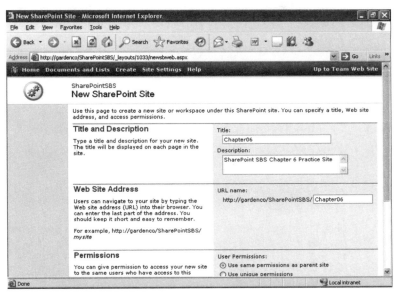

16 Click the **Create** button to display the **Template Selection** page.

17 In the **Template** list, choose the name of the template that you just uploaded, for example SharePoint SBS Chapter 6 Starter, and then click the **OK** button.

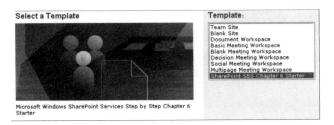

The Home page of the new practice site is displayed.

CLOSE the browser.

(*Optional*) Removing the STP Site Templates

To remove the chapter starter templates from the site template gallery, perform the following steps:

BE SURE TO verify that you have sufficient rights to delete a site template from the top-level site template gallery. If in doubt, see the Appendix on page 260.

OPEN the top-level SharePoint site where you previously uploaded the site template STP files. If prompted, type your user name and password, and then click OK.

1 On the top link bar, click **Site Settings** to display the **Site Settings** page.

2 In the **Administration** section, click **Go to Site Administration** to display the **Site Administration** page.

3 In the **Site Collection Galleries** section, click **Manage site template gallery** to display the **Site Template Gallery** page.

Note If you see a Go to Top-level Site Administration link in the Site Collection Administration section at the bottom of the page, you are not on the top-level site administration page. A site template can only be removed from the site template gallery on a top-level site. To display the Site Administration page for the top-level site, click Go to Top-level Site Administration and then repeat the previous step.

Edit

4 Click the **Edit** icon to display the details for the site template.

5 Click **Delete** to remove the site template. You will be prompted to confirm your request. Click **OK** to complete the deletion and redisplay the **Site Template Gallery**.

6 Repeat the edit and delete steps to remove each site template that you no longer want available for the creation of practice sites.

CLOSE the browser.

(*Optional*) Deleting a Practice Site

If you created a practice site that you no longer want, you can delete it. Perform the following steps to delete a practice site:

BE SURE TO verify that you have sufficient rights to delete a site. If in doubt, see the Appendix on page 260.

OPEN the parent SharePoint site where you previously created the practice site. If prompted, type your user name and password, and then click OK.

1 On the top link bar, click **Site Settings** to display the **Site Settings** page.

2 In the **Administration** section, click **Manage sites and workspaces** to display the **Sites and Workspaces** page.

Delete

3 In the list of sites, click the **Delete** icon to delete the site and to display the **Delete Web Site** page.

4 Click the **Delete** button to delete the site.

CLOSE the browser.

Conventions and Features

You can save time when you use this book by understanding how the *Step by Step* series shows special instructions, keys to press, buttons to click, and so on.

Convention	Meaning
1 **2**	Numbered steps guide you through hands-on exercises in each topic.
●	A round bullet indicates an exercise that has only one step.
(CD icon)	This icon at the beginning of a chapter reminds you to install the files used in the exercises.
Tip	These paragraphs provide a helpful hint or shortcut that makes working through a task easier.
Important	These paragraphs point out information that you need to know to complete the procedure.
Troubleshooting	These paragraphs show you how to fix a common problem that might prevent you from continuing with the exercise.
⊠ Close	When a button is referenced in a topic, a picture of the button appears in the left margin.
Alt + Tab	A plus sign (+) between two key names means that you must hold down the first key while you press the second key. For example, "press Alt + Tab" means "hold down the Alt key while you press the Tab key."
Black bold type	In steps, program items that you click or press are in black bold type.
Blue italic type	Terms explained in the glossary are shown in blue italic type.
Blue bold type	Text that you will type appears in blue bold type in the procedures.
Italic type	Folder paths, URLs, and emphsized words appear in italic type.
BE SURE TO	These words are found at the beginning of paragraphs preceding or following step-by-step exercises. They point out items you should check or actions you should carry out either before beginning an exercise or after completing an exercise.
USE OPEN	These words are found at the beginning of paragraphs preceding step-by-step exercises. They draw your attention to practive files that you'll need to use in the exercise.
CLOSE	This word is found at the beginning of paragraphs following step-by-step exercises. They give instructions for closing open files or programs before moving on to another topic.

Quick Reference

3   In the **Links** tool pane, make your modifications.

4   Click **Apply** to apply the modification, and then click **OK**.

Chapter 3   **Creating and Managing Sites**

Page 32   **To create a child site**

1   On the top link bar, click **Site Settings**.

2   On the **Site Settings** page, in the **Administration** section, click **Manage sites and workspaces**.

3   On the **Sites and Workspaces** page, click **Create**.

4   On the **New SharePoint Site** page, specify the settings for the new site.

5   Click the **Create** button.

6   On the **Template Selection** page, select a template from the **Template** list, and then click **OK**.

Chapter 4   **Working with Lists**

Page 60   **To browse the lists for a site**

1   On the top link bar, click **Documents and Lists**.

2   On the **Documents and Lists** page, explore the lists.

60   **To browse list templates available**

1   On the top link bar, click **Create**.

2   On the **Create Page** page, explore the list templates.

62   **To create a list**

1   On the top link bar, click **Create**.

2   On the **Create Page** page, in the **Lists** section, click a list template.

3   On the **New List** page, specify settings for the list, and then click the **Create** button.

62   **To modify the settings for a list**

1   Open the list for which you want to modify the settings.

2   On the left side of the page in the **Actions** section, click **Modify settings and columns**.

3   On the **Customize** page, in the **General Settings** section, click **Change general settings**.

4   On the **List Setting** page, modify the settings for the list, and then click **OK**.

65   **To add a new item to a list**

   1   Open the list to which you want to add a new item.

   2   On the list page, click **New Item**.

   3   On the **New Item** page, specify the settings for the new item.

   4   Click **Save and Close** to save the list item.

65   **To edit an item in a list**

   1   Open the list for which you want to edit an item.

   2   On the list page, move your mouse over the list item, and then click the down arrow that appears.

   3   In the menu, click **Edit Item**.

   4   On the item page, edit the settings for the new item.

   5   Click **Save and Close** to save the list item.

65   **To delete an item in a list**

   1   Open the list for which you want to delete an item.

   2   On the list page, move your mouse over the list item, and then click the down arrow that appears.

   3   In the menu, click **Delete Item**.

   4   In the dialog box that appears, click **OK** to confirm the deletion.

70   **To attach a file to a list item**

   1   Open the list to which you want to attach a file.

   2   On the list page, move your mouse over the list item, and then click the down arrow that appears.

   3   In the menu, click **Edit Item**.

   4   On the item page, click **Attach File**.

   5   On the page to add attachments, click **Browse**.

   6   In the **Choose File** dialog box, select a file, and then click the **Open** button. Once selected, the location of the selected document is displayed in the **Name** text box.

   7   Click **OK** to attach the document to the list item.

   8   Click **Save and Close** to complete the process of attaching the document to the list item.

75 **To add a new column to a list**

1 Open the list to which you want to add a new column.

2 On the left side of the page in the **Actions** section, click **Modify settings and columns**.

3 On the **Customize** page, in the **Columns** section, click **Add a new column**.

4 On the **Add Column** page, in the **Column name** text box, type a name for the new column.

5 Select a column type.

6 In the **Optional Setting for Column** section, specify other column settings.

7 Click **OK** to add the new column to the list.

75 **To edit a column in a list**

1 Open the list for which you want to edit a column.

2 On the left side of the page in the **Actions** section, click **Modify settings and columns**.

3 On the **Customize** page, in the **Columns** section, click the name of the existing column you want to edit.

4 On the **Change Column** page, edit the settings for the column.

5 Click **OK** to save the changes to the column.

75 **To delete a column in a list**

1 Open the list for which you want to delete a column.

2 On the left side of the page in the **Actions** section, click **Modify settings and columns**.

3 On the **Customize** page, in the **Columns** section, click the name of the existing column you want to delete, and then click the **Delete** button.

4 In the dialog box that appears, click **OK** to delete the column.

75 **To change the order of the columns displayed on the new and edit list item pages**

1 Open the list for which you want to change the column order.

2 On the left side of the page in the **Actions** section, click **Modify settings and columns**.

3 On the **Customize** page, in the **Columns** section, click **Change the order of the fields**.

4 On the **Change Field Order** page, use the drop-down lists to change the order of the columns, and then click **OK** to save the change.

79 **To sort items in a list**

1 Open the list you want to sort.

2 Click on the column name you want to sort. The list items are sorted in ascending order.

3 Click on the column name again. The list items are sorted in descending order.

79 **To filter items in a list**

1 Open the list you want to filter.

2 Click **Filter**. Drop-down menus appear above each column.

3 In the drop-down menu above a column, click a filter to filter the list.

4 To change the filter, click **Change Filter**. Drop-down menus reappear above each column.

81 **To create a new list view**

1 Open the list for which you want to create a new view.

2 On the left side of the page in the **Actions** section, click **Modify settings and columns**.

3 On the **Customize** page in the **Views** section, click **Create a new view**.

4 On the **Create View** page, click a type of view.

5 On the next **Create View** page, specify the setting for the view.

6 Click **OK** to save the list view.

81 **To modify a list view**

1 Open the list for which you want to modify a view.

2 On the left side of the page in the **Actions** section, click **Modify settings and columns**.

3 On the **Customize** page in the **Views** section, click the name of the view you want to modify, and then on the **Edit View** page, modify the view settings.

4 Click **OK** to save the changes.

86 **To create an alert that notifies you of changes to a list**

1 Open the list for which you want to create an alert.

2 On the left side of the page in the **Actions** section, click **Alert me**.

3 On the page that appears, specify the e-mail alert settings.

4 Click **OK** to create the e-mail alert.

86 **To delete an alert**

1 Open the list for which you want to delete an alert.

2 On the left side of the page in the **Actions** section, click **Alert me**.

3 On the **New Alert** page, in the **Alert Frequency** section, click **View my existing alerts on this site**.

4 On the **My Alerts on this Site** page, add a check mark next to the alert you want to delete, and then click **Delete Selected Alerts**.

5 In the dialog box that appears, click **OK** to confirm the deletion.

88 **To delete a list**

1 Open the list you want to delete.

2 On the left side of the page in the **Actions** section, click **Modify settings and columns**.

3 On the **Customize** page, in the **General Settings** section, click **Delete this list**.

4 In the dialog box that appears, click **OK** to confirm the deletion.

Chapter 5 **Creating and Managing Libraries**

Page 92 **To create a new document library**

1 On the top link bar, click **Create**.

2 On the **Create Page** page, in the **Document Libraries** section, click **Document Library**.

3 On the **New Document Library** page, specify the settings for the new document library, and then click the **Create** button.

94 **To create a new form library**

1 On the top link bar, click **Create**.

2 On the **Create Page** page, in the **Document Libraries** section, click **Form Library**.

3 On the **New Form Library** page, specify the settings for the new form library.

4 Click the **Create** button.

94 **To associate a form template with a form library**

1 Open the form library you want to delete.

2 On the left side of the page, in the **Select a View** section, click **Explorer View**.

3 Double-click the **Forms** folder.

4 Copy your form template from your computer to the **Forms** folder.

5   On the left side of the page, in the **Actions** section, click **Modify Settings and Columns**.

6   On the **Customize** page, in the **General Settings** section, click **Change General Settings**.

7   On the **Form Library Settings** page, in the **Form Template** section, type the file name of the template you want to use, and click **OK**.

97   **To create a picture library**

1   On the top link bar, click **Create**.

2   On the **Create Page** page, in the **Picture Libraries** section, click **Picture Library**.

3   On the **New Picture Library** page, specify the settings for the new picture library.

4   Click the **Create** button.

98   **To add documents to a document library**

1   Open the document library to which you want to add a document.

2   On the document library page, click **Upload Document**.

3   On the **Upload Document** page, click the **Browse** button.

4   In the **Choose File** dialog box, browse to the file you would like to upload, click **Open**, and then click **Save and Close** to upload the document.

99   **To add pictures to a picture library**

1   Open the picture library to which you want to add pictures.

2   On the picture library page, click **Add Picture**.

3   On the Add Picture page, click the **Browse** button.

4   In the **Choose File** dialog box, browse to the file you would like to upload, click **Open**, and then click **Save and Close** to add the picture to the library.

100   **To create a new folder in a library**

1   Open the library in which you want to add a new folder.

2   On the library page, click **New Folder**.

3   On the **New Folder** page, in the **Name** box, type the name of the folder you would like to create, and then click **Save and Close** to create the new folder.

101   **To check out a document from the document library**

1   Open the document library from which you want to check out a document.

2   On the document library page, move your mouse over the document you would like to check out, click the down arrow that appears, and then click **Check Out**.

101 **To check in a document to the document library**

1 Open the document library to which you want to check in a document.

2 On the document library page, move your mouse over the document you want to check in, click the down arrow that appears, and then click **Check In**.

3 On the **Check In** page, select **Check In Document**, and then in the **Check In comments** box, type any comments you want to add, and then click **OK**.

103 **To check out a document from Word 2003**

1 Open the document library from which you want to check out a document.

2 On the document library page, move your mouse over the document that you would like to check out and edit, and then click the down arrow that appears.

3 Click **Edit in Microsoft Office Word**, and then in the dialog box that displays a warning, click **OK**.

4 In Word 2003, click **File**, and then click **Check Out**.

103 **To check in a document being edited in Word 2003**

1 In Word 2003, click **File**, and then click **Check In**.

2 In the **Check In Comments** dialog box, type any comments.

3 Click **OK**, and then close Word 2003.

104 **To view a document's version history and restore back to a previous version**

1 Open the document library that has a document that you want to restore back to a previous version.

2 On the document library page, move your mouse over the document for which you want to see the version history, and then click the down arrow that appears.

3 Click **Version History**.

4 On the **Version saved for** document page, move the mouse over the date of the document you want to restore, click the down arrow that appears, and then click **Restore**.

5 In the dialog box indicating that you are about to replace the current version with the selected version, click **OK**.

106 **To delete a document that is no longer in use**

1 Open the document library that has a document that you want to delete.

2 On the document library page, move your mouse over the document you would like to delete, click the down arrow that appears, and then click **Delete**.

3 In the dialog box that appears, click **OK** to confirm the deletion.

1 Open the document library that has a document for which you want to set up an alert.

2 Move your mouse over the document for which you would like an alert set up, click the down arrow that appears, and then click **Alert Me**.

3 On the **New Alert** page, specify the e-mail alert settings.

4 Click **OK** to create the e-mail alert.

Chapter 6 **Working with Library Settings**

1 On the top link bar, click **Documents and Lists**.

2 On the **Documents and Lists** page, in the **Document Libraries** section, click the document library you want to access.

3 On the left side of the page, under **Actions**, click **Modify settings and columns**.

4 On the **Customize** page, in the **General Settings** section, click **Change general settings**.

5 On the **Document Library Settings** page, in the **Navigation** section, select **Yes** when asked whether you want to display a library on the Quick Launch bar, and then click **OK**.

1 On the top link bar, click **Documents and Lists**.

2 On the **Documents and Lists** page, in the **Document Libraries** section, click the document library you want to access.

3 On the document library page, under **Actions**, click **Modify settings and columns**.

4 On the **Customize** page, in the **General Settings** section, click **Change general settings**.

5 On the **Document Library Settings** page, in the **Content Approval** section, select **Yes** to the question **Require content approval for submitted items?**.

6 Click **OK**.

1 Open the document library that has a document to which you want to add a column.

2 On the left side of the page, under **Actions**, click **Modify settings and columns**.

3 On the **Customize** page, under the **Columns** section, click **Add a new column**.

4   On the **Add Column** page, specify the settings for adding a new column, and then click **OK**.

116   **To modify a column in a document library**

1   Open the document library that has a column you want to modify.

2   On the document library page, under **Actions**, click **Modify settings and columns**.

3   On the **Customize** page, in the **Columns** section, click the title of the column you want to modify.

4   On the **Change Column** page, specify the settings you want to modify, and then click **OK**.

118   **To add metadata to a document**

1   Open the document library that has a document to which you want to add metadata.

2   On the document library page, move your mouse over the document name, and then click the down arrow that appears.

3   Click **Edit Properties**.

4   On the page that appears, enter any information in the available fields.

5   Click **Save and Close**.

120   **To change the view for your document library**

1   Open the document library that has a view you want to change.

2   On the left side of the page under **Actions**, click **Modify settings and columns**.

3   On the **Customize** page in the **Views** section, click **Create a new view**.

4   On the **Create View** page, click a view type.

5   On the next **Create View** page, specify settings for the view, and then click **OK**.

122   **To grant users permissions to documents in a library**

1   Open the library for which you want to change permissions.

2   On the library page under **Actions**, click **Modify settings and columns**.

3   On the **Customize** page in the **General Settings** section, click **Change permissions for this** *<form or document>* **library**, and then click **Add Users**.

4   On the **Add Users** page, specify users and select their permissions.

5   Click the **Next** button.

6   On the second **Add Users** page, review the user and e-mail settings, and then click the **Finish** button.

125 **To create a Web Folder that points to your SharePoint site**

1 Click **Start**, click **My Computer**, and then on the left side of the screen, click **My Network Places**.

2 If the **Network Tasks** pane appears on the left, click **Add a network place**; otherwise, double-click the **Add Network Place** icon.

3 In the **Add Network Place Wizard**, click **Next**.

4 Click **Choose another network location**, and then click **Next**.

5 In the **Internet or Network Address** box, type the address of your SharePoint site, and then click **Next**.

6 In the **Type a name for this network place** box, type the name of your SharePoint site, click **Next**, and then click **Finish**.

128 **To add a discussion comment to a document**

1 Open the document library that has a document to which you want to add a discussion comment.

2 On the document library page, move your mouse over the document, click the down arrow that appears, and then **click Discuss**.

3 In the **File Download** dialog box, click **Open**.

4 In the lower-left corner on the **Discuss** bar, click **Discussions**, and then select **Insert about the Document**.

5 In the **Enter Discussion Text** dialog box, specify a discussion subject and discussion text, and then click **OK**.

130 **To delete a library**

1 Open the library you want to delete.

2 On the left hand side, under **Actions**, click **Modify settings and columns**.

3 On the **Customize** page, in the **General Settings** section, click **Delete this** *<form>* **library**.

4 In the dialog box that appears asking if you are sure, click **OK**.

Chapter 7 Working with Document Workspaces

Page 134 **To create a Document Workspace from an existing document within SharePoint**

1 Open the document library that has a document for which you want to create a Document Workspace.

2 On the document library page, move your mouse over the document, and then click the down arrow that appears.

3 Click **Create Document Workspace**.

4 On the **Create Document Workspace** page, click **OK**.

137 **To create a new document and generate a new Document Workspace from Word 2003**

1 Open the document library to which you want to add a new document.

2 Click **New Document**, and then when a dialog box appears indicating that some files can harm your computer, click **OK**.

3 In Word 2003, type some information into the document.

4 Click **File**, and then click **Save**.

5 In the **File name** box, type the name of the document, and then click the **Save** button.

6 Click **View**, and then click **Task Pane** to open the task pane.

7 At the top of the task pane, click **Getting Started**, and then select **Shared Workspace**.

8 In the **Shared Workspace** task pane, click the **Documents** tab.

9 Move your mouse over the document name, and then click the down arrow that appears.

10 Click **Create Document Workspace**.

11 In the dialog box that appears, click **Yes**, and then close Word 2003.

140 **To browse to a Document Workspace for a document.**

1 On the top link bar, click **Documents and Lists**.

2 On the **Documents and Lists** page on the left side of the page under **See Also**, click **Document Workspaces**.

3 On the **Sites and Workspaces** page under **Document Workspaces**, click the Document Workspace you would like to access.

142 **To add a user to a Document Workspace from within Word 2003**

1 On the top link bar, click **Documents and Lists**.

2 On the **Documents and Lists** page on the left side of the page under **See Also**, click **Documents Workspaces**.

3 On the **Sites and Workspaces** page, click a document workspace.

4 On the document workspace page, move your mouse over the document name, and then click the down arrow that appears.

5 Click **Edit in Microsoft Office Word**.

6 In the dialog box that appears, click **OK**.

7   In Word 2003, if the **Shared Workspace** task pane does not appear on the right side of the screen, click **View**, and then click **Task Pane**.

8   On the **Shared Workspace** task pane, click the **Members** tab.

9   Toward the bottom of the task pane, click **Add New Members**.

10   In the **Add New Members** dialog box, in the **Enter e-mail addresses or user names, separated by semicolons** box, type the e-mail address or user name of a user you want to add.

11   Click **Next**, and then click **Finish**.

12   In the **Add New Members** dialog box, clear or select the check box to send an e-mail invitation to the new members, and then click **OK**.

142   **To add a task to the Document Workspace from within Word 2003**

1   In Word 2003 with the **Shared Workspace** task pane open, click the **Tasks** tab.

2   In the bottom section of the pane, click **Add New Task**.

3   In the **Task** dialog box in the **Title** box, type a name for the task.

4   In the **Assigned To** box, select a user to whom to assign the task.

5   In the **Description** box, type a description for the task.

6   In the **Due Date** box, select the due date for the task, and then click **OK**.

142   **To check document information from within Word 2003**

●   In Word 2003, with the **Shared Workspace** task pane open, click the Info tab.

146   **To publish a document from the Document Workspace back to the document library**

1   On the top link bar, click **Documents and Lists**.

2   On the **Documents and Lists** page on the left side of the page under **See Also**, click **Document Workspaces**.

3   On the **Sites and Workspaces** page, click a document workspace.

4   On the document workspace page, move your mouse over the document name, and then click the down arrow that appears.

5   Click **Publish to Source Location**.

6   On the **Publish to Source Location** page, click **OK**.

148   **To delete a document's Document Workspace**

1   On the top link bar, click **Documents and Lists**.

2   On the **Documents and Lists** page on the left side of the page under **See Also**, click **Document Workspaces**.

3 On the **Sites and Workspaces** page, under the **Delete** column, click the delete icon that corresponds to your document name.

4 On the **Delete Web Site** page, click the **Delete** button.

Chapter 8 Working with Meeting Workspaces

To create a Meeting Workspace by using the Basic Meeting Workspace template

1 On the top link bar, click **Create**.

2 On the **Create Page** page, in the **Web Pages** section, click **Sites and Workspaces**.

3 On the **New SharePoint Site** page, specify the information for the new site.

4 Click the **Create** button.

5 On the **Template Selection** page, in the **Template** box, select **Basic Meeting Workspace**, and then click **OK**.

To create a Meeting Workspace for an event

1 Under the **Events** Web Part, click one of the events.

2 On the **Events** page, click **Edit Item**.

3 On the next **Events** page, select the **Use a Meeting Workspace to organize attendees, agendas, documents, minutes, and other details for this event.** check box.

4 Click **Save and Close**.

5 On the **New or Existing Meeting Workspace** page, review the settings and then click **OK**.

6 On the **Template Selection** page, in the **Template** box, select **Basic Meeting Workspace**, and then click **OK**.

To add a topic as an objective to a Meeting Workspace

1 Open a meeting workspace.

2 Under the **Objectives** Web Part, click **Add new item**.

3 On the **Objectives: New Item** page, in the **Objective** box, type the meeting objective.

4 Click **Save and Close**.

To create an agenda for a Meeting Workspace

1 Open a meeting workspace.

2 Under the **Agenda** Web Part, click **Add new item**.

3 On the **Agenda: New Item** page, specify the agenda information.

4 Click **Save and Close**.

179 **To view survey responses**

1   On the Quick Launch bar under **Surveys**, click the name of the survey.

2   On the survey page on the left side under **Select a View**, click **Graphical Summary**.

3   On the survey page on the left side under **Select a View**, click **All Responses**.

179 **To edit any responses in your survey**

1   On the Quick Launch bar, under **Surveys**, click the name of the survey.

2   On the survey page on the left side under **Select a View**, click **All Responses**.

3   Point to the survey item, click the down arrow, and then in the drop-down list, click **Edit Item**.

4   Edit the response, and then click **Save and Close**.

179 **To export results of the survey to an Excel 2003 spreadsheet**

1   On the Quick Launch bar, under **Surveys**, click the name of the survey.

2   On the survey page on the left side under **Select a View**, click **Overview**.

3   Click **Export Results to a spreadsheet**.

4   If the **File Download** dialog box appears with a warning that some files can harm your computer, click the **Open** button.

5   In the **Opening Query** dialog box, click the **Open** button.

6   If a Microsoft Excel dialog box appears with a warning about hidden or read-only columns, click **OK**.

184 **To create a new discussion board**

1   On the Quick Launch bar, click **Discussions**.

2   On the **Documents and Lists** page, click **Create Discussion Board**.

3   On the **Create Page** page, in **the Discussion Boards** section, click **Discussion Board**.

4   On the **New Discussion Board** page, specify the settings for the new discussion board.

5   Click the **Create** button.

184 **To add a new topic to a discussion board**

1   Open a discussion board.

2   Click **New Discussion**.

3   On the **New Item** page, specify the discussion topic information.

4   Click **Save and Close**.

184 **To reply to a discussion topic**

    1 Open a discussion board.

    2 Point to a discussion topic, click the down arrow, and in the drop-down list, click **Reply**.

    3 On the **New Item** page, specify the discussion topic reply.

    4 Click **Save and Close**.

184 **To delete a discussion topic**

    1 Open a discussion board, and on the left side under **Select a View**, click **Flat**.

    2 Point to the topic you want to remove, click the down arrow, and then in the drop-down list, click **Delete Item**.

    3 In the Microsoft Internet Explorer dialog box asking if you are sure you want to delete the item, click **OK**.

184 **To delete a discussion board**

    1 Open a discussion board.

    2 On the left side under **Actions**, click **Modify settings and columns**.

    3 On the **Customize** page, in the **General Settings** section, click **Delete this discussion board**.

    4 In the Microsoft Internet Explorer dialog box asking if you are sure you want to delete it, click **OK**.

Chapter 10 **Using Windows SharePoint Services with Outlook 2003**

Page 190 **To import the contact information from your Outlook 2003 Address Book to a contacts list on a SharePoint site**

    1 On the Quick Launch bar, under the **Lists** section, click **Contacts**.

    2 On the **Contacts** page, click **Import Contacts**.

    3 If the **Choose Profile** dialog box is displayed, select the profile that corresponds to your e-mail account, and then click **OK**.

    4 In the **Select Users to Import** dialog box, from the **Show Names from the:** drop-down list under **Outlook Address Book**, select **Contacts**.

    5 Select the users you wish to import, and then click **OK**.

    6 If a **Microsoft Office Outlook** warning dialog box appears stating that a program is trying to access e-mail addresses you have stored in Outlook 2003, click the **Allow access for:** check box, and then select **5 minutes** from the drop-down list.

    7 Click **Yes**.

192 **To export contacts from a contacts list on a SharePoint site into Outlook 2003**

    1   On the Quick Launch bar, under the **Lists** section, click **Contacts**.

    2   On the **Contacts** page, move your mouse over the name of the user you want to export, and then click the down arrow that appears.

    3   Click **Export Contact**.

    4   In the **File Download** dialog box, click **Open** to open the VCF file you want to export.

    5   In the **Contact** dialog box, if the **Full Name** field is blank, type the name of the contact. If the **File as:** field is blank, click the down arrow to the right of the field and select an appropriate value.

    6   Click **Save and Close**.

195 **To copy events to your Outlook 2003 calendar folder from the events list on the SharePoint site.**

    1   Click **Events** on the Events bar.

    2   On the **Events** page, click **Link to Outlook**.

    3   In the dialog box that appears asking if you want to add the folder to Outlook 2003, click **Yes**.

    4   In Outlook 2003, on the Standard toolbar, click the **Month** button. If the current calendar view does not contain any event items, use the scroll bar until you can see them.

    5   To update the Outlook 2003 copy, right-click the **Events** Calendar folder, and in the drop-down menu, click **Refresh**.

198 **To view both your personal Outlook 2003 calendar and a linked SharePoint events list**

    1   Open Outlook 2003 in Calendar view.

    2   In the Outlook 2003 navigation pane, under **My Calendars**, select the **Calendar** check box.

    3   In the Outlook 2003 navigation pane, under **Other Calendars**, select the **Events** check box.

199 **To copy an event from a linked SharePoint Events calendar to your personal calendar**

    1   In Outlook 2003, with your personal Calendar and linked SharePoint Events Calendar visible, double-click an appointment in the **Events** calendar that you want to copy to your own personal calendar.

    2   In the **Appointment** dialog box on the Standard toolbar, click the **Copy to Personal Calendar** button once, and then close the **Appointment** dialog box.

201 **To manage SharePoint alerts in Outlook 2003**

1 Open Outlook 2003 in Mail view.

2 Click the **Tools** menu, and then click **Rules and Alerts**.

3 In the **Rules and Alerts** dialog box, click the **Manage Alerts** tab, and then click **New Alert**.

4 In the **New Alert** dialog box in the **Web site Address** text box, type the URL of a SharePoint site for which you want to create alerts, and then click **Open**.

5 In the **New Alert** site that appears, select a list or document library you want to be alerted about, and then click the **Next** button.

6 On the next **New Alert** page, in the **Send Alerts To** section, type your e-mail address if it doesn't already appear. Review the other settings, and then click **OK**.

7 Close all the Internet Explorer windows.

8 Switch to Outlook 2003 and the new alert should be listed in the **Rules and Alerts** dialog box. If the alert does not appear, click **OK**, close Outlook, restart Outlook, and reopen the **Rules and Alerts** dialog box.

205 **To create a Meeting Workspace from Outlook 2003**

1 In Outlook 2003 on the Standard toolbar, click the down arrow to the right of **New**, and then click **Appointment**.

2 In the Appointment dialog box, on the Standard tool bar, click **Invite Attendees**.

3 In the **To** text box, type the e-mail addresses of people you want to invite to this meeting.

4 In the **Subject** text box, type a subject and in the **Location** text box, type a location.

5 Click the **Meeting Workspace** button.

6 In the **Meeting Workspace** task pane, in the **Create a workspace** section, click **Change settings**.

7 Click the down arrow next to **Select a location**, and then select **Other**.

8 In the **Other Workspace Server** dialog box, type the URL of a SharePoint site, and then click **OK**.

9 In the **Meeting Workspace** task pane, click **OK**, and then click **Create**.

10 On the **Standard** toolbar, click **Send**.

Chapter 11 **Using Windows SharePoint Services with Excel 2003 and Access 2003**

Page 212 **To import data from an Excel 2003 spreadsheet to a list in SharePoint**

1 On the top link bar, click **Create**.

2 On the **Create Page** page, in the **Custom Lists** section, click **Import Spreadsheet**.

3 On the **New List** page, in the **Name** text box, type a name for the list and in the **Description** text box, type a description.

4 In the **Import from Spreadsheet** section, click the **Browse** button.

5 In the **Choose file** dialog box, select an Excel 2003 spreadsheet, and then click the **Open** button.

6 On the **New List** page, click the **Import** button.

7 In the **Import to Windows SharePoint Services list** dialog box from the **Range Type** drop-down list select **Range of Cells**, then press D.

8 In the spreadsheet, select the range of cells that has data you want to import, and then on the dialog box, click the **Import** button.

216 **To add a new list item, edit an existing list item, and delete an existing list item in Datasheet view**

1 Open a list you want to modify.

2 Click **Edit in Datasheet** to display the list in Datasheet view.

3 In the last row of the list, in the column, type the information for a new list item.

4 In a cell you want to edit, click in the cell and modify the contents.

5 In a list item you want to delete, click on the far left cell to select the entire list item.

6 Press the A key to permanently remove the list item from the list.

7 Click **Yes** to confirm the deletion.

216 **To add a new column to a list in Datasheet view**

1 Open a list to which you want to add a new column.

2 Click **Edit in Datasheet** to display the list in Datasheet view.

3 Right-click on the column to the left of where you want the new column to appear, and then click **Add Column** in the context menu.

4 On the **Add Column** page, specify the name and setting for the new column, and then click **OK**.

220 **To export a list from a SharePoint site to an Excel 2003 spreadsheet**

1 Open a list you want to export to an Excel 2003 spreadsheet.

2 On the left side under **Actions**, click **Export to spreadsheet**.

3 If the **File Download** box is displayed, click the **Open** button.

4 In the **Opening Query** dialog box, click the **Open** button.

220 **To synchronize data in the spreadsheet with the contents of the list on the SharePoint site**

1   Edit your list in Excel 2003.

2   On the **Lists** toolbar, click the **Synchronize List** button.

3   Switch back to the list page in SharePoint, click the Internet Explorer **Refresh** button, and then verify changes made in Excel 2003 are synchronized with the SharePoint list.

223 **To publish a spreadsheet to a SharePoint list by using Excel 2003**

1   Open a spreadsheet in Excel 2003.

2   Click any cell within the data.

3   On the **Data** menu, point to **List**, and then click **Create List**.

4   In the **Create List** dialog box, verify the settings, and then click **OK**.

5   On the **List** toolbar, click the **List** button, and from the menu, click **Publish List**.

6   In the **Publish List to SharePoint Site** Wizard, in the **Address** box, type your site address.

7   Select the **Link to the new SharePoint list** check box.

8   In the **Name** box, type a name for the list and in the **Description** box type a description.

9   Click the **Next** button, and then click the **Finish** button.

10   In the **Windows SharePoint Services** dialog box, click the link to the new list.

227 **To export data from an Access 2003 database to a SharePoint list**

1   Open the Access 2003 database from which you want to export data.

2   In the **Database** window, click **Tables**.

3   Right-click the table you want to export and from the context menu click **Export**.

4   In the **Export Table** dialog box, from the **Save as type** drop-down list, select **Windows SharePoint Services()**.

5   In the **Export to Windows SharePoint Services Wizard** on the **Specify site and list information** page in the **Site** drop-down list, type or select your site.

6   In the **List Name** text box, type a name for the list.

7   Leave the **Open the list when finished** check box selected.

8   Click the **Finish** button.

9   In the dialog box that appears indicating that Access 2003 has finished exporting the table, click **OK**.

229 **To import data from a SharePoint list into an Access 2003 table**

1   In Access 2003, on the **File** menu, point to **Get External Data**, and then click **Import**.

2   In the Import dialog box, from the **Files of type** drop-down list, select **Windows SharePoint Services()**.

3   In the **Import from Windows SharePoint Services Wizard** on the **Select a site** page in the **Sites** text box, type in your SharePoint site address, and then click **Next**.

4   On the **Select Lists** page, in the **Lists** text box, select a list, select the **Import one or more lists** option, and then click the **Next** button.

5   On the **Select related lists** page, select the **Create linked tables to selected lists** option.

6   Click the **Next** button, and then click **Finish**.

7   In the dialog box that indicates the import is finished, click **OK**.

232 **To link a table to a SharePoint list**

1   In Access 2003, on the **File** menu, point to **Get External Data**, and then click **Link Tables**.

2   In the **Link** dialog box, from the **Files of type** drop-down list, select **Windows SharePoint Services()**.

3   In the **Link to Windows SharePoint Services Wizard** on the **Select a site** page in the **Sites** text box, type your site address, and then click the **Next** button.

4   On the **Select lists** page, in the **Lists** text box, select a list, and then select the **Link to one or more views of a list** option.

5   Clear the **Retrieve IDs for lookup columns** check box, and then click the **Next** button.

6   On the **Select views** page, in the **Views** text box, select a view.

7   Click the **Next** button, click **Finish**, and then click **OK**.

8   In the dialog box that indicates the link is finished, click **OK**.

Chapter 12   Working with Web Parts

Page 240   **To remove a Web Part from a page**

1   Open a page that has a Web Part you want to remove.

2   Verify that the link in the upper-right corner of the page is **Modify Shared Page**, indicating that you have the Web Part in shared view.

3   Click the down arrow on the Web Part title bar you want to remove, and from the Web Part menu, click **Close**, temporarily removing the Web Part from the page.

240 **To delete a Web Part from a page**

1 Open a page with a Web Part you want to delete.

2 In the upper-right corner of the page, click **Modify Shared Page** and from the Web Part Page menu, click **Design this Page**.

3 Click the down arrow on the Web Part title bar you want to delete, and from the Web Part menu, click **Delete**.

4 When a Microsoft Internet Explorer dialog box appears asking if you want to delete this Web Part, click **OK**.

5 In the upper-right corner of the page, click **Modify Shared Page**, and then click **Design this Page** from the Web Part Page menu.

243 **To add a Web Part to a page**

1 Open a page to which you want to add a Web Part.

2 In the upper-right corner of the page, click **Modify Shared Page**, point to **Add Web Parts**, and then click **Browse**.

3 When the **Add Web Parts** tool pane appears, locate a Web Part you want to add.

4 In the **Add Web Parts** tool pane, move the mouse over the icon to the left of the Web Part so that the mouse pointer changes to a four-way arrow.

5 While holding down the mouse button, drag the Web Part to a location on the page. As you move the Web Part, a dark blue horizontal line shows you where the Web Part will be added.

6 On the **Add Web Parts** tool pane title bar, click the **Close** button.

243 **To restore a Web Part from the Web Part Page Gallery**

1 Open a page that has a Web Part you want to restore.

2 In the upper-right corner of the page, click **Modify Shared Page**, point to **Add Web Parts**, and then click **Browse**.

3 On the **Add Web Parts** tool pane, click **Web Part Page Gallery**.

4 In the **Web Part List**, add Web Part to the page by dragging or using the **Add** button.

5 On the **Add Web Parts** tool pane title bar, click the **Close** button.

248 **To customize the Content Editor Web Part**

1 Open a page that has a Content Editor Web Part you want to customize.

2 Click the down arrow on the title bar of the **Content Editor Web Part**, and then click **Modify Shared Web Part**.

3 In the **Content Editor Web Part** tool pane, click the **Rich Text Editor** button.

4 In the **Rich Text Editor – Web Page** dialog box, enter your content. For example, you can type and format text, insert pictures, and insert hyperlinks.

5 In the lower-right corner, click the **Save** button.

6 Using the **Content Editor Web Part** tool pane, specify additional settings for the **Content Editor Web Part**.

7 In the **Content Editor Web Part** tool pane, click **OK** to close the tool pane.

248 **To customize a SharePoint List View Web Part**

1 Open a page that has a List View Web Part you want to customize.

2 On the title bar of the list view Web Part, click the down arrow, and then click **Modify Shared Web Part**.

3 In the list view tool pane below the **Selected View** drop-down list, click the **Edit the current view** link.

4 On the **Edit View** page specify settings to modify the list view, and then click **OK**.

5 Click the down arrow on the title bar of the list view Web Part, and then from the Web Part menu, click **Modify Shared Web Part**.

6 In the list view tool pane, specify additional settings for the list view **Web Part**.

7 In the list view tool pane, click **OK**.

254 **To move a Web Part on a page**

1 In the upper-right corner of the page, click **Modify Shared Page**, and from the Web Part Page menu, click **Design this Page**.

2 Move the mouse over the title bar of the Web Part so that the pointer changes to a four-way arrow. While holding down the mouse button, drag the Web Part to another location on the page.

3 In the upper-right corner of the page, click **Modify Shared Page**, and then from the Web Part Page menu, click **Design this Page**.

256 **To create a document library to store Web Part Pages**

1 On the top link bar, click **Create**.

2 On the **Create Page** page, in the **Document Libraries** section, click **Document Library**.

3 On the **New Document Library** page, in the **Name** text box, type a name for the document library.

4 In the **Document Template** section in the **Document template:** drop-down list, select **Web Part Page**.

5 Click the **Create** button.

256 **To create a new Web Part Page**

1 On the top link bar, click **Create**.

2 On the **Create Page** page, in the **Web Pages** section, click **Web Part Page**.

3 On the **New Web Part Page** page, in the **Name** text box, type a file name for the Web Part page.

4 In the **Layout** section select a layout.

5 In the **Save Location** section in the **Document Library** drop-down list, select the document library to which you want to save Web Part Pages.

6 Click the **Create** button.

Using Windows SharePoint Services with InfoPath 2003

To create a new SharePoint form library from InfoPath 2003

1 Open InfoPath 2003.

2 Switch to Design mode by clicking the **File** menu and then clicking **Design a Form**.

3 In the **Design a Form** pane, under **Open a form in a design mode**, click **On My Computer**.

4 Select an InfoPath form template, and then click **Open**.

5 On the **File** menu, select **Publish**.

6 In the **Publishing Wizard** on the **Welcome** page, click **Next**.

7 On the page listing the shared locations, select **To a SharePoint form library** and click **Next**.

8 On the next page, select **Create new form library (recommended)**,and then click **Next**.

9 On the page to specify the location of the SharePoint site where you want to create the form library, type the URL of your SharePoint site. Click **Next**.

10 On the name and description page, in the **Name** box, type the name for the form library and in the **Description** box, type a description. Click **Next**.

11 Click **Finish**.

12 On the wizard's last page, verify that the form template was successfully published, and then click **Close**.

To modify the existing form library from InfoPath 2003

1 Open InfoPath 2003.

2 From the **File** menu, select **Design a Form**.

3   In the **Design a Form** pane, under **Open a form in design mode**, click **On a SharePoint site**.

4   In the **Open from SharePoint Site** dialog box, in the location box, type the URL of the SharePoint site where the existing library is located. Click **Next**.

5   On the page listing form libraries, select the form library, and then click **Open**.

6   On the **File** menu, select **Publish**.

7   In the **Publishing Wizard**, on the **Welcome** page, click **Next**.

8   On the page listing the shared locations, select **To a SharePoint form library**. Click **Next**.

9   On the next page, click **Modify existing form library**, and then click **Next**.

10   On the page to specify the location of the existing library, type the URL of your SharePoint site. Click **Next**.

11   On the page listing libraries you can modify, select the form library, and then click **Next**.

12   Use the **Add**, **Remove**, and **Modify** buttons to modify the table layout for the form library.

13   When finished, click **Finish**.

14   On the wizard's last page, verify that the form template was successfully published, and then click **Close**.

To modify an existing form library from a SharePoint site

1   On the top link bar, click **Document and Lists**.

2   On the **Documents and Lists** page, in the **Document Libraries** section, click the form library.

3   On the form library page, in the left pane, **under Actions**, click **Modify settings and columns**.

4   On the **Customize** page, in the **General Settings** section, to the right of the **Template** location, click **(Edit Template)**. The form template opens in InfoPath 2003 in Design mode.

5   In InfoPath 2003 modify the form as needed.

6   On the **File** menu, click **Save** to save the changed form template to the SharePoint site.

To create a new form and save it to the SharePoint form library

1   On the top link bar, click **Document and Lists**.

2   On the **Documents and Lists** page, in the **Document Libraries** section, click a form library.

3   On the form library page, click **Fill Out This Form**. InfoPath 2003 opens the form in **Fill out a form** mode.

4   Add text to the form fields as needed.

5   From the **File** menu, select **Save As**.

6   In the Save As dialog box, in the **File Name** box, type a name, and then click **Save** to save the form to the SharePoint form library.

To edit an existing form and save it back to the form library

1   On the top link bar, click **Document and Lists**.

2   On the **Documents and Lists** page, in the **Document Libraries** section, click the name of your form library.

3   On the form library page, move the mouse over the name of the form you want to edit. Click the arrow, and then click **Edit in Microsoft Office InfoPath**.

4   In InfoPath 2003, make any edits as needed.

5   From the **File** menu, click **Save**.

Finding Information on the SharePoint Site

To search for content on an entire SharePoint Web site

1   In the upper-right corner of the Home page of the site, in the Search box, type a keyword. Then press F or click on the green **Go** button.

2   On the **Search Results** page, browse through the results of your search and click on a link to view the entire content.

3   Optionally, search for another keyword directly from the **Search Results** page.

To search for content on a specific list

1   Open a list where you would like to search for content.

2   In the upper-right corner of the default list view in the Search box, type a keyword. Then press F or click on the green **Go** button.

To set up a Web folder to search

1   In Windows Explorer, in the Folders pane on the left, click **My Network Places**.

2   If you don't see an option to **Add a Network Place**, deselect the **Folders** button in the Windows Explorer toolbar. Click **Add a Network Place**.

3   On the first page of the **Add a Network Place Wizard**, click the **Next** button.

4 On the second page of the **Add a Network Place Wizard**, click **Choose another network location**, and then click the **Next** button.

5 On the third page of the **Add a Network Place Wizard**, type the address for the document library where you want to search. Click **Next**.

6 If prompted, enter the credentials you use to access the document library.

7 On the fourth page of the **Add a Network Place Wizard**, type the name you would like to see in Office 2003. Click **Next**.

8 Click the **Finish** button.

9 Close the Web folder and Windows Explorer.

To search for documents using the File Search option in an Office 2003 application, for example Word 2003

1 Open Word 2003.

2 From the **File** menu, click **File Search**.

3 In the **Basic File Search** tool pane, in the **Search text:** box, type the keywords you want to search for.

4 In the **Selected locations** drop-down list, deselect **My Computer**, expand **My Network Places**, and then select the Web folder you just created.

5 Click the **Go** button. Found documents will be displayed in the **Search Results** tool pane.

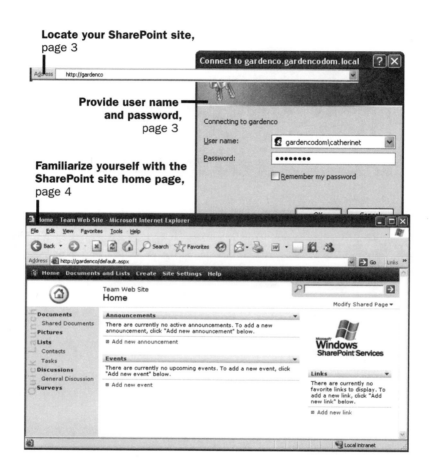

Locate your SharePoint site,
page 3

**Provide user name
and password,**
page 3

**Familiarize yourself with the
SharePoint site home page,**
page 4

Chapter 1 at a Glance

1 Introduction to Windows SharePoint Services

In this chapter you will learn:

✔ What Windows SharePoint Services is.

✔ How Windows SharePoint Services enables team collaboration and sharing.

✔ How Microsoft Office integrates with Windows SharePoint Services.

✔ What user rights on Windows SharePoint Services are.

✔ How Windows SharePoint Services relates to SharePoint Portal Server.

In the modern business environment, with its distributed workforce that assists customers at any time and in any location, team members need to be in closer contact then ever before. Effective collaboration is becoming more and more important. However, it is often difficult to achieve. Microsoft Windows SharePoint Services addresses this problem by incorporating essential collaboration and communication technologies into a single Web-based environment that integrates easily with desktop applications such as Microsoft Office.

In this chapter, you will learn what Windows SharePoint Services is and how it works with Microsoft Office applications, providing enhanced productivity environments for users and teams. You will also learn about the relationship between Windows SharePoint Services and Microsoft SharePoint Portal Server 2003, and learn how to decide which product is right for you.

See Also Do you need only a quick refresher on the topics in this chapter? See the Quick Reference entries on page xvi.

Important The exercises in this book use a fictitious business called *The Garden Company*. In the scenarios used in the book, The Garden Company is setting up a SharePoint environment for team collaboration and information sharing. There are three people involved in setting up and providing content for this environment: Catherine Turner, the owner of The Garden Company; Mike Galos, her assistant; and Kim Yoshida, the head buyer.

What Is Windows SharePoint Services?

Windows SharePoint Services is a component of Microsoft Windows Server 2003. It is provided as a free download, and gives you a powerful toolset for organizing information, managing documents, and providing efficient collaboration environments.

With Windows SharePoint Services, teams can create Web sites to share information and foster collaboration with other users. You can access content stored within a SharePoint site from a Web browser and through desktop applications such as Microsoft Office.

Tip   Windows SharePoint Services and SharePoint Portal Server 2003 are known collectively as Microsoft SharePoint Products and Technologies.

Team Collaboration and Sharing

SharePoint sites provide places to capture and share ideas, information, communication, and documents. The sites facilitate team participation in discussions, shared document collaboration, and surveys. The document collaboration features allow for easy checking in and checking out of documents, and document version control.

A SharePoint site can have many *subsites*, the hierarchy of which, on Web servers, resembles the hierarchy of folders on file systems—it is a tree-like structure. Similar to storing your files in folders on file systems, you can store your files within SharePoint sites. However, SharePoint sites take file storage to a new level, providing communities for team collaboration and making it easy for users to work together on documents, tasks, contacts, events, and other information. This team collaboration environment can greatly increase individual and team productivity.

The collaborative tools provided by Windows SharePoint Services are easy to use, so you can share files and information and communicate more effectively with your coworkers. You can create and use SharePoint sites for any purpose. For example, you can build a site to serve as the primary Web site for a team, or you can create a site to facilitate organizing a meeting. A typical SharePoint site might include a variety of useful tools and information, such as shared document libraries, contacts, calendars, task lists, discussions, and other information sharing and visualizing tools.

SharePoint site users can find and communicate with key contacts and experts, both with e-mail and with instant messaging. Site content can be easily searched, and users can also receive alerts to tell them when existing documents and information have been changed, or when new ones have been added. You can customize site content and layout to present targeted information to specific users on precise topics.

In this exercise, you will locate your SharePoint site and familiarize yourself with its home page.

OPEN the browser.
BE SURE TO know the location of your SharePoint site. If in doubt, check with your SharePoint administrator.

1 In the browser **Address** box, type the URL, or location, of your SharePoint site, http://<**yourservername/path**>.

The *yourservername* portion is the name of the SharePoint server you will be using for the exercises in this book. The *path* portion might be empty, or might include one or more levels in the site hierarchy on your SharePoint server.

Important For exercises in this book, we use a site located at the server *gardenco*. Its URL is *http://gardenco*. However, in your environment you will be using a different site installed on a different server. You will need to use your site location http://<*yourservername/path*> in place of *http://gardenco* throughout the book.

2 If prompted, type your user name and password.

3 Click **OK**.

The home page of your site appears. Although it might look somewhat different than the typical SharePoint team site The Garden Company starts with, it is still likely to include links to a variety of information, as well as the information sharing tools provided by Windows SharePoint Services.

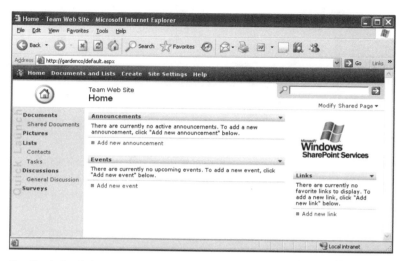

On the left of the page, you might see links to one or more of the following: Documents, Pictures, Lists, Discussions, and Surveys. The area that contains these links is called a *Quick Launch bar;* it enables you to navigate straight to the information and tools that you require.

The top link bar is a bar that appears at the top of each page. It includes various links, such as Home, Documents and Lists, Create, Site Settings, and Help. These links typically do not change so it is an easy way to quickly navigate a site.

CLOSE the browser

See Also For more information on SharePoint site navigation, refer to Chapter 2, "Navigating a SharePoint Site."

Microsoft Office Integration with Windows SharePoint Services

Many Microsoft Office menus and features are integrated closely with Windows SharePoint Services features. You can use SharePoint Services functionality from within your Office applications. For example, you can create a new SharePoint site and save your files to it without leaving your Office application.

A SharePoint site's collaborative content—including documents, lists, events, task assignments, and membership rosters—can be read and edited within Microsoft Office Word 2003, Microsoft Office Excel 2003, and Microsoft Office PowerPoint 2003. Microsoft Office Outlook 2003 allows SharePoint site event calendars to be viewed side-by-side with personal calendars, and you can also create meeting-specific workspaces on the SharePoint site from Outlook 2003.

There are different levels of integration between different versions of Office and Windows SharePoint Services. The Microsoft Office System provides feature-rich integration with Windows SharePoint Services, while Office 2000 provides only basic integration, and Office XP provides some additional integration features to Office 2000.

Office 2000 provides simple file save integration with Windows SharePoint Services. For example, you can open and save files stored on SharePoint sites from your Office 2000 applications and receive alerts in Outlook 2000. However, Office 2000 users cannot use some advanced features of Windows SharePoint Services, and some features may require additional steps.

Office XP provides additional data integration capabilities, including the ability to have interactive access to data stored on SharePoint sites. For example, you can export list data from SharePoint sites to Excel 2002, and view properties and metadata for files that are stored on SharePoint sites. However, Office XP is not integrated fully with some of the features of Windows SharePoint Services. For example, you cannot use Office XP applications to create document workspace sites, meeting workspace sites, or shared attachments in Outlook 2002.

Tip You can perform these tasks on the SharePoint site by using the browser.

With Office 2003, you can use Windows SharePoint Services to create documents and workspaces, to organize team meetings and activities, and to access and analyze data from SharePoint sites. Furthermore, you can use data integration between Office 2003 and Windows SharePoint Services, moving data to and from the SharePoint site and creating databases linked to data stored on SharePoint sites. In addition, Windows SharePoint Services integrates with the newer members of the Office System, such as Microsoft OneNote and Microsoft InfoPath. With InfoPath, teams and organizations can develop and deploy dynamic forms; InfoPath is designed to be able to store and aggregate forms on SharePoint sites.

Office 2003 provides many features for teams with members in different locations. The tight integration between SharePoint Services sharing tools and Office 2003 can help these teams improve their productivity. For example, analysts and other users who need live, up-to-date access to data can use Office 2003 applications to work with live data stored on SharePoint sites.

The following table provides an integration comparison for general business tasks that users perform every day between Windows SharePoint Services and different versions of Office.

Task	Office 2000	Office XP	Office 2003
Save and open files from SharePoint sites	Yes	Yes	Yes
Create new documents from the SharePoint site	No	Yes	Yes
Track document versions	No	No	Yes
Check out and check in documents	No	No	Yes
Upload multiple documents	No	No	Yes
Participate in inline discussions	Yes	Yes	Yes

To share a particular task, document, or project, Windows SharePoint Services provides a specific site environment called a *Document Workspace.* You can create a Document Workspace site from an Office 2003 application or a browser.

Many organizations use e-mail and shared network folders as their primary document sharing tools. When a user creates a document, they send the document, or a link to the document, to co-authors and reviewers in an e-mail message. With Office 2003, you can automatically create a Document Workspace site and a shared attachment when you use e-mail to send a document to other users for review. A *shared attachment* is a document that is stored on a SharePoint site and linked to an e-mail message. When you create a shared attachment, Windows SharePoint Services stores the document, and you can then configure the Document Workspace to track document versions. When you turn on version tracking, users can view previous versions of the document, and you can roll back changes if necessary.

See Also   For more information on working with Document Workspaces, refer to Chapter 7, "Working with Document Workspaces."

The following table compares how different versions of Office work with Document Workspaces.

Feature	Office 2000	Office XP	Office 2003
Shared attachments	No	No	Yes, with Outlook attachments
Create Document Workspace sites automatically	No	No	Yes, with shared attachments
Shared Workspace task pane	No	No	Yes
Document updates for shared attachments	No	No	Yes
View and edit shared attachments	Yes	Yes	Yes

Windows SharePoint Services integrates with Outlook 2003 much more than with the previous versions of Outlook. For example, you can keep a local copy of your team's calendars and contacts lists that is synchronized with the SharePoint site. You can also import contacts from your Outlook Address Book into a contacts list on a SharePoint site and export individual contacts or events from a SharePoint site to your Outlook Contacts or Calendar folders.

See Also For more information about integration between Windows SharePoint Services and Outlook 2003, refer to Chapter 10, "Using Windows SharePoint Services with Outlook 2003."

The following table compares the integration features between different versions of Outlook and Windows SharePoint Services.

Feature	Outlook 2000	Outlook 2002	Outlook 2003
Synchronize calendar and contact lists	No	No	Yes
Receive alerts	Yes	Yes	Yes
Alert integration with Outlook	No	No	Yes

Integration between Windows SharePoint Services and Excel 2003 enables you to export and import data to and from SharePoint lists. Excel 2003 also provides two-way synchronization between Excel spreadsheets and SharePoint lists, so you can work offline and then synchronize the changes when you reconnect.

See Also For more information about integration between Windows SharePoint Services and Excel 2003, refer to Chapter 11, "Using Windows SharePoint Services with Excel 2003 and Access 2003."

The following table compares the integration features between different versions of Excel and Windows SharePoint Services.

Feature	Excel 2000	Excel 2002	Excel 2003
Two-way synchronization with SharePoint lists	No	No	Yes
Export list data to Excel spreadsheets	No	Yes	Yes
Create custom lists from Excel spreadsheets	No	No	Yes

Similar to Excel 2003, integration between Windows SharePoint Services and Access 2003 enables you to export and import data to and from SharePoint lists. In addition, linking Access 2003 tables to SharePoint lists provides you with live, up-to-date access to data. You can use Access 2003 to analyze and manipulate live data stored on SharePoint sites.

See Also   For more information about integration between Windows SharePoint Services and Access 2003, refer to Chapter 11, "Using Windows SharePoint Services with Excel 2003 and Access 2003."

The following table compares the integration features between different versions of Access and Windows SharePoint Services.

Feature	Access 2000	Access 2002	Access 2003
Link tables to SharePoint lists	No	No	Yes
Export list data to Access database tables	No	No	Yes
Create custom lists from Access database tables	No	No	Yes

Windows SharePoint Services User Rights

In Windows SharePoint Services, access to sites is controlled through a role-based membership system. This membership system uses *site groups.* Each SharePoint site user belongs to at least one site group, either directly or indirectly.

Site groups specify what rights users have on a SharePoint site. These rights determine what specific actions users can perform on the site; in essence, each site group is a collection of rights. Windows SharePoint Services has five default user site groups, which include the following:

- **Guest.** By default, the Guest site group does not include any rights.
- **Reader.** Members of the Reader site group can browse the SharePoint site.

- **Contributor.**   In addition to the Reader group rights, the Contributor site group includes rights that allow its members to add, edit and delete items on the site, for example, Word documents.

- **Web Designer.**   In addition to the Contributor group rights, members of the Web Designer site group can modify pages on the site.

- **Administrator.**   Members of the Administrator site group have full administrative access to the site.

Important   For most of the exercises in this book you will need Reader or Contributor rights. We will tell you to verify if you have sufficient rights before the exercises where you need higher level of access, such as Web Designer or Administrator. If you are not sure what rights you have on your SharePoint site, check with your SharePoint administrator.

See Also   For more information about site groups, refer to Chapter 3, "Creating and Managing Sites." A full list of rights and their associated permissions is provided in the Appendix.

Windows SharePoint Services and SharePoint Portal Server

Both SharePoint Portal Server 2003 and Windows SharePoint Services, known together as SharePoint Products and Technologies, facilitate collaboration within an organization and with partners and customers.

As mentioned earlier, Windows SharePoint Services is a collection of services for Microsoft Windows Server 2003 that you can use to share information and collaborate with other users.

SharePoint Portal Server 2003 is an enterprise portal server built upon Windows SharePoint Services that you can use to aggregate multiple SharePoint sites, information, and applications in your organization into a single, easy-to-use portal.

Because SharePoint Portal Server 2003 requires Windows SharePoint Services, all features of Windows SharePoint Services are available in SharePoint Portal Server 2003. However, SharePoint Portal Server provides additional enterprise-level functionality.

Additional Features in SharePoint Portal Server 2003

In addition to the features of Windows SharePoint Services, SharePoint Portal Server 2003 includes the following features:

- News and Topics areas on the portal Home page
- A personal site, called *My Site*, for portal users that has personal and public views and a link to your personal site on the portal Home page

- Enterprise-level searching that includes searching across file shares, Web servers, multiple SharePoint sites, Exchange Public Folders, and Lotus Notes

- The ability to target information to specific audiences

- Alerts that notify you when changes are made to relevant information, documents, or applications

- Single sign-on for enterprise application integration

Deciding Between Windows SharePoint Services and SharePoint Portal Server

To decide if you need Windows SharePoint Services by itself or with SharePoint Portal Server 2003, you need to assess how your requirements are met by the features and functionality of these products.

The following table may assist you in your decision process. It shows the comparison between feature sets of Windows SharePoint Services and SharePoint Portal Server 2003.

Feature	Windows SharePoint Services	SharePoint Portal Server 2003
Alerts	Yes	Yes
Browser-based customization	Yes	Yes
Discussion boards	Yes	Yes
Document libraries	Yes	Yes
Document Workspace	Yes	Yes
Meeting Workspace	Yes	Yes
Lists	Yes	Yes
Microsoft BizTalk integration	No	Yes
FrontPage integration	Yes	Yes
InfoPath integration	Yes	Yes
Surveys	Yes	Yes
Templates	Yes	Yes
Web Part pages	Yes	Yes
Automatic categorization	No	Yes
Audiences	No	Yes
Topic areas	No	Yes

Feature	Windows SharePoint Services	SharePoint Portal Server 2003
News	No	Yes
Personal sites	No	Yes
Shared Services	No	Yes
Single sign-on	No	Yes
Site Directory	No	Yes
User profiles	No	Yes

Key Points

- Windows SharePoint Services provides a powerful set of tools for information sharing and document collaboration.

- SharePoint Web sites provide places to capture and share ideas, information, communication, and documents.

- You can access content stored within a SharePoint site both from a Web browser and through desktop applications such as Microsoft Office.

- There are different levels of integration between different versions of Office and Windows SharePoint Services, with Office 2003 providing the closest integration.

- Access to a SharePoint site is controlled through a role-based membership system that is based on site groups. There are five default site groups: Guest, Reader, Contributor, Web Designer, and Administrator.

- SharePoint Portal Server 2003 is built upon Windows SharePoint Services. All features of Windows SharePoint Services are available in SharePoint Portal Server 2003 and provide additional enterprise-level functionality.

- SharePoint Portal Server 2003 and Windows SharePoint Services are known collectively as SharePoint Products and Technologies.

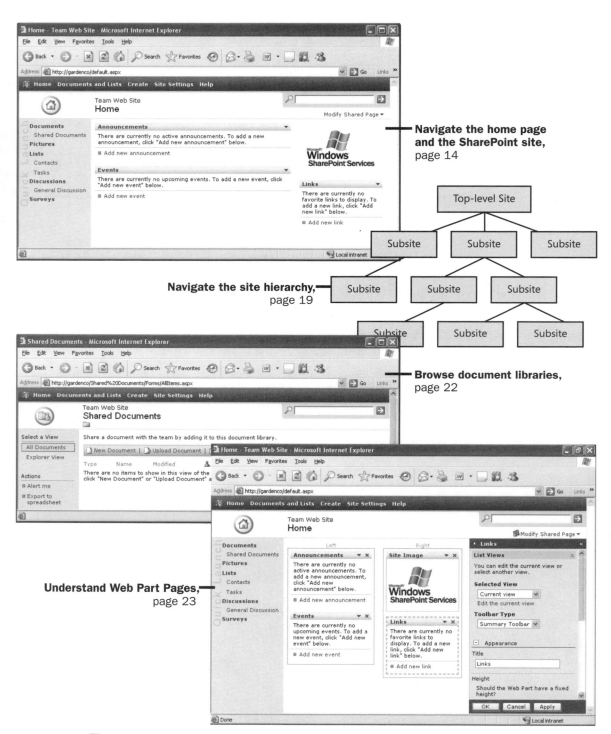

Navigate the home page and the SharePoint site, page 14

Navigate the site hierarchy, page 19

Browse document libraries, page 22

Understand Web Part Pages, page 23

Chapter 2 at a Glance

2 Navigating a SharePoint Site

A typical Microsoft Windows SharePoint Services Web site provides you with an infrastructure where your team can communicate, share documents and data, and work together. Different types of SharePoint sites have different infrastructures, such as a team site, a blank site, a Document Workspace and a Meeting Workspace. The team site infrastructure includes the following components:

- **Libraries.**   Document, picture, and form libraries are collections of files that you share and work on with your team members. A typical team site includes a built-in document library called Shared Documents. You can create your own document, picture and form libraries when needed.

- **Lists.**   With SharePoint lists, you and your team members can work with structured, tabular data on the Web site. A typical team site includes five built-in lists: Announcements, Contacts, Events, Links, and Tasks. There are other lists provided by Windows SharePoint Services that you can add to your site if required. You can also create custom lists.

- **Discussion boards.**   Discussion boards provide a forum where you and your team members can post comments and reply to each others' comments. By default, a typical team site comes with a built-in discussion board named *General Discussion*. You can create your own discussion boards when needed.

- **Surveys.**   Surveys provide a way of polling team members. SharePoint sites don't have a built-in survey, but you can create your own.

In this chapter, you will learn how to navigate the SharePoint site infrastructure. You will start with the home page of a typical SharePoint site, then learn how to browse the site hierarchy. You will also learn how to navigate the lists and libraries on your SharePoint site, as well as understand the concept of Web Part Pages.

See Also   Do you need only a quick refresher on the topics in this chapter? See the Quick Reference entries on pages xvi–xvii.

Important   Remember to use your SharePoint site location in place of *http://gardenco* in the exercises.

Navigating the Home Page and the SharePoint Site

A *home page* is the main page of a SharePoint Web site; it provides a navigational structure that links the site components together. Typically, a home page of a SharePoint site has two main navigation areas: the *top link bar* at the top of the page and the *Quick Launch bar* at the left of the page.

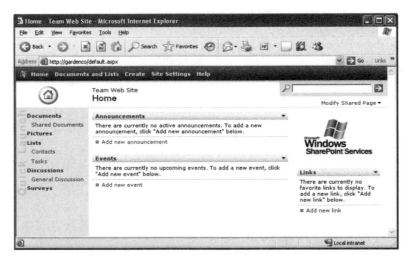

The top link bar is displayed on all pages within the SharePoint site and provides the following links:

- **Home.**   The Home link opens the home page for a site.
- **Documents and Lists.**   The Documents and Lists link opens the Document and Lists page, which lists all the libraries, lists, discussion boards, and surveys on your site. The Document and Lists page also provides links to the child sites and workspaces; it is your main navigational aid for the site.

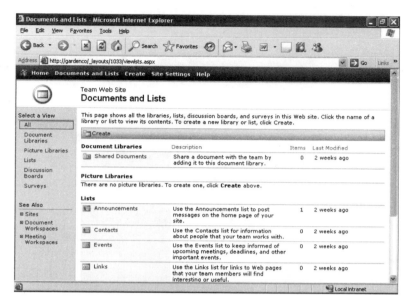

- **Create.** The Create link opens the Create Page page, which enables you to add a new library, list, discussion board, survey, or Web page to your site.

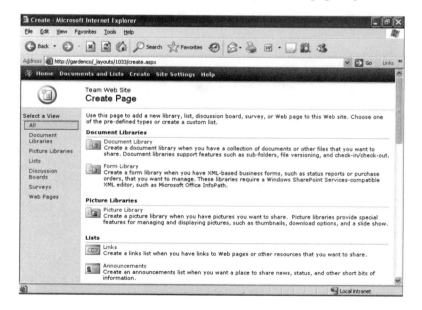

■ **Site Settings.** The Site Settings link opens the Site Settings page, which enables you to administer and customize your site.

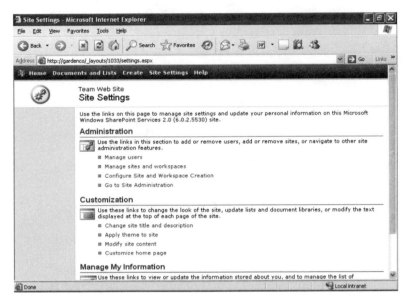

■ **Help.** The Help link opens Windows SharePoint Services Help, which is launched in a separate window. The content displayed in this window is context-specific and depends on the page you are viewing.

Depending on the site, the Quick Launch bar has one or more links to the subsets of information contained in the Documents and Lists page. These subsets, referred to as *views*, are created by filtering the information contained within this page. The Quick Launch bar can also contain links to site components created by you and your team members, for example, document libraries or lists. Usually, the Quick Launch bar contains the following links:

■ **Documents.**   The Documents link opens a view of a Document and Lists page, which shows all the document and form libraries in your site.

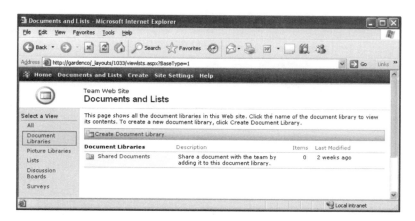

On a typical team site, the Quick Launch bar also provides a second level link to a Shared Documents library.

■ **Pictures.**   The Pictures link opens a view of a Document and Lists page that shows all picture libraries in your site.

■ **Lists.**   The Lists link opens a view of a Document and Lists page that shows all lists in your site. On a typical team site, the Quick Launch bar also provides two second level links to Contacts and Tasks lists.

■ **Discussions.**   The Discussions link opens a view of a Document and Lists page that shows all discussion boards in your site. On a typical team site, the Quick Launch bar also provides a second level link to a General Discussion board.

■ **Surveys.**   The Surveys link opens a view of a Document and Lists page that shows all surveys in your site.

In addition to the top link bar and the Quick Launch bar, a home page of a typical SharePoint team site includes views of the following lists:

■ Announcements

■ Events

■ Links

Each of these lists is presented within its own page component called a Web Part. You can add items to these lists by clicking Add item within the list's Web Part.

In this exercise, you will navigate to the Surveys page, and then go back to the home page.

OPEN your SharePoint site, for example, *http://gardenco*. If prompted, type your user name and password, and then click OK.

1 On the **Quick Launch** bar, click **Surveys**.

The Document and Lists page opens in the Surveys view.

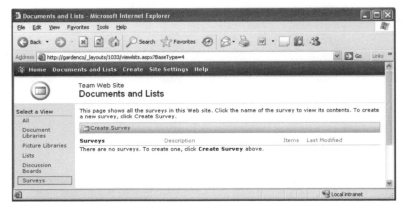

2 Explore the page.

Notice that the top link bar hasn't changed. However, there is no Quick Launch bar. Instead, there is a menu of actions specific to the functionality of the page: in this case, the menu enables you to view other components of your SharePoint site.

The main part of the page lists the surveys on the site. The Garden Company site hasn't created a survey yet, so this page doesn't display any surveys.

3 Click **Home** on the top link bar to go back to the site's home page.

CLOSE Internet Explorer.

See Also For more information on working with surveys, refer to Chapter 9, "Working with Surveys and Discussion Boards."

Navigating the Site Hierarchy

A SharePoint site can have many subsites, the hierarchy of which, on Web servers, resembles the hierarchy of folders on file systems. Sites that do not have a parent site are referred to as *top-level sites*. Top-level sites can have multiple subsites, and these subsites can have multiple subsites, down as many levels as you need. The entire hierarchical structure of a top-level site and all of its subsites is called a *site collection*.

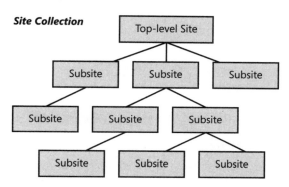

If you have Administrator rights on the parent site, you can view the list of all subsites to the parent site. This list displays only the immediate subsites for the current site (one level down).

In this exercise, you will view a list of subsites to your SharePoint site. You will browse to this list in two different ways. You will also navigate the sites' hierarchy.

OPEN the SharePoint site to which you'd like to view the subsites. If prompted, type your user name and password, and then click OK.

BE SURE TO verify that you have sufficient rights to view the subsites. (For this exercise, Administrator rights are required.) If in doubt, see the Appendix on page 260.

1   On the top link bar, click **Site Settings**.

2   On the **Site Settings** page, under **Administration**, click **Manage sites and work-spaces**.

3   On the **Sites and Workspaces** page, under **Sites**, explore the list of the subsites to your site.

4   On the top link bar, click **Home**.

You will now browse to the list of subsites in different way.

5   On the top link bar, click **Documents and Lists**.

6   On the **Documents and Lists** page, on the left pane under **See Also**, click **Sites**.

You might need to scroll down to see this link.

7   On the **Sites and Workspaces** page under **Sites**, click a subsite.

Each subsite within the site hierarchy, apart from the top-level site, has the link to the parent site displayed on the top link bar.

8   On the subsite's home page, on the right side of the top link bar, click the link that points up to the parent site, such as **Up to Team Web Site**.

9   You are taken back to the home page of the parent site.

CLOSE Internet Explorer.

> **See Also**   For more information on working with sites, refer to Chapter 3, "Creating and Managing Sites."

Browsing the Lists on a SharePoint Site

SharePoint lists are Web-based, editable tables. SharePoint lists provide you and your team with the ability to work with structured data. As we have discussed, the typical team Web site provides five default lists, all of which appear by default on the team site home page:

- **Announcements.**   The Announcements list is a place to post information for the team.

- **Contacts.**   The Contacts list stores information such as name, telephone number, e-mail address, and street address for people who work with your team.

- **Events.**   The Events list is a place to post important dates.

- **Links.**   The Links list displays hyperlinks to Web pages of interest to team members.

- **Tasks.**   The Tasks list provides a to-do list for team members.

In addition to these default lists, you can create your own lists when required. When creating a new list, you might choose to place a link to this list on the Quick Launch bar.

See Also   For more information on working with lists, refer to Chapter 4, "Working with Lists."

In this exercise, you will view a list of all SharePoint lists that exist on your site. You will then navigate to a list, and then back to the home page.

OPEN the SharePoint site in which you'd like to view the existing lists. If prompted, type your user name and password, and then click OK.

1   On the top link bar, click **Documents and Lists**.

On the Documents and Lists page under Lists, links to all existing lists in your site are displayed.

2   Click a list, for example, **Announcements**.

The Announcements page appears.

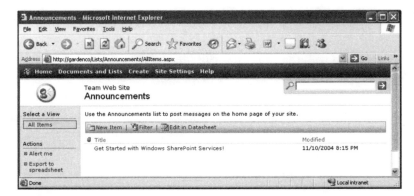

3 On the list page, view the list items. For example, the **Announcements** list on The Garden Company site has only one default item.

4 To go back to the site's home page, click **Home**.

CLOSE Internet Explorer.

Browsing the Document Libraries

SharePoint libraries not only store files, but provide a flexible collaboration environment for you and your team to work on files.

A SharePoint library page lists each file in this library as well as its properties, and provides a link to each file. By default, the team site comes with a built-in document library named Shared Documents that is listed on the Quick Launch bar.

In addition to the Shared Documents library, you can create your own document, picture, and form libraries when required. When creating a new library, you might choose to place a link to this library on the Quick Launch bar.

See Also For more information on working with documents in the document libraries, refer to Chapter 5, "Creating and Managing Libraries." For more information on configuring the document libraries, refer to Chapter 6, "Working with Library Settings."

In this exercise, you will view a list of all SharePoint libraries that exist on your site. You will then navigate to a Shared Documents library.

OPEN the SharePoint site in which you'd like to view the list of existing libraries. If prompted, type your user name and password, and then click OK.

1 On the top link bar, click **Documents and Lists**.

On the Documents and Lists page under Document Libraries, links to all existing document and form libraries are displayed.

2 Click a link, for example, **Shared Documents**.

The Shared Documents page appears.

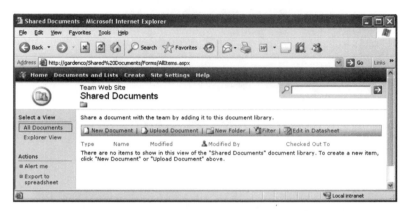

3 On the **Shared Documents** page, view the list of files in this library. In this example, The Garden Company team members haven't put any documents in this library as yet.

4 To go back to the site's home page, click **Home**.

CLOSE Internet Explorer.

Understanding Web Part Pages

A *Web Part Page* is a special type of page on a SharePoint site that contains one or more Web Parts. A *Web Part* is an independent component that can be reused, shared, and personalized by all users who have permission to access it. Web Parts are the basic building blocks of a Web Part Page; each Web Part occupies its own rectangular area within the page.

For example, the home page of a typical team site contains four Web Parts. Three of them display the default lists: Announcements, Events, and Links. The fourth Web Part displays a Windows SharePoint Services logo.

Web Part Pages often contain several Web Parts that might be connected together if required. Using Web Parts, you can organize disparate information and consolidate data–such as lists and charts–and Web content–such as text, links and images–into a single Web page.

See Also For more information on Web Part Pages, refer to Chapter 12, "Working with Web Parts."

The Links Web Part can prove to be particularly useful for you when you consider making the navigation of your site easy. For example, you can add links to the Links list that are displayed within the Links Web Part.

See Also For more information on how to add items to a list, refer to Chapter 4, "Working with Lists."

In this exercise, you will modify the title of the Links Web Part on the home page of the team site.

OPEN the SharePoint site home page, for example, *http://gardenco*. If prompted, type your user name and password, and then click OK.

BE SURE TO verify that you've got sufficient rights to modify the Web Parts. If in doubt, see the Appendix on page 260.

1 In the upper-right corner of the page underneath the top link bar, click **Modify Shared Page**.

2 In the menu that appears, point to **Modify Shared Web Parts**, and then in the sub-menu that appears, click **Links**.

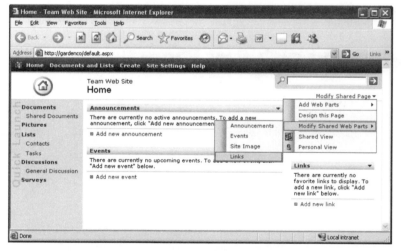

3 The Links Web Part is displayed with the dashed yellow line surrounding it. In addition, a Web Part tool pane is displayed on the right of the browser window.

4 To expand the appearance options for the Links Web Part, within the tool pane, click **Appearance**.

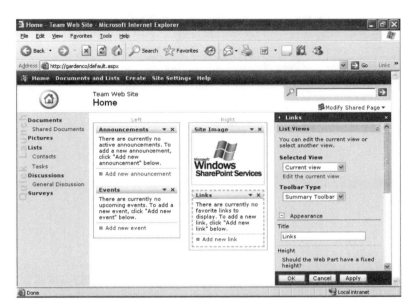

5 Under **Appearance**, in the **Title** box, delete the current Web Part title **Links** and type the new title The Garden Company Links.

6 Click **Apply**, and then verify that the new title is displayed in the Web Part title bar.

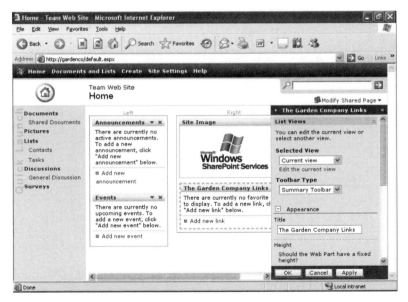

7 Click **OK**.

The modified Web Part is displayed on the home page.

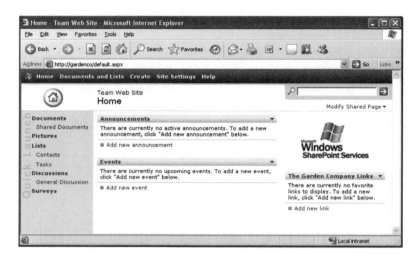

CLOSE Internet Explorer.

Key Points

- The infrastructure of a typical SharePoint site includes the following components: document, form, and picture libraries; lists; discussion boards; and surveys.

- A home page of a SharePoint site has two main navigation areas: the top link bar at the top of the page and the Quick Launch bar at the left of the page.

- The top link bar is displayed on all pages within the site.

- A SharePoint site can have many subsites, the hierarchy of which, on Web servers, resembles the hierarchy of folders on file systems.

- Sites that do not have a parent site are referred to as top-level sites. Top-level sites can have multiple subsites, and these subsites can have multiple subsites, down as many levels as you need.

- The Documents and Lists page that is linked from the top link bar displays all the libraries, lists, discussion boards, and surveys on your site. The Document and Lists page also provides links to the child sites and workspaces.

- A home page of a typical SharePoint site has one or more Web Parts. To assist navigation, you might consider modifying the Links Web Part.

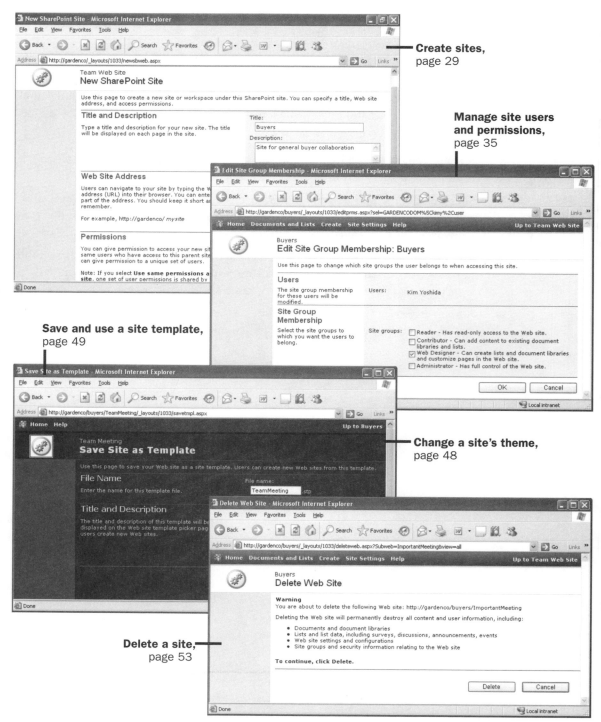

Create sites,
page 29

**Manage site users
and permissions,**
page 35

Save and use a site template,
page 49

Change a site's theme,
page 48

Delete a site,
page 53

Chapter 3 at a Glance

3 Creating and Managing Sites

In this chapter you will learn to:

✔ Create sites.

✔ Manage site users and permissions.

✔ Manage sites and child sites.

✔ Change a site's theme.

✔ Save and use a site template.

✔ Delete a site.

Microsoft Windows SharePoint Services *sites* and *workspaces* are containers for *Web Part Pages*, *Web Parts*, *lists*, and *document libraries*. You can use any site as a single container for your data or you can create as many child sites as you need to make your data easier to find and manage. You might find yourself frequently creating sites to secure a place for a given group of people to collaborate on its contents. For example, you might create a site to manage a new team or project, collaborate on a document, or prepare for and follow up on a meeting. As containers, sites can be used to secure their contents.

Site templates are used in Windows SharePoint Services as a blueprint to jump start a new site's usefulness by auto-generating the Web Part Pages, Web Parts, lists, and document libraries that will likely be most useful in a given situation. In this chapter, you will learn how to create a site using one of the site templates that are available from a default installation and the steps necessary to manage and administrate this site. You might want to differentiate a site by the way it is presented to the user, so you will also learn how to apply a *theme* to your site.

See Also   Do you need a quick refresher on the topics in this chapter? See the Quick Reference entries on page xvii.

Important   Remember to use your SharePoint site location in place of *http://gardenco* in the exercises.

Creating Sites

The catalyst for organizing your data into different site containers will often be the same catalyst for creating multiple subdirectories on the file system. Perhaps you just have too much information to use a single container and still easily find what you are looking for. Imagine if all your files were kept in the root of the hard drive along with the operating system files and the files for all your other programs. The list of files would be difficult to sort through, work with, and manage. Just as you would create subdirectories to organize your file system data, you will likely create child sites to help organize your SharePoint data in logical ways.

The initial site created in a SharePoint *site collection* is called the *top-level site*. Although the top-level site is functionally the same as its child sites, it is created from within *SharePoint Central Administration*. This is because it doesn't have a parent site. The top-level site in a site collection exclusively contains administrative links on the Site Administration page to manage site collection functionality.

To create a child site you must navigate to the New SharePoint Site page of the would-be parent site. See the following sidebar, "http://[site]/_layouts/1033/ Directory," for details about how to gain direct access to the destination directly from the browser's address bar.

http://[site]/_layouts/1033/ Directory

Most SharePoint administration pages are kept in a common folder called *_layouts*. Using *http://[site]/_layouts/1033/* in the address bar of your browser, you can quickly navigate to administrative pages that may be buried relatively deep in a site's administrative links.

1033 is the Locale Culture ID (LCID) for the English language. Contents like date, time, and currency are displayed according to the location or region that the LCID identifies. If you use a language other than English, your LCID will be different than 1033.

The following table shows examples typically found in the top link bar of every SharePoint site.

Web site address (URL)	Administrative Page
http://[site]/_layouts/1033/viewlsts.aspx	Documents and Lists
http://[site]/_layouts/1033/create.aspx	Create Page
http://[site]/_layouts/1033/settings.aspx	Site Settings

The following table shows the same examples for a child site.

Web site address (URL)	Administrative Page
http://[site]/[childsite]/_layouts/1033/viewlsts.aspx	Documents and Lists
http://[site]/[childsite]/_layouts/1033/create.aspx	Create Page
http://[site]/[childsite]/_layouts/1033/settings.aspx	Site Settings

Note how the suffix for each Web site address is the same regardless of how deep into the site hierarchy you go. So, you can directly access the New SharePoint Site page by typing the following Web site address directly into your browser's address bar:

http://gardenco/_layouts/1033/newsbweb.aspx

When you are initially creating anything in Windows SharePoint Services, you are establishing two name values: the display name, usually labeled *Name* or *Title*, and the URL name, also known as the *internal name*. Occasionally, as is the case with sites, there is an option to provide the URL name separately. In any case, only the display name can be changed after an item is created.

Best practices to follow when initially naming anything in Windows SharePoint Services include the following:

- The initial name should be descriptive, intuitive, and easy to remember.

- The initial name should be kept short. There is a limit of 260 total characters available for the entire Web site address, so if you consistently use long names you will eventually have problems.

- The initial name should not contain spaces. Spaces in the address bar are replaced with %20 so they take up three characters each. Spaces also make the Web site address difficult to use in an e-mail and difficult for others to read.

- The initial name should be consistently used throughout the site.

Tip When the URL name is not prompted for on a SharePoint create page, the display name, usually labeled *Title*, is used to populate both the display name and the URL name. There are certainly other best practices that could be established for a specific organization. It would be wise to establish your own naming conventions early on.

With Microsoft Office FrontPage 2003 both the display name and the URL name can be changed after an item is created.

When creating a new site there are two permission options available. The default option, "Use same permissions as parent site," checks the parent site's permission every time the user visits the child site to determine what the user is allowed to do on that site. As the permissions on the parent site change over time, the permissions on the child site reflect those changes. If you select the "Use unique permissions" option instead, you, as the site's creator, initially will be the only user with access to the site and you will be associated with the Administrator site group.

Tip If you select "Use same permissions as parent site," it is possible to have the right to create a new site but not have the right to delete it. However, if you select "Use unique permissions," you will be the site's administrator and, as such, will always have the right to delete the new site.

From the Template Selection page, you can populate your site using one of the eight built-in templates. Each template provisions Web Part Pages, Web Parts, lists, and document libraries using the navigation best suited for the purpose of the template.

The first three templates listed—Team Site, Blank Site, and Document Workspace—all have the same latent capabilities and *Quick Launch bar* navigation. The *Team Site* provisions a Shared Documents library and five lists: Announcements, Contacts, Events, Links, and Tasks. The *Blank Site*, as you might surmise, has no lists or document libraries and only the Site Image Web Part. The *Document Workspace* provisions the same document libraries and lists as the Team Site, but makes the Shared Documents library more prominent by placing a Web Part for it on the default home page for the site. It also places a Members Web Part on the default home page.

The five meeting workspace templates are named Basic Meeting Workspace, Blank Meeting Workspace, Decision Meeting Workspace, Social Meeting Workspace, and Multi-page Meeting Workspace. These sites are variations on a single theme. They show *Page tabs* across the top of each page rather than a Quick Launch bar on the left. In addition to some of the traditional list types, such as Tasks, Meeting Workspaces can also provision unique lists, such as Agenda, Attendees, Decisions, Objectives, and Things To Bring.

Tip The eight built-in templates are actually *configurations* of the two underlying *site definitions*.

Additional configurations and even alternate site definitions can be created in the underlying files by the people that manage your Web servers. The eight built-in configurations can also be removed or altered.

You will likely focus, at least initially, on utilizing these built-in site templates. However, it is possible to save sites that you create as templates that you and others can select from the Template Selection page.

In the following exercise, you will create a child site that the buyers at The Garden Company will use to collaborate. As a team, the buyers need a centralized place to consolidate their announcements, links, and general discussions as well as track the status of their purchases and the list of current suppliers. You will use the Team Site template to initially populate the new child site.

OPEN the SharePoint site that you'd like to create a new child site within, for example: *http://gardenco*. If prompted, type your user name and password, and then click OK.
BE SURE TO verify that you have sufficient rights to create a site. If in doubt, see the Appendix on page 260.

1   On the top link bar, click **Site Settings**.

2   In the **Administration** section, click **Manage sites and workspaces**.

3   Click **Create**, to display the **New SharePoint Site** page.

4   In the **Title** text box, type Buyers, to establish a display name for the new site.

5   In the **Description** textbox, type a description, such as Site for general buyer collaboration, to help users understand the purpose for the new site.

6   In the **URL name** textbox, type buyers for the Web Site Address.

This will determine the value in the browser's address bar that people will see when they visit the site. See the tip on naming conventions earlier in this section for best practices regarding naming.

7   Click the option button that defines the type of permissions you want to initially use on the site. For the Buyers site, use the default option **Use same permissions as parent site**.

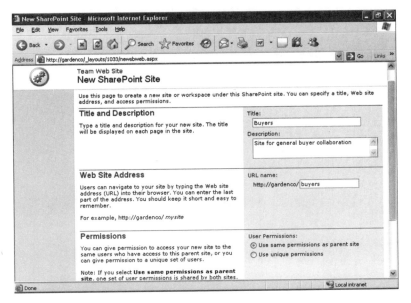

8   Click the **Create** button.

Note   Clicking the Cancel button will return you to the previous page and will not create the site.

The Template Selection page appears.

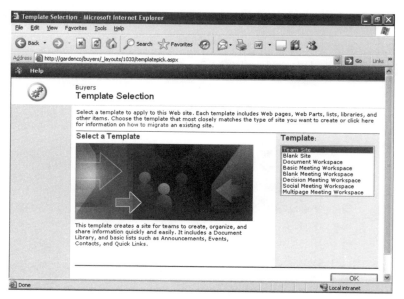

9 In the **Template** list, click **Team Site**.

10 Click **OK** to create the new site with a default set of Web Part Pages, Web Parts, lists, and document libraries for the buyers to use on the new site.

The Buyers Home page appears.

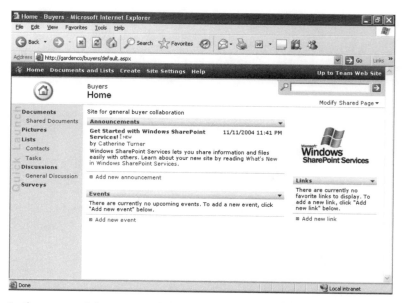

11 In the upper-right corner, click **Up to Team Web Site**, to return to the parent site.

CLOSE the browser.

Managing Site Users and Permissions

Information in Windows SharePoint Services is either secured at the site level or at the list level. By default, all lists inherit the permissions of the site that contains them. You can delve deeper into list security in Chapter 4, "Working with Lists."

There are two obvious permission options available for a child site. The default option, "Use same permissions as parent site," checks the parent site's permission every time the user visits the child site, while the other option, "Use unique permissions initially," provides the site's creator sole access to the new site as its administrator.

Because permissions can be changed after the site is created, there are really two additional permission options that may not be evident. The third option is to use the same permissions, but then after the site is provisioned, change the new site to use unique permissions. This effectively copies the permissions of the parent site to the child site. Future changes to the parent site then would not be reflected on the child site. And finally, if you do use unique permissions, you will have complete control over the site as its sole administrator while you set it up, and then later you can change it back to use the same permissions as the parent site.

Tip   You can switch indefinitely between these options by using the "Manage permission inheritance" link on the Site Administration page.

Once a site uses unique permissions, you can use the "Manage users" link on the Site Settings page. Because there is no tie to the parent site, you can add and remove users from the site regardless of whether they have permissions on any other site. When users are added to a site, they must be associated with at least one *site group*.

Think of site groups as a named collection of rights. There are five site groups that Windows SharePoint Services makes available on every site, as described in the following table.

Site Group	Description of rights	Actual rights
Guest	Rights given on lists or document libraries by way of per-list permissions are automatically added to the Guest site group. The Guest site group cannot be customized or deleted. Changes to list permissions define this site group.	Varies
Reader	Has read-only access to the site.	View Items View Pages

Site Group	Description of rights	Actual rights
Contributor	Can add content to existing document libraries and lists.	All Reader rights plus: Add Items Edit Items Delete Items Browse Directories Manage Personal Views Add/Remove Private Web Parts Update Personal Web Parts Create Cross-site Groups
Web Designer	Can create lists and document libraries and customize pages in the site.	All Contributor rights plus: Manage Lists Cancel Check-Out Add and Customize Pages Apply Themes and Borders Apply Style Sheets
Administrator	Has full control of the Web site. This cannot be changed.	All Web Designer rights plus: Manage List Permissions Manage Site Groups View Usage Data Create Subsites Manage Web Site

Tip   Although you can create your own site groups and you can even alter all site groups except for the Administrator site group, you likely will find these groups to be adequate.

Not only can you associate individual users with site groups but you can also associate *Windows groups* (*Windows NT groups*, *Active Directory groups* or *local machine groups*) with site groups. This is a very practical approach to providing tight security with minimum maintenance. However, you may not have control over the Windows groups created in the operating system. If that is the case, *cross-site groups* may be your ideal solution. Cross-site groups are a named collection of users, similar to Windows groups. Cross-site groups are maintained in each SharePoint site collection and can also be associated with site groups in any site in that site collection.

Rather than restrict people from collaborating on your new site, you may want to provide everyone some level of access. Anonymous users can be granted up to Contributor level access to the lists and document libraries in a site. Anonymous Access must be enabled on the SharePoint server before it can be enabled for individual sites.

Tip   You will also find an option to provide all authenticated users a default level of access on the Anonymous Access page.

After all the people and groups are assigned to various site groups, it is possible, and even likely, that someone will be associated at various levels with more than one site group. Rather than enforcing the most restrictive site group, all associated rights are aggregated and the cumulative list of unique rights applied.

In this exercise, you will change the permissions for a child site from inheriting permissions from its parent site to using unique permissions. Then you will add users that represent The Garden Company buyers to the child site as Contributors.

OPEN the buyer child site created in the previous exercise from the address bar of your browser: *http://gardenco/buyers*. If prompted, type your user name and password, and then click OK.
BE SURE TO verify that you have sufficient rights to alter the site's permissions. If in doubt, see the Appendix on page 260.

1   On the top link bar, click **Site Settings**.

There is no "Manage users" link anywhere on the page because users are being managed at the parent site.

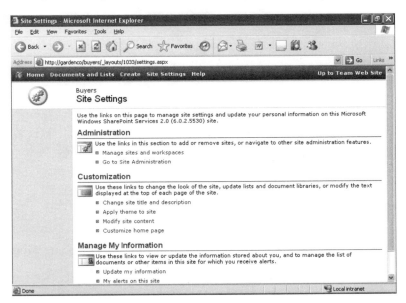

2   In the **Administration** section, click **Go to Site Administration**.

Again, there is no "Manage users" link anywhere on the page; only the "Manage permission inheritance" link.

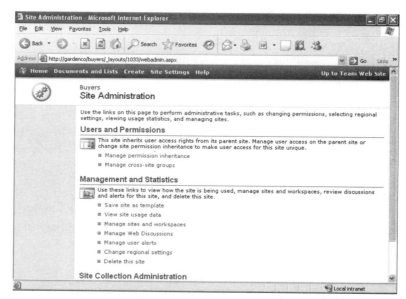

3 In the **Users and Permissions** section, click **Manage permission inheritance**.

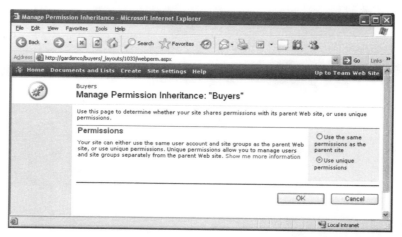

4 Click **Use unique permissions**, and then click **OK** to apply the change and redisplay the **Site Settings** page.

Notice how this page has changed. You now have a copy of the users and permissions that the parent previously managed.

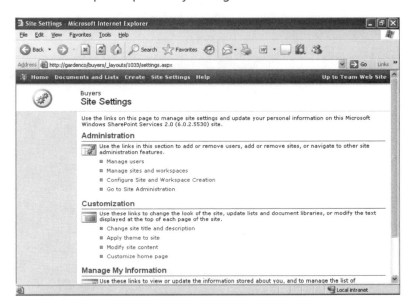

Tip The Configure Site and Workspace Creation option in the Administration section can be used to add the *Create Subsites* right to select site groups, allowing users associated with them to create sites and workspaces.

5 In the **Administration** section, click **Go to Site Administration**, to redisplay the **Site Administration** page.

Notice the plethora of new options, including a "Manage users" link, available to you in the Users and Permissions section. Of course, you could change the permission inheritance back to inherit user permissions for the site from the parent site. But now you can manage the users of this site from here instead.

Tip The "Manage users" link here and the "Manage users" link on the Site Settings page both link to the same administration page.

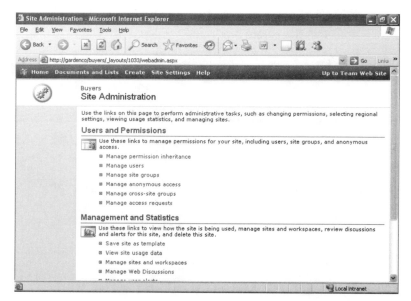

Also note that the links to "Manage site groups," "Manage anonymous access," and "Manage cross-site groups" previously discussed in this section are now available.

6 In the **Users and Permissions** section, click **Manage users**.

The Manage Users page appears.

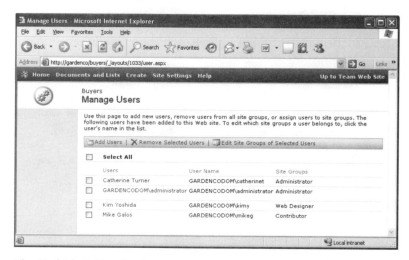

Kim Yoshida is The Garden Company's Head Buyer, so she will need to be associated with the Administrator site group. Mike Galos does not need to collaborate with the buyers, so he can be removed. And finally, you need to add the **Buyers** Windows group and associate it with the Contributors site group.

Important   Your site will not have Catherine Turner, Kim Yoshida, and Mike Galos as users. If you want to modify the permissions for your list of users, you can continue to follow along with these steps, replacing the names as appropriate. The permission changes you make in the Buyers site will not affect the permissions in the parent site. Also, you will not have the Buyers Windows group. If your domain has a Windows group that you can use, you can use that group instead.

7   Click **Kim Yoshida**.

The Edit Site Group Membership: Buyers page appears.

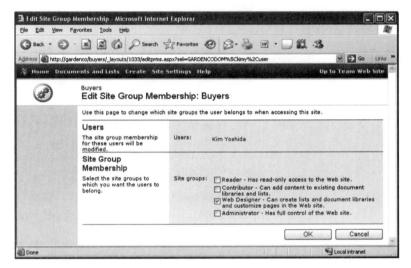

8   Select the **Administrator** check box, deselect the **Web Designer** check box, and then click **OK** to apply the change.

9   Select the **Mike Galos** check box, and then click **Remove Selected Users**.

A warning dialog box appears.

10 Click **OK** to remove the user.

Clicking the Cancel button would discard the removal request.

11 On the **Manage Users** page, click **Add Users**.

The Add Users: Buyers page appears.

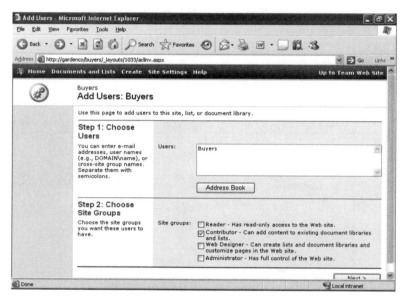

12 Type Buyers as the Windows group that you want to associate with the Contributor site group, click the **Contributor** site group, and then click **Next**.

Note   Typically you will add users and Windows groups using a format like *domainname\username* or *domainname\groupname*. Fortunately, Windows SharePoint Services searches the domain for users and Windows groups that match even if the proper naming convention isn't provided.

Windows SharePoint Services locates the Windows group and determines if there is an e-mail address associated with it. If you provide an e-mail address in the E-mail Address box, the send e-mail option will be enabled and you can notify the new members of your site about their membership.

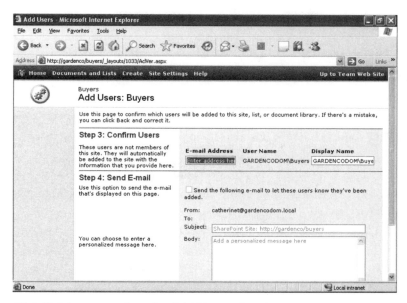

13 Click **Finish** to complete the **Add Users** wizard.

The Manage Users page appears.

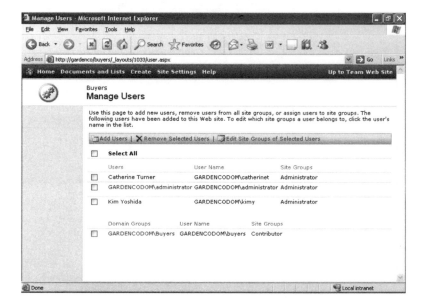

Tip It is wise to at least associate every user in the various child sites to a site collection with the Reader site group in the top-level site. Users will be unable to use custom site templates and list templates imported into a site collection unless they are associated with one of the four built-in site groups in the top-level site.

CLOSE the browser.

Managing Sites and Child Sites

Your child sites have been created, site templates have been applied, and users have been given proper permissions. How do you get back to your child sites? How can you create another child site from your child site? How will you find child sites that others have created?

In this exercise, you will create a meeting workspace child site of the Buyers child site. Since you must be in a site to create a child site, you will first see how to navigate to the Buyers child site. Then you will view the entire site collection's site hierarchy from the top-level site.

OPEN the parent for the Buyers site from the address bar of your browser: *http://gardenco*. If prompted, type your user name and password, and then click OK.
BE SURE TO verify that you have sufficient rights to create a new site. If in doubt, see the Appendix on page 260.

1 On the top link bar, click **Site Settings**.

2 In the **Administration** section, click **Manage sites and workspaces**.

A list of all the child sites, grouped by site type, are displayed.

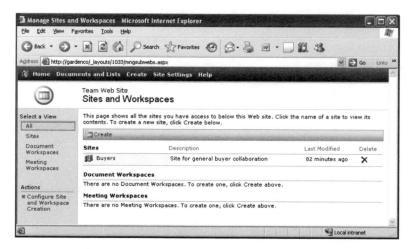

Tip The Configure Site and Workspace Creation option in the Actions section on the Quick Launch bar can be used to add the *Create Subsites* right to select *site groups*, allowing users associated with them to create sites and workspaces.

3 Click **Buyers** to display the child site.

4 On the top link bar, click **Site Settings**.

5 In the **Administration** section, click **Manage sites and workspaces**.

Tip Alternatively, you could type the entire site hierarchy directly into the browser's address bar. At first this seems a little odd, but Microsoft Internet Explorer will learn the places that you type often and it can be a real time saver rather then clicking through the user interface. To see the child sites of the current site, append /_layouts/1033/mngsubwebs.aspx to the current site's Web site address.

6 Click **Create** to display the **New SharePoint Site** page.

You were at this page earlier in this chapter when we created the Buyers child site. However, this time you are creating a child of the Buyers site rather then a child of the starting site.

7 In the **Title** text box, type Team Meeting, to establish a display name for the new site.

8 In the **Description** text box, type a description, such as Site for monthly team meeting details, to help users understand the purpose of the new site.

9 In the **URL name** text box, type TeamMeeting for the Web Site Address. Remember the naming conventions listed earlier in this chapter.

10 Keep the default permissions by using the **Use same permissions as parent site** option.

11 Click the **Create** button to display the **Template Selection** page.

12 In the **Template** list, click **Basic Meeting Workspace**.

13 Click **OK** to create and display the new meeting workspace.

Notice how different Meeting Workspaces look from team sites. Page tabs, such as the Home tab, replace the Quick Launch bar. Documents and Lists, Create, and Site Settings do not show on the top link bar. Site Settings now is on the bottom of the Modify This Workspace menu, which is just below the search box.

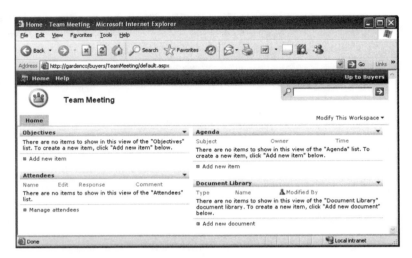

Next we navigate back to the top-level site to see the entire hierarchy of child sites.

Note To navigate to the top-level site, you could click Up to Buyers located in the upper-right corner to return to the parent site, and then on the Buyers site, click Up to Team Web Site to return to its parent; continue this process until you get to the top-level site. Using the **Go to Top-level Site Administration** link at the bottom of the Site Administration page for any child site is a quicker way to navigate directly to the top-level administration page.

14 From the **Modify This Workspace** menu, click **Site Settings**.

15 In the **Administration** section, click **Go to Site Administration**.

The Site Administration page appears.

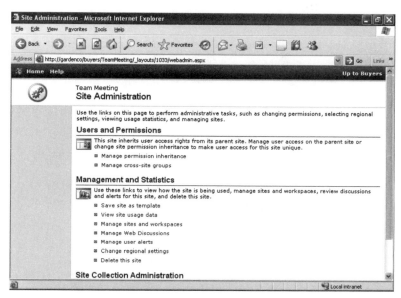

16 At the bottom of the Team Meeting **Site Administration** page click, **Go to Top-level Site Administration**.

The Top-level Site Administration page appears.

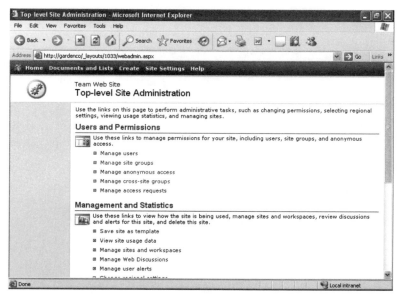

17 Near the bottom of the page in the **Site Collection Administration** section, click **View site hierarchy**, to display the View Site Hierarchy page.

> **Note** Depending on your permissions, you might not be able to access this page.

This page shows you all the flattened out, fully qualified child sites in the entire hierarchy. You can click on the site name to display the site or click on the Manage link to display the Site Administration page for the associated child site.

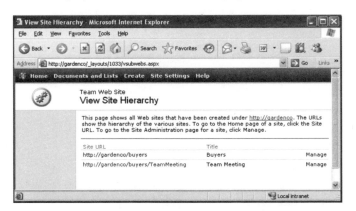

CLOSE the browser.

Changing a Site's Theme

The blue SharePoint sites initially are fine, but they eventually blur together because they look too similar. With Windows SharePoint Services you can apply a theme to your sites. Themes can radically affect display items, such as colors, graphics, text, banners, and borders. You can choose from nearly 80 built-in themes. Each SharePoint site can have its own theme, or you could set up several sites to all have a common theme so that they visually relate.

> **Tip** With Microsoft Office FrontPage 2003 you can gain even more control over how themes are applied to your site. You can choose to only apply themes to specific pages or even create your own custom themes.

Perhaps the buyers at The Garden Company want to create a theme for their Team Meeting child site so that it stands out from the other sites. In this exercise, you will navigate to the Team Meeting site and apply a theme.

OPEN the Team Meeting site from the address bar of your browser: *http://gardenco/buyers /TeamMeeting*. If prompted, type your user name and password, and then click OK.
BE SURE TO verify that you have sufficient rights to set up a site's theme and view the site hierarchy. If in doubt, see the Appendix on page 260.

1 On the **Team Meeting** child site from the **Modify This Workspace** menu just below the search box, click **Site Settings**.

2   In the **Customization** section, click **Apply theme to site** to display the **Apply Theme to Web site** page.

3   In the **Select a Theme** list, click **Breeze**.

4   Click the **Apply** button to apply a theme and then redisplay the **Site Settings** page of the **Team Meeting** site.

5   Click **Home** to display the new home page theme of the **Team Meeting** site.

The Team Meeting site appears with its new theme.

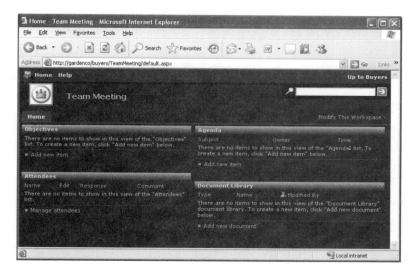

CLOSE the browser.

Saving and Using a Site Template

After working with a site for a while, you might want to save it just the way it is so that it can be re-created repeatedly. Windows SharePoint Services facilitates this activity by letting the Web Designers and Administrators save a site as a custom template. *Custom templates* are a way of packaging a set of changes to an existing site definition and making that package available as a template for new sites and lists. Custom templates behave in much the same way that the five built-in templates do in that they provision Web Part Pages, Web Parts, lists, and document libraries best suited for the purpose of the template. In fact, everything in a site except security related information is saved in a custom site template, including its theme and navigation. You can even optionally retain the data in all the site's lists and document libraries.

Note   The STP files on this book's CD-ROM that are used to recreate the solutions for each chapter are actually custom site templates saved to a file.

Important There is currently a 10 MB limit on the total size of any custom template.

Every custom template is based on an underlying site definition and saved as a file in the *site collection site gallery* document library in the root of the site collection. Once saved, a custom site template is made immediately available throughout the entire site collection in which it was saved. When creating a new child site, any user that is associated with one of the default site groups (excluding the Guest site group) in the top-level site will see the saved custom site template as an option on the Template Selection page. To use a custom site template when creating a new top-level site from *SharePoint Central Administration*, it must be placed into the *central template gallery* using a command-line tool on the Web server rather than just in the site collection site gallery.

Let's say that the unique look that The Garden Company buyers created for their Team Meetings site has caught on and they want to be able to use the theme repeatedly. In this exercise, you will save the Team Meeting site as a custom site template and then use it to create another meeting site as a child of the Buyers child site.

OPEN the Team Meeting site from the address bar of your browser: *http://gardenco/buyers /TeamMeeting*. If prompted, type your user name and password, and then click OK.
BE SURE TO verify that you have sufficient rights to save a site template and create a new site. If in doubt, see the Appendix on page 260.

1 On the **Team Meeting** child site, from the **Modify This Workspace** menu, click **Site Settings**.

2 In the **Administration** section, click **Go to Site Administration**.

3 In the **Management and Statistics** section, click **Save site as template** to display the **Save Site as Template** page.

4 In the **File name** text box, type TeamMeeting to establish a name for the STP file.

5 In the **Template title** text box, type Team Meeting Template to establish the name that will show in the list of templates to choose from on the **Template Selection** page.

6 In the **Description** text box, type a description, such as Cool blue site for team meetings that the buyers created, to help site creators understand the intended purpose of the custom site template.

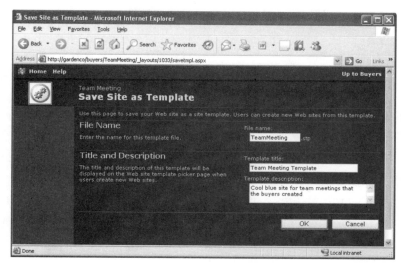

7 Click **OK**, to save the custom site template into the site collection site template gallery and to display the **Operation Completed Successfully** page.

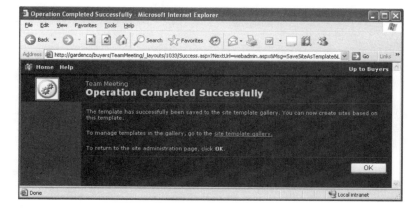

Tip If you want to see where the custom site template was placed, you can click on the "site template gallery" link on the Operation Completed Successfully page.

8 Click **OK** to acknowledge the page and redisplay the **Team Meeting Site Administration** page.

9 In the upper-right corner, click **Up to Buyers** to display the **Buyers** child site.

10 On the top link bar, click **Site Settings** to display the **Site Settings** page.

11 In the **Administration** section, click **Manage sites and workspaces** to display the **Sites and Workspaces** page.

12 Click **Create** to display the **New SharePoint Site** page.

13 In the **Title** text box, type Important Meeting to establish a display name for the new site.

14 In the **Description** textbox, type a description, such as Site for that important meeting, to help users understand the purpose of the new site.

15 In the **URL name** text box, type ImportantMeeting for the Web Site Address. Remember the naming conventions listed earlier in this chapter.

16 Keep the default permissions by using the **Use same permissions as parent site** option.

17 Click the **Create** button, to display the **Template Selection** page.

The **Team Meeting Template** is now available in the **Template** list. Also note that the description given to the custom site template is displayed below the image when it is selected.

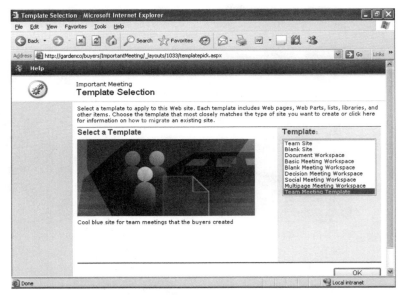

18 On the **Template** list, click **Team Meeting Template**.

19 Click **OK** to apply the template and display the new meeting workspace.

The new site **Important Meeting** site will be identical to the original **Team Meeting** site.

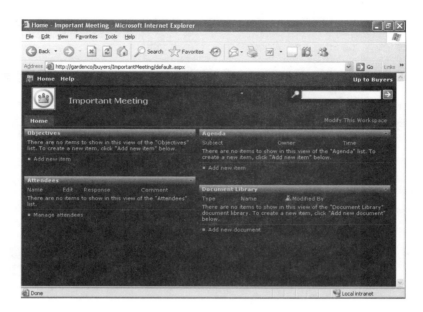

CLOSE the browser.

Deleting a Site

As always, if you can create something, you also need to be able to uncreate it. Windows SharePoint Services generates all the necessary user interface elements to create, review, update, delete, and manage. However, proceed with some prudence because once something in Windows SharePoint Services is deleted, it cannot be undeleted. You can put very good backup and recovery practices in place, but like a file on your file system, if something is created and deleted before a backup is run, it cannot be restored. There isn't anything like a recycle bin available for Windows SharePoint Services yet.

Tip It is possible to delete an entire site collection full of sites from SharePoint Central Administration.

Sometimes you will want to remove a site that you either created in error or no longer need. In fact, the creator of the Important Meeting child site at The Garden Company changed priorities and the site is no longer needed. So, in this exercise, you will delete the Important Meeting child site from the Buyers child site.

OPEN the Buyers site from the address bar of your browser: *http://gardenco/buyers*. If prompted, type your user name and password, and then click OK.
BE SURE TO verify that you have sufficient rights to delete a site. If in doubt, see the Appendix on page 260.

1   On the top link bar, click **Site Settings**.

2 In the **Administration** section, click **Manage sites and workspaces**.

The Sites And Workspaces page appears.

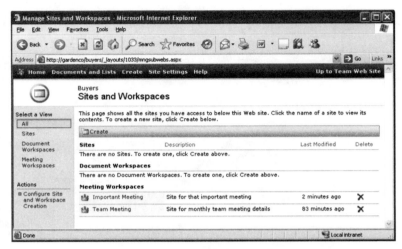

X
Delete

3 On the far right of the **Important Meeting** line, click the **Delete** icon, to begin the site deletion process.

The Delete Web Site page appears.

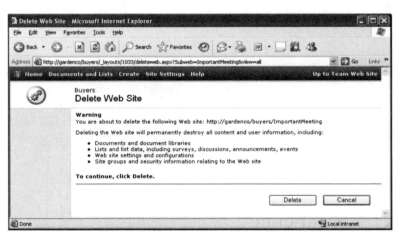

4 Click the **Delete** button to confirm the deletion request, complete the deletion process, and return to the **Sites and Workspaces** page.

The Important Meeting site is no longer displayed.

Tip   It is also possible to delete the site that you are in by clicking "Delete this site" in the "Management and Statistics" section near the bottom of any site's Site Administration page. This is an effective way to delete a top-level site.

CLOSE the browser.

Key Points

- Sites are containers for Web Part Pages, Web Parts, lists, and document libraries.
- The initial site created in a SharePoint site collection is called the top-level site.
- To create a child site you must navigate to the New SharePoint Site page.
- Don't use spaces in site names and keep them short and intuitive.
- Sites are easy to create and secure.
- Only after a site is using unique permissions can you manage its users.
- Site groups are a named collection of rights.
- Cross-site groups are a named collection of users (similar to Windows groups).
- All associated rights are aggregated and the cumulative list of unique rights applied.
- Clicking Up to [Parent Site] in the upper-right corner of a child site will return the user to the parent site.
- Each site can have its own theme.
- Sites can be saved as custom templates and immediately used to create other clone sites in a site collection.
- Deleting a site is permanent; there is no recycle bin in Windows SharePoint Services.

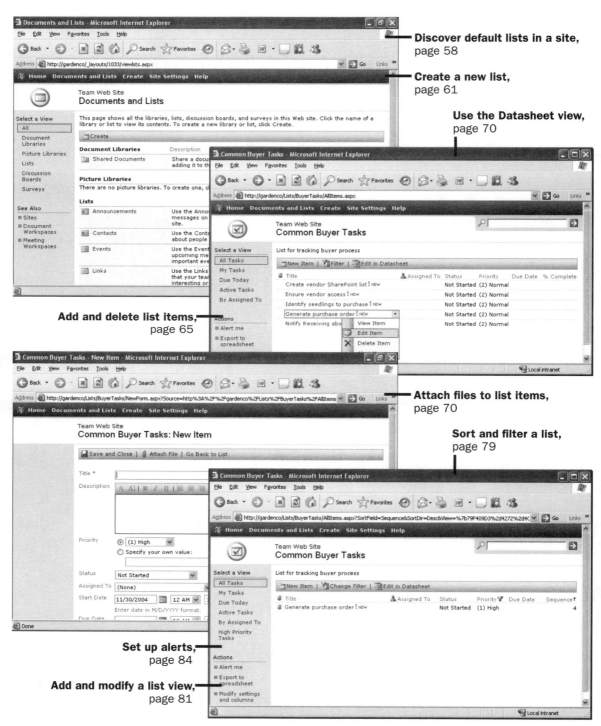

Discover default lists in a site, page 58

Create a new list, page 61

Use the Datasheet view, page 70

Add and delete list items, page 65

Attach files to list items, page 70

Sort and filter a list, page 79

Set up alerts, page 84

Add and modify a list view, page 81

Chapter 4 at a Glance

4 Working with Lists

In this chapter you will learn to:

✔ Discover default lists in a site.

✔ Create a new list.

✔ Add, edit, and delete list items.

✔ Use the Datasheet view.

✔ Attach files to list items.

✔ Add, edit, and delete list columns.

✔ Sort and filter a list.

✔ Add and modify a list view.

✔ Set up alerts.

✔ Delete a list.

You can think of the *lists* in Microsoft Windows SharePoint Services as editable, Web-based tables that facilitate concurrent, multi-user interactions against a common, centralized, extensible set of columns and rows. SharePoint lists empower users to provision their own repositories of structured information using *list items* that behave like rows with labeled *columns* named by you. The Web pages necessary to create, review, update, delete, and manage these lists and their data are automatically and dynamically generated by Windows SharePoint Services.

Tip   Unstructured information is typically stored as a document with associated columns in a document library. Document libraries are discussed at length in Chapters 5 and 6.

In this chapter, you will discover default lists that are already on your site, create new lists, and alter existing lists. Many lists are provisioned on your behalf and you need only to begin using them. But there will come a time when the lists that are provided do not quite meet a need. So, this chapter will also explore the Web pages that enable you to alter existing lists and create your own lists.

See Also   Do you need only a quick refresher on the topics in this chapter? See the Quick Reference entries on pages xvii–xxi.

Important   Before you can use the practice files provided for this chapter, you need to install them from the book's companion CD to their default locations. See "Using the Book's CD-ROM" on page vii for more information.

Important   Remember to use your SharePoint site location in place of *http://gardenco* in the exercises.

Discover Default Lists in a Site

Many default lists are provided by Windows SharePoint Services. When you need to create a list, you can use the default *list templates* to generate a new list with a static set of pre-defined columns. As explained later in this chapter, after a list has been created, additional columns can be added and most of the default columns can be altered or deleted. The list templates built into Microsoft Windows SharePoint Services are described in the following table.

	List template	Site Type	Description
	Agenda	Meeting Workspaces	Create an agenda list when you want to outline the meeting topics, determine who will cover the topics, and how much time each presenter is allotted.
	Announcements	All Sites	Create an announcements list when you want a place to share news, status, and other short bits of information.
	Contacts	All Sites	Create a contacts list when you want to manage information about people that your team works with, such as customers or partners. You can share information between your contacts list and Windows SharePoint Services-compatible contacts programs.
	Custom List	All Sites	Create a custom list when you want to specify your own columns. The list opens as a Web page, to which you can add or edit items one at a time.
	Custom List in Datasheet View	All Sites	Create a custom list when you want to specify your own columns. The list opens in a spreadsheet-like environment for convenient data entry, editing, and formatting. It requires a Windows SharePoint Services-compatible list datasheet control and ActiveX control support.
	Decisions	Meeting Workspaces	Create a decisions list when you want to keep track of all decisions made at the meeting. Attendees and others can then review the results of the meeting.

	List template	Site Type	Description
	Events	All Sites	Create an events list when you want a calendar-based view of upcoming meetings, deadlines, and other important events. You can share information between your events list and Windows SharePoint Services-compatible events programs.
	Import Spreadsheet	All Sites	Import a spreadsheet when you want to create a list that has the same columns and contents as an existing spreadsheet. Importing a spreadsheet requires a spreadsheet application compatible with Windows SharePoint Services.
	Issues	All Sites	Create an issues list when you want to manage a set of issues or problems. You can assign, prioritize, and follow the progress of issues from start to finish.
	Links	All Sites	Create a links list when you have links to Web pages or other resources that you want to share.
	Objectives	Meeting Workspaces	Create an objectives list when you want to let your attendees know your goals for the meeting. Every meeting should begin with a purpose in mind.
	Tasks	All Sites	Create a tasks list when you want to track a group of work items that you or your team needs to complete.
	Text Box	Meeting Workspaces	Create a text box when you want to insert custom text, such as instructions or motivational quotes, into the meeting.
	Things To Bring	Meeting Workspaces	Create a list of things that attendees should bring to be prepared for the meeting, such as notebooks, handouts, or something to eat.

Tip   The Text Box is an odd list, having only a single column and only supporting a single row. It can also be shared across multiple meetings in a repeating group.

As discussed in Chapter 3, "Creating and Managing Sites," Microsoft Windows SharePoint Services provisions some of these lists for you when you create a new site, depending on which site template you use. The *Blank Site* has no lists or document libraries, whereas the *Team Site* and *Document Workspace* provision a Shared Documents library and five lists: Announcements, Contacts, Events, Links, and Tasks. The Meeting Workspace templates provision unique lists, such as Agenda, Attendees, Decisions, Objectives, and Things To Bring.

See Also For more information about Document Workspaces, refer to Chapter 7, "Working with Document Workspaces." For more information about Meeting Workspaces, refer to Chapter 8, "Working with Meeting Workspaces."

In the following exercise, you will browse to the lists that have been created for The Garden Company's top-level site. Subsequently, you will browse to the Create page to see the list templates available when you create a new Team Site.

OPEN a newly created SharePoint Team Site to explore, for example *http://gardenco*. If prompted, type your user name and password, and then click OK.
BE SURE TO verify that you have sufficient rights to browse the site. If in doubt, see the Appendix on page 260.

1 On the top link bar, click **Documents and Lists**.

This site has one default document library, called *Shared Documents*, a discussion board called *General Discussion*, and five default lists: Announcements, Contacts, Events, Links, and Tasks.

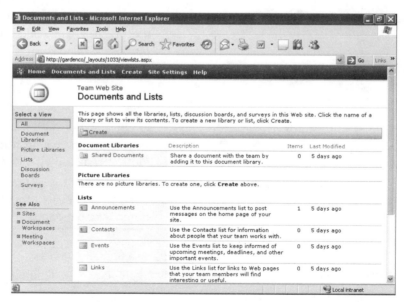

 2 Click **Create** to display the **Create** page.

Tip   Don't be confused by the naming convention. The names for the list templates are identical to the names for the default lists that are generated by Windows SharePoint Services. However, they are radically different from each other. Each list template shown on the Create page could be used to create one of more uniquely named instances in the Documents and Lists page. For instance, if the Announcements list template was used to create the Announcements list, the resulting list could be called something else, such as *Sales Notices*. The names do not have to be the same.

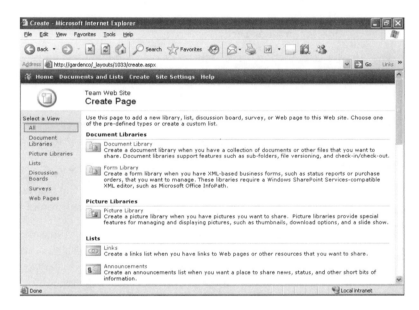

CLOSE the browser.

Creating a New List

The first step in creating a new list is to ask yourself, "What kind of information do I want to gather?" The answer to this question will help you to determine which list template to choose. Perhaps you want to start with a list that is close to your end goal and then add, delete, and alter columns to give you just the solution you are trying to achieve. For example, if you plan to collect information like names and addresses, you might choose the Contact list template to create your initial list, and then modify it. Or perhaps you will want to start with a bare-bones list and build it entirely from scratch. In that case, you would choose the Custom List list template.

Tip   If the list items in the list you want to create always begin with a document, consider using a document library instead of a list. Document libraries are discussed at length in Chapters 5 and 6.

In the following exercise, you will create a list for the buyers at The Garden Company to track the status of tasks in the buying process. This task list will be based on the Tasks list template. After the list is created, you will alter the display name so that it displays Common Buyer Tasks.

OPEN the SharePoint site from which you'd like to create the new list, for example, *http://gardenco*. If prompted, type your user name and password, and then click OK.
BE SURE TO verify that you have sufficient rights to create lists. If in doubt, see the Appendix on page 260.

1   On the top link bar, click **Create**.

2   In the **Lists** section, click **Tasks** to display the **New List** page.

You will use this page to create a task list based upon the Tasks list template. You can name your new task list anything you want.

Tip   There is no restriction on the number of copies of any list template you can create in a site. For example, you can have as many task lists as you like.

3   In the **Name** text box, type BuyerTasks to establish a display name for the new list.

Because no text box is provided for the URL name, the Name text box also supplies the value that Windows SharePoint Services uses for internal names.

Note   When you initially create a list in Windows SharePoint Services, you establish two name values: the display name, usually labeled *Name* or *Title*, and the URL name, also known as the *internal* name. However, you can only change the display name after the item is created. When the URL name is not prompted for separately on a SharePoint create page, the display name, usually labeled *Title*, is used to populate both names.

Tip   Follow these best practices when initially naming a list in Windows SharePoint Services:

- The initial name should be descriptive, intuitive, and easy to remember.

- The initial name should be kept short. A limit of 260 total characters is available for the entire Web site address, so if you consistently use long names you will eventually have problems.

- The initial name should not contain spaces. Spaces in the address bar are replaced with "%20," which takes up three characters for each space. Spaces also make the Web site address difficult to use in an e-mail message and difficult for others to read.

- The initial name should be consistently used throughout the site.

Your organization might have specific naming conventions that you want to follow.

4   In the **Description** text box, type a description, such as List for tracking buyer process to help users understand the purpose for the new list.

5   In the **Navigation** section, Verify that the **Yes** option is selected indicating that you want this new list to appear on the Quick Launch bar.

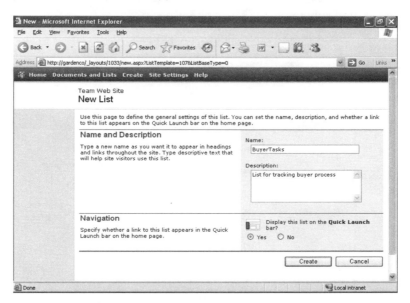

6   Click the **Create** button to complete the list creation.

The BuyerTasks page is displayed in All Tasks view.

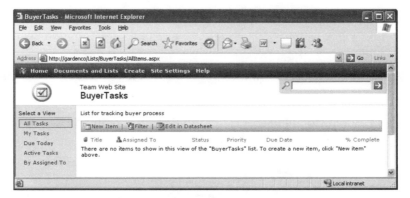

    7   On the top link bar, click **Home** to display the **Home** page for the site.

The new **BuyerTasks** list now appears in the Quick Launch bar.

Because this list was named without a space, it would be useful to change the display name so that it has a space in it.

8 On the Quick Launch bar, click **BuyerTasks** to redisplay the **BuyerTasks** page.

9 On the left side of the page in the **Actions** section, click **Modify settings and columns**.

The Customize Buyer Tasks page appears.

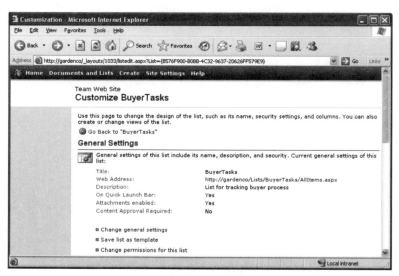

10 In the **General Settings** section, click **Change general settings**.

The List Settings: BuyerTasks page appears.

11 In the **Name** text box, replace *BuyerTasks* with Common Buyer Tasks (including spaces).

12 Scroll to bottom of the page and click the **OK** button to save the change.

The Customize Common Buyer Tasks page is displayed.

13 At the top of the page, click **Go Back to "Common Buyer Tasks"** to redisplay the **Common Buyer Tasks** page.

The bold title at the top of this page and all other pages associated with this list now reflects the modified display name. However, you can see that the browser's address bar still reflects the initial name (internal name) given to this list.

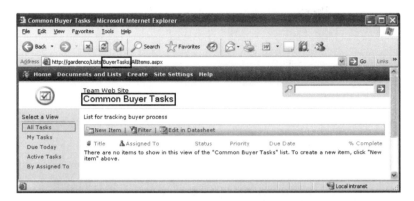

14 On the top link bar, click **Home** to display the **Home** page for the site.

The Quick Launch bar displays the new **Common Buyer Tasks** display name.

CLOSE the browser.

Adding, Editing, and Deleting List Items

Creating a SharePoint list generates the pages needed to view the list, view a *list item*, add a new list item, and edit an existing list item. The interface also provides options to delete a list item, subscribe to an *alert* for the list or a list item, and other options, such as the import and export of list items.

See Also For more information about subscribing to alerts, see the section "Setting Up Alerts" later in this chapter. For more information about importing and exporting list items, refer to Chapter 11, "Using Windows SharePoint Services with Excel 2003 and Access 2003."

Tip Frequently, multiple list views are generated when a new list is created. The Common Buyer Tasks list, created using the Tasks list template, has the following five list views: All Tasks, My Tasks, Due Today, Active Tasks, and By Assigned To.

You can navigate to a list's default *list view* page by clicking on its name in the Quick Launch bar or by clicking on the link at the top of any *List View Web Part* for that list.

In this exercise, you will add several task list items for the buyers at The Garden Company to use in their buying process, modify one of the list items, and delete another. Mike would also like to get their Public Workshops onto the calendar. So, you will add one recurring event to the Events list.

OPEN the SharePoint site where you previously created the Common Buyer Tasks list, for example: *http://gardenco*. If prompted, type your user name and password, and then click OK.
BE SURE TO verify that you have sufficient rights to alter list items. If in doubt, see the Appendix on page 260.

1 On the Quick Launch bar, click **Common Buyer Tasks**.

2 Click **New Item** to display the **Common Buyer Tasks: New Item** page.

3 In the **Title** text box, type Create vendor SharePoint list.

4 Leave the default values for **Priority**, **Status**, **% Complete**, and **Assigned To** fields.

5 In the **Description** text box, type List for vendor to submit seedlings offered this year.

6 Delete today's date from the **Start Date** text box.

7 Leave the **Due Date** text box empty.

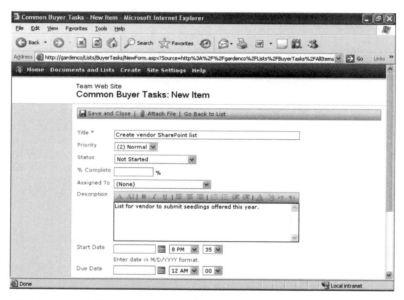

8 Click **Save and Close** to save the list item and redisplay the **Common Buyer Tasks** page.

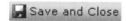

I NEW The newly created list item appears in the body of the page. A small image with an exclamation mark and the word NEW is displayed to the right of the Title text indicating that this list item was recently created.

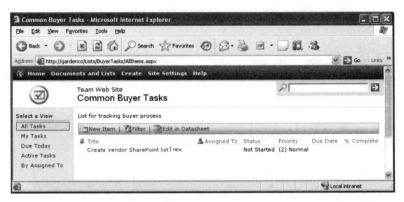

9 Using steps 2 through 8 as a guide, create list items using the values in the following table:

Title	Description
Ensure vendor access	Ensure vendor has access to add a list item for each seedling offered.
Identify seedlings to purchase	Identify which vendor seedlings to purchase.
Generate purchase order	Use Microsoft Word mail merge to generate a purchase order from the filtered list.
Notify Receiving about purchase	Notify Receiving about the anticipated arrival of vendor seedlings.

Tip When you need to create several items for a list, creating one item at a time can get tedious. Instead, you can create multiple list items using a Datasheet view. This option is covered briefly in the following section and covered in detail in Chapter 11, "Using Windows SharePoint Services with Excel 2003 and Access 2003."

Mike suggests that generating the purchase should be changed to a high priority task.

1 To implement Mike's suggestion, move your mouse over the **Generate purchase order** list item, and then click the down arrow that appears.

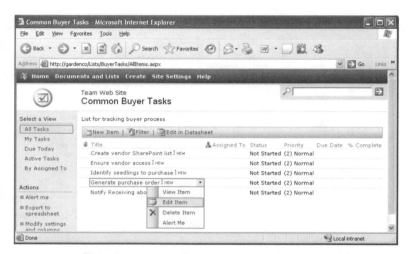

2 In the menu, click **Edit Item** to display the **Common Buyer Tasks: Generate purchase order** page.

3 Change the **Priority** drop-down list from (2) **Normal** to (1) **High**, and then click **Save and Close**.

Mike also suggests that creating the vendor SharePoint list is done only when a new vendor is established rather than for each buying cycle. So, he wants it removed.

4 To implement Mike's suggestion and remove the list item, move your mouse over the **Create vendor SharePoint list** list item, click the down arrow that appears, and then click **Delete Item**.

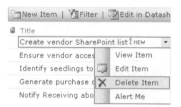

You will be prompted to confirm the deletion.

Tip Once a list item is deleted it cannot be undeleted.

5 Click **OK** to confirm the deletion.

To add a recurring Public Workshop to the Events list, you need to navigate to the Events list.

1 On the top link bar, click **Document and Lists**.

2 In the **Lists** section, click **Events** to display the **Events** list.

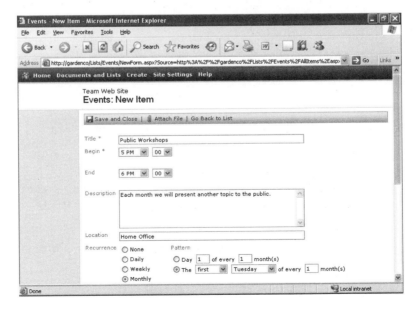

3 Click **New Item** to display the **Events: New Item** page.

4 In the **Title** text box, type Public Workshops.

5 Leave the default value for the **Begin** date but change the time to 5 PM.

6 Leave the **End** date blank but change the time to 6 PM.

The monthly meeting is set to last one hour.

7 In the **Description** text box, type Each month we will present another topic to the public.

8 In the **Location** text box, type Home Office.

9 In the **Recurrence** section, select the **Monthly** option.

Many user interface changes occur when Recurrence is changed from the default of None to Monthly. Note that the dates for Begin and End are removed leaving just the time fields. The Begin date is also moved to the Start Date of the Date Range section.

10 In the **Pattern** section, select **The** first Tuesday **of every** 1 month(s).

11 Leave the default values for all other fields.

    12   Click **Save and Close** to save the list item and redisplay the **Events** page.

CLOSE the browser.

Using the Datasheet View

If you have Microsoft Office 2003 installed, you can use an optional Datasheet view of the list that can be a huge productivity boost. Creating one item at a time requires several clicks and can get tedious. The Datasheet view presents all the list items of a list in a grid and facilitates editing across the entire table. Yet, drop-down lists, checkboxes, and column edits are all still maintained. Using the Datasheet view is a lot like editing a table in Microsoft Access. You can use your cursor keys or your mouse to move from cell to cell to make changes to any row in the list. When you move off of a row, changes are saved automatically. The last row in the datasheet view is used to add additional list items to the list.

An entire task pane on the right edge of the Datasheet view enables powerful integration between Microsoft Windows SharePoint Services, Microsoft Excel 2003, and Microsoft Access 2003.

See Also   For more information about the Datasheet view, refer to Chapter 11. For more information about SharePoint integration with Microsoft Office, refer to both Chapters 10 and 11.

Attaching Files to List Items

Sometimes, you might have one or more documents that you want to attach to a list item. By default, all SharePoint lists allow attachments. However, if every list item has one and only one document, reconsider the use of a list and opt for a document library.

Tip   It is possible to disable attachments to list items. To do this, on the "Change general settings" page for your list, click "Modify settings and columns," click Change general settings, and then click the Disabled option in the Attachments section.

In the following exercise, you will create a simple Microsoft Word document to simulate a purchase order and attach it to an existing list item in the Common Buyer Tasks list.

OPEN the SharePoint site where you previously created the Common Buyer Tasks list, for example *http://gardenco*. If prompted, type your user name and password, and then click OK.
BE SURE TO verify that you have sufficient rights to alter list items. If in doubt, see the Appendix on page 260.

    1   Open Microsoft Word, and then in the blank document, type Purchase Order.

    2   On the **File** menu, click **Save As**. Save the document in the **My Documents** folder on your hard drive and name it GardenCoPurchaseOrder.doc.

3 Close Microsoft Word.

4 In the browser on the Quick Launch bar, click **Common Buyer Tasks**.

The Common Buyer Tasks default list view page is displayed.

5 Move your mouse over the **Generate purchase order** list item, click the down arrow that appears, and then click **Edit Item** to display the **Common Buyer Tasks: Generate purchase order** page.

6 Click **Attach File** to display the page to add attachments.

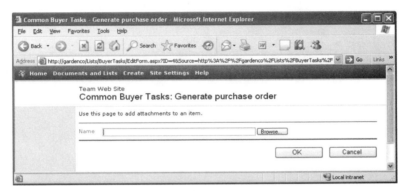

7 Click **Browse** to display the **Choose File** dialog box.

Tip If you use the Choose File dialog box, you might need to navigate to My Documents to find the GardenCoPurchaseOrder.doc that you created earlier in this chapter. Alternatively, type the location of the document to attach in the Name text box.

8 Select GardenCoPurchaseOrder.doc, and then click the **Open** button, or double-click the document to open it.

Once selected, the location of the selected document is displayed in the Name text box.

9 Click **OK** to attach the document to the list item.

The Common Buyer Tasks: Generate purchase order edit page is displayed. The attachment is listed at the bottom of the page. A Delete link also appears that can be used to remove the attachment anytime this page is displayed.

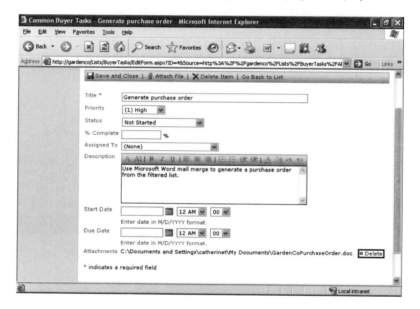

Important At this point, the document is just associated with the list item. Closing the browser or clicking Go Back to List will abandon the attachment.

Tip Multiple attachments are supported on each list item. You may click Attach File repeatedly and attach as many documents as you want. However, the interface only supports attaching a single document at a time.

10 Click **Save and Close** to complete the process of attaching the document to the list item.

The Common Buyer Tasks page is displayed.

Attachment

Each list item in the list that has one or more attachments will be displayed with an attachment icon in the leftmost column.

CLOSE the browser.

Adding, Editing, and Deleting List Columns

The list templates provided by Windows SharePoint Services are a great start to generate a list with very little effort. However, should you need to customize them, Windows SharePoint Services enables you to add, edit, and delete the columns in any list.

A plethora of column types exist when you want to extend a list with an additional column. Once you name your new column, you need to select one of the column types displayed in the following table.

Tip Most, but not all, column types have both Required and Default value options. If Required is set to true, the user must enter a value into the column when creating or editing a list item. If the user doesn't enter a value, the Default value will be used.

Note Because every column type has a Description option and an Add to default view option, these options are not explicitly listed in the table.

Column Type	Used To	Options	Edit Using
Single line of text	Enter a few words	Required Maximum number of characters Default value	Single-line text box
Multiple lines of text	Enter one or more sentences	Required Number of lines to display Allow rich HTML text	Multiple-line text box with a toolbar to edit text
Choice	Select one or more choices from a static list	Required List of choices Display options Allow 'fill-in' choices Default value	Drop-down list, option buttons, or a group of checkboxes
Number	Enter a number	Required Minimum and Maximum values Number of decimal places Default value Show as percentage	Single-line text box
Currency	Enter a monetary value	Required Minimum and Maximum values Number of decimal places Default value Currency format	Single-line text box

Column Type	Used To	Options	Edit Using
Date and Time	Enter date and/or time-of-day	Required Date format Default value	Date text box with a pop-up calendar and drop-down lists for hours and minutes
Lookup	Select one member of the site or list item from a list in the site	Required Get information from In this column Include presence information	Drop-down list
Yes/No	Enter true or false	Default value	A single check box
Hyperlink or Picture	Enter a link to a page or picture	Required Format URL as	Single-line text box
Calculated	Calculate information from columns on this list, columns on another list, dates, or numbers using standard mathematical operators	Formula The data type returned from this formula is	Single-line text box

After you've added a column, you can make some changes to it. You can change the display name but the internal name cannot be changed. Most other column options can be changed even after data has already been entered into the list. If changing an option will potentially result in the loss of information, Windows SharePoint Services will prompt you to confirm the change before proceeding.

Tip You can also change a field from not required to required after data has already been entered. The underlying data is not affected unless someone attempts to edit an existing record. The new required rule is enforced and the list item cannot be saved without providing a value in the required column.

Most columns in the list can be deleted. However, all lists have at least one column that cannot be removed, typically the Title column. Certain lists also prevent the deletion of columns so that the list can display properly or so that they integrate with the Microsoft Office System properly. For example, the Assigned To, Status, and Category columns of any list based on the Issues list template cannot be deleted, and all of the default columns in any list based on the Event list template cannot be deleted.

Five columns are automatically created and cannot be changed: ID, Created, Created By, Modified, and Modified By. The ID column ensures that the list item is unique in the list. It contains a sequential number beginning with 1 and increments by 1 for each new list item. Windows SharePoint Services automatically captures when the list item was created, who it was created by, when it was modified, and who it was modified by. Initially, the Created and the Modified columns are equal, as are the Created By and Modified By columns.

In the following exercise, you will enhance the Common Buyer Tasks list by adding a Sequence column, by editing the Priority column to include an additional option, and by deleting the % Complete column. Finally, you will change the order of the columns on the New, Display, and Edit pages to show the Description column immediately after the Title column.

OPEN the SharePoint site where you previously created the Common Buyer Tasks list, for example, *http://gardenco*. If prompted, type your user name and password, and then click OK.
BE SURE TO verify that you have sufficient rights to manage the list. If in doubt, see the Appendix on page 260.

1   On the Quick Launch bar, click **Common Buyer Tasks**.

2   On the left side of the page in the **Actions** section, click **Modify settings and columns**.

The Customize Common Buyer Tasks page appears.

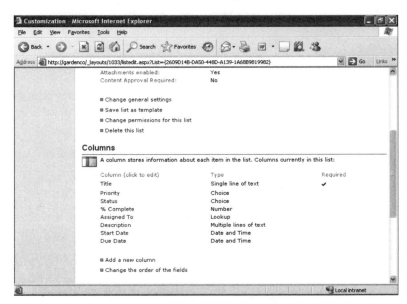

3   In the **Columns** section, click **Add a new column** to display the **Common Buyer Tasks: Add Column** page.

4   In the **Column name** text box, type Sequence.

5 In the list of column types, click **Number**.

6 In the **Description** text box, type Used to order tasks..

7 Leave the default values for the rest of the column's settings.

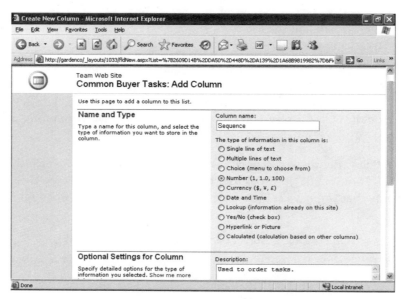

8 Scroll to the bottom of the page, and click **OK** to finish adding the **Sequence** column to the list.

The Customize Common Buyer Tasks page is displayed.

The buyers commonly have some tasks that are very low on the task list and would like to add an option to the Priority column to reflect this. They typically use Medium rather than Normal to rank their tasks and they would like to allow people to enter priorities other than High, Medium, Low, or Very Low.

1 To edit the settings for the existing column, in the **Columns** section, click **Priority**.

2 In the **Type each choice on a separate line** text box, type (4) Very Low as the last line to add an additional option to the drop-down list.

3 In the **Type each choice on a separate line** text box, replace (2) Normal with (2) Medium in the second line to alter the existing option in the drop-down list.

Tip Any list items that previously had the option (2) Normal chosen will need to be manually changed to the new option, (2) Medium. Also, if you don't change the Type each choice on a separate line text box, the Default value will change to the first choice on the list, (1) High in this case. If you want the Default value to remain as the second option, you need to type (2) Medium into the Default value text box. For this exercise, you can use the default (1) High.

4   In the **Allow 'Fill-in' choices** column, click **Yes** to allow values that are not included in the column's list of choices to be entered.

Tip   Optionally, choose to display the choices using the Radio Buttons option or "Checkboxes (allow multiple selections)" option. Selecting the Checkboxes option will allow multiple values to be selected.

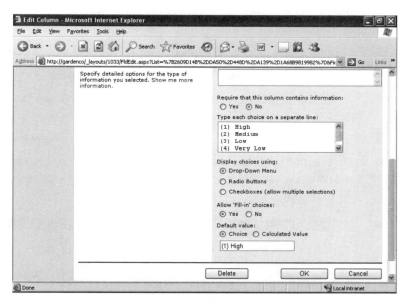

5   Click **OK** to save changes to the **Priority** column.

The Customize Common Buyer Tasks page is displayed.

The buyers don't plan on using the % Complete column, so it can be deleted. In the next part of the exercise, you will delete this column from the list.

1   In the **Columns** section, click **% Complete** to delete the existing column.

2   At the bottom of the page, click **Delete** to initiate deletion of the **% Complete** column from the list and display the deletion confirmation dialog.

A dialog box appears, asking you if you're sure you want to delete the column.

3   Click **OK** to delete the **% Complete** column.

The Customize Common Buyer Tasks page is displayed.

When creating or editing list items, the buyers would like to show the Description column immediately after the Title column. In the next part of the exercise, you will change the order of the columns displayed on the New, Display, and Edit pages.

1 In the **Columns** section, click **Change the order of the fields**.

2 To the right of the **Description** column, select **2** from the drop-down list to change the sequence of the fields so that the **Description** column comes immediately after the **Title** column.

3 Click **OK** to save the sequence change.

The Customize Common Buyer Tasks page is displayed.

4 At the top of the page, click **Go Back to "Common Buyer Tasks"** to return to the default list view page.

5 Click **New Item** to display the **Common Buyer Tasks: New Item** page.

6 On the modified **Common Buyer Tasks: New Item** page, verify that the order of the columns has changed and the Description column comes immediately after the Title column.

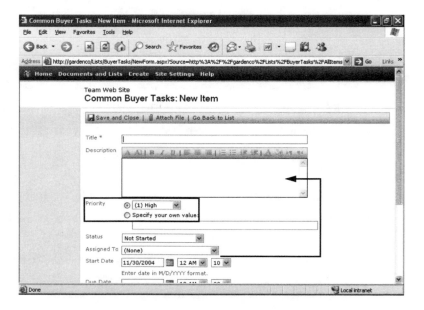

CLOSE the browser.

Sorting and Filtering a List

As the list grows, it eventually becomes difficult to see the entire list on a single page. To this end, Windows SharePoint Services provides built-in sorting and filtering capabilities. On any standard list view page, individual column headers can be used to alphabetically sort the entire list, first ascending and then descending.

Filtering on the list view page works similar to the way Microsoft Excel auto-filter works. Once the filter is enabled, a unique list of the values for each column is generated and presented as a drop-down list above each column. The filters are cumulative.

Tip   In the Datasheet view, sorting and filtering are available from the drop-down arrow on the top right corner of every column.

In this exercise, you will sort and filter the Common Buyer Tasks list.

OPEN the SharePoint site where you previously created the Common Buyer Tasks list, for example, *http://gardenco*. If prompted, type your user name and password, and then click OK.
BE SURE TO verify that you have sufficient rights to view the list. If in doubt, see the Appendix on page 260.

1   On the Quick Launch bar, click **Common Buyer Tasks**.

2   Edit each list item as indicated in the following table:

Title	Sequence
Ensure vendor access	1
Notify Receiving about purchase	2
Identify seedlings to purchase	3
Generate purchase order	4

3   Move the mouse over the **Sequence** column and wait for about a second.

The column will be immediately underlined and a ToolTip will appear that reads Sort by Sequence.

4   Click on the **Sequence** column.

↓
Ascending Sort

A down arrow icon is displayed to the right of the column name, and the list items are displayed in ascending numerical order.

5   Click on the **Sequence** column again.

↑
Descending Sort

An up arrow icon appears to the right of the column name, and the list items are displayed in descending numerical order.

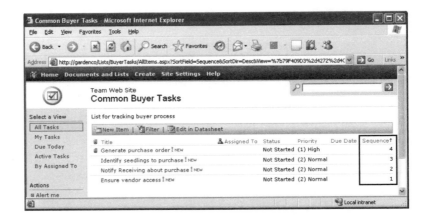

Tip Clicking on another column will abandon the sort on the current column. You must use a list view to get more than one column sorted.

6 Click **Filter**.

Drop-down menus above each column are displayed.

7 In the drop-down above **Priority**, click **(1) High**.

The page immediately redisplays the filtered list with only those list items that are set to a high priority.

Filtered

The Filtered icon appears to the right of each column that has an auto-filter applied.

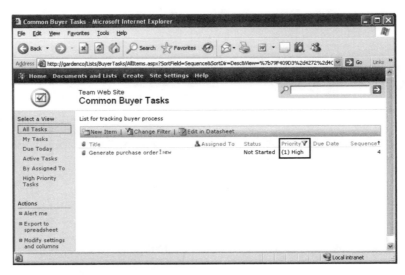

8 Click **Change Filter**.

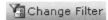

The list is redisplayed with drop-down menus above each column so that additional columns can be filtered.

Tip   To return to a full list, either click on one of the list views to the left of the page or return all filter to (All).

CLOSE the browser.

Adding and Modifying a List View

Sorting and filtering directly on a list view page's columns is only temporal. However, you can use the list views to provide permanent definition of how the information in the list is displayed. List views define which columns to show in a list and in what sequence these columns are displayed. The sequence is defined from left to right. They may also define the order of rows to be presented, which rows to reveal, and how the list items will be grouped, totaled, styled, and paginated. List views can be created using one of the three starter views defined in the following table.

Starter View	Description
Standard View	View data in a standard table and easily switch to Datasheet View.
Datasheet View	View data in an editable spreadsheet and easily switch to Standard View.
Calendar View	View data in a calendar format and easily switch from day view, to week view, and to month view.

Every time a new list view is created for a specific list, it begins as one of these starter views. Once created, it is placed to the left of the page with the other list views.

There are two kinds of list views: Public and Personal. *Public* list views can be seen by everyone that can view the list, whereas, *Personal* list views can be viewed only by the creator. Readers and contributors cannot create Public list views. Everyone can create their own personal list views on a list.

In this exercise, you will create a Public list view called *High Priority Tasks* for the buyers to see only the tasks that are currently set to a (1) High priority along with their current status. You will use the Datasheet view starter so that all the list items can be easily updated simultaneously.

OPEN the SharePoint site where you previously created the Common Buyer Tasks list, for example, *http://gardenco*. If prompted, type your user name and password, and then click OK.
BE SURE TO verify that you have sufficient rights to manage the list. If in doubt, see the Appendix on page 260.

1   On the Quick Launch bar, click **Common Buyer Tasks** to display the **Common Buyer Tasks** page in standard view.

2 On the left side of the page in the **Actions** section, click **Modify settings and columns** to display the **Customize Buyer Tasks** page.

3 At the bottom of the page in the **Views** section, click **Create a new view**.

The Common Buyer Tasks: Create View page appears.

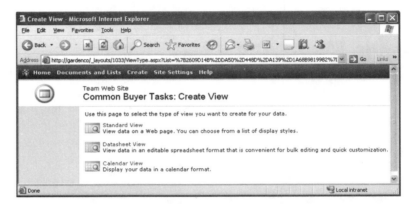

4 Click **Datasheet View** so that the new list view has an editable spreadsheet as its default view and displays the **Common Buyer Tasks: Create Datasheet View** page.

5 In the **View Name** text box, type HighPriorityTasks.

6 In the **Audience** section, verify that **Create a Public View** is selected.

7 Uncheck all check boxes in the **Display** column except the **Title (linked to item with edit menu)** column and the **Status** column.

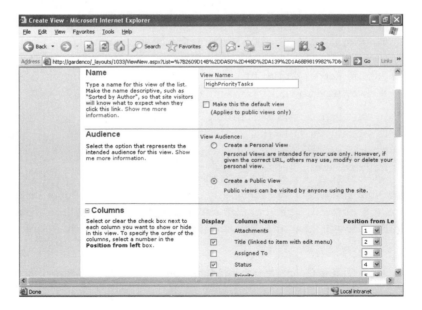

The Title column is currently set to 2 and the Status column is currently set to 4. Therefore, the Title column will be displayed before the Status column.

Tip There are three Title columns listed in the Columns section. They all represent the same value, but each one is displayed in a special way. The selected "Title column: Title (linked to item with edit menu)" not only shows the text value of the Title column but also includes a drop-down menu that can be accessed by moving your mouse over the text and clicking on the down arrow. "Title (linked to item)", currently unselected and at the bottom of the Columns section, simply presents the text value in the Title column as a link to the View page for each list item. And finally, the actual Title column, also currently unselected, is just like any other column; it shows only the text captured for the Title column for each list item.

8 In the **Sort** section in the **First sort by the column** drop-down list, click **Sequence** to order the list using the value in the **Sequence** column.

By default, it appears in ascending order.

9 In the **Filter** section in the **Show the items when column** drop-down list, click **Priority** to set up a row filter.

10 Leave **is equal to** as the selected option for the filter condition.

11 In the text box just below the filter condition, type (1) High.

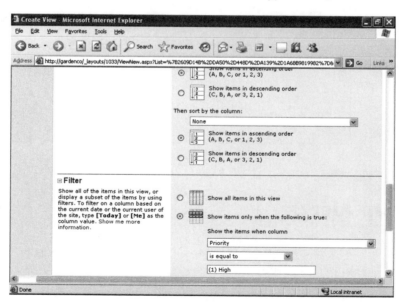

12 Click **OK** to save the list view and redisplay the **Customize Common Buyer Tasks** page.

Now that the list view has been created you can go back and change the display name.

1   At the bottom of the page in the **Views** section, click **HighPriorityTasks** to display the **Common Buyer Tasks: Edit Datasheet View** page.

2   In the **View Name** text box, replace HighPriorityTasks with High Priority Tasks (including spaces) to change the name that is displayed at the left of the list view page.

3   Scroll to the bottom of the page, and then click **OK** to redisplay the **Customize Common Buyer Tasks** page.

4   Near the top of the page, click **Go Back to "Common Buyer Tasks"** to return to the default list view page for the list.

5   On the left side of the page, click on **High Priority Tasks** to display the list using the rules that we established in this exercise.

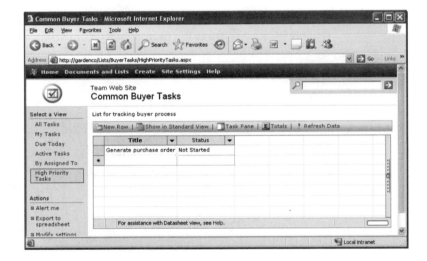

CLOSE the browser.

Setting Up Alerts

Windows SharePoint Services includes a handy feature that sends an e-mail notification whenever changes are made to site content, including changes made to list items in a list. The setup for an e-mail notification is called an alert. No alerts are set up automatically, so you must sign up for the alerts you want.

Alerts are quite easy to set up. Every list in a SharePoint site displays an Alert Me link in the Actions section at the left of the page. By clicking on this link, you can subscribe to a list level alert. A similar Alert Me option is available when viewing any list item in the list. As you might suspect, with this link you can subscribe to a list item level alert.

Alerts specify to whom the alert is sent and the kind of changes and frequency for which the alert is sent. By default, the alert is sent to the e-mail address of the user setting up the alert. If no e-mail address has been established for the authenticated user, the Send Alerts To section prompts for one. Once provided, the e-mail address will be remembered for subsequent subscriptions. Should the e-mail address provided need to be changed later, a link called "Change my e-mail address" is included in the Send Alerts To section.

You have some choices when setting up alerts as to the type of change that you want to be alerted about. List level alerts allow subscriptions for All Changes to any list item changes or alternatively for Added items only, Changed items only, or Deleted items only. If you want to see added items and changed items but not deleted items, you need to set up two alerts. List item level alerts, on the other hand, allow alerts only for Changed items. This is logical because you can only set up this alert once the list item already exists; a deletion is considered a change to the list item.

Tip Document libraries support the additional ability to set up alerts when Web discussion updates occur. For more information about document libraries, refer to Chapters 5 and 6.

You must also specify the alert frequency. You have three choices for any type of alert: Send e-mail immediately, Send a daily summary, or Send a weekly summary. Choosing to receive an alert immediately queues the notice to be sent as soon as the next job runs or whenever the alert is triggered. By default, the alert job runs every five minutes but could be configured by your administrator to wait as long as 59 minutes. The daily and weekly summary stores all changes made to the list or the list item and sends a summary at the end of the period chosen. By default, daily summary alerts are generated at midnight each night and weekly summary alerts are generated at midnight on Sunday night each week.

Lists created using the Issues list template have an additional, special alert that can be enabled at the bottom of the general list settings for the list. When enabled, a supplementary notice is sent to the user in the Assigned To column of the issue whenever the list item is changed.

Tip Administrators of the SharePoint environment can establish quotas for the total number of alerts that any user can subscribe to. By default, this quota is set to 50. This number can be changed or even set to unlimited. Alerts can also be turned off entirely.

You can view and manage all of the alerts that you have previously set up using the "View my existing alerts on this site" link in the Alert Frequency section instructions. To add or delete alerts, you can use the Add Alerts or Delete Selected Alerts links.

Important Alerts must be manually deleted when users are removed from a site, otherwise the alerts are orphaned. Also, if a user has set up alerts for themselves, they will continue to receive them even if they are removed from access to the list. It is important to delete these alerts to prevent unauthorized users from having access to site and user information.

In this exercise, you will create a new alert that notifies you of all changes to the Common Buyer Tasks list. After testing the alert, you will delete it.

OPEN the SharePoint site where you previously created the Common Buyer Tasks list, for example, *http://gardenco*. If prompted, type your user name and password, and then click OK.
BE SURE TO verify that you have sufficient rights to manage the list. If in doubt, see the Appendix on page 260.

1 On the Quick Launch bar, click **Common Buyer Tasks**.

2 On the left side of the page in the **Actions** section, click **Alert me** to display the **New Alert: Common Buyer Tasks: All items** page.

3 Leave the default settings of **All changes** and **Send e-mail immediately**.

4 Click **OK** to create the e-mail alert and return to the **Common Buyer Tasks** page.

Important   If your server is not configured to send e-mail, an Error page appears. If this page appears, you will not be able to complete the rest of the steps in this exercise.

5 Edit the **Notify Receiving about purchase** item, and then change the **Priority** to **(1) High**. Be sure to click **Save and Close** after making the change.

6 After a few minutes, you should receive an e-mail message that looks like the following:

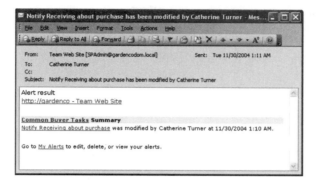

Now you will delete the alert.

7   On the **Common Buyer Tasks** page on the left side of the page in the **Actions** section, click **Alert me** to display the **New Alert: Common Buyer Tasks: All items** page.

8   In the **Alert Frequency** section, click **View my existing alerts on this site** to display the **My Alerts on this Site** page.

9   Add a check mark next to **Common Buyer Tasks: All items**.

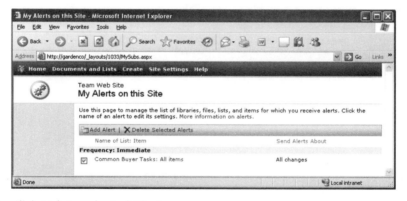

10   Click **Delete Selected Alerts**.

✗ Delete Selected Alerts

The "Are you sure you want to delete this alert?" dialog box is displayed.

11   Click **OK** to confirm the deletion.

CLOSE the browser.

Delete a List

It is important to know how to get rid of an obsolescing list or perhaps one created in error. But be forewarned, deleting a list permanently removes the list and all the list items contained within it. Once it's gone, it's gone. There is no recycle bin.

That said, The Garden Company buyers are happy with their new Common Buyer Tasks task list and no longer need the Tasks task list that was created when the site was originally provisioned. In this exercise, you will delete the surplus list.

OPEN the SharePoint site where you previously created the Common Buyer Tasks list, for example, *http://gardenco*. If prompted, type your user name and password, and then click OK.
BE SURE TO verify that you have sufficient rights to delete the list. If in doubt, see the Appendix on page 260.

1 On the Quick Launch bar, click **Tasks**.

2 On the left side of the page in the **Actions** section, click **Modify settings and columns** to display the **Customize Tasks** page.

3 In the **General Settings** section, click **Delete this list**.

The "Are you sure you want to delete this list?" dialog box is displayed.

4 Click **OK** to confirm the deletion.

The Documents and Lists page appears. The Tasks list is no longer shown on the Documents and Lists page.

CLOSE the browser.

Key Points

■ Lists are like editable, Web-based tables.

■ List templates can be used to generate a new list with a static set of default columns. There are 14 built-in, default list templates: Agenda, Announcements, Contacts, Custom List, Custom List in a Datasheet, Decisions, Events, Import Spreadsheet, Issues, Links, Objectives, Tasks, Text Box, and Things To Bring.

■ You can create SharePoint lists using descriptive, easy to remember, consistent names.

■ One or more documents can be optionally attached to a list item.

■ With Windows SharePoint Services, you can add, edit, and delete the columns in any list.

■ List views define how the list items in the list are displayed. Lists can be sorted and filtered manually or through the use of named list views.

■ Public list views can be seen by everyone, whereas Personal list views can only be seen by their creator.

■ You can create alerts for a list when you want to know that an item in a list has been changed.

■ Deleting a list permanently removes the list and all the list items from the site.

Create document, form, and picture libraries, page 92

Add documents to a library, page 97

View document versions, page 104

Get alerted when a document changes, page 108

Chapter 5 at a Glance

5 Creating and Managing Libraries

In this chapter you will learn to:

✔ Create libraries.

✔ Add documents.

✔ Add pictures.

✔ Create a new folder in a library.

✔ Check documents in and out from the document library.

✔ Check documents in and out from Office 2003.

✔ Work with version history.

✔ Delete documents.

✔ Use alerts.

One of the most compelling features Microsoft Windows SharePoint Services provides is *libraries*. Libraries are a great place to store documents or forms. In a business, being able to quickly and effectively find and access information in documents is of paramount importance. You learned in the previous chapters that lists are a great way to work with structured data; libraries function similarly for unstructured data like Word documents. With SharePoint document libraries, you can filter and group documents, as well as see metadata for documents stored in the library.

In this chapter and the next, you will learn how to work with documents in SharePoint Services. This chapter focuses on creating libraries, adding documents and pictures to them, and working with documents in document libraries. In Chapter 6, "Managing Libraries," we will focus on modifying and configuring document libraries; you will use the libraries and views created in this chapter's exercises for the exercises in Chapter 6.

See Also Do you need only a quick refresher on the topics in this chapter? See the Quick Reference entries on pages xxi–xxiv.

 Important Before you can use the practice files provided for this chapter, you need to install them from the book's companion CD to their default locations. See "Using the Book's CD-ROM" on page vii for more information.

Important Remember to use your SharePoint site location in place of *http://gardenco* in the exercises.

91

Creating Libraries

You can use libraries to store your documents on a SharePoint site rather than on your local computer's hard drive so that other employees can more easily find and work with them. Libraries are similar to lists, but they are used instead to store files. Like lists, libraries have metadata, which lets you easily filter, sort, and group items in the libraries.

Creating Document Libraries

When you create a new SharePoint site, a generic *document library* called *Shared Documents* is created for you. You might not want to use this library because it lacks a descriptive name. Instead, you should create new libraries for a particular category or subject of your business. For instance, in the examples used in this book, Catherine Turner of The Garden Company could create a document library for documents describing the different plant types that the company carries, or one for company newsletters. You want to make sure that the name of a document library is descriptive and that each library has a specific topic to make it easier to find the documents. Storing all documents together in the Shared Documents document library defeats the purpose of using SharePoint sites to make information easier to find.

In this exercise, you will open your SharePoint site and create a new document library called *Plant Descriptions*.

OPEN the SharePoint site in which you'd like to create a document library. If prompted, type your user name and password, and then click OK.
BE SURE TO verify that you have sufficient rights to create a document library. If in doubt, see the Appendix on page 260.

1 On the top link bar, click **Create**.

The Create Page page appears.

2 In the **Document Libraries** section, click **Document Library**.

The New Document Library page is displayed.

3 In the **Name** box, type the name that you want to give the document library, for example Plant Descriptions.

4 In the **Description** box, type the description of the document library, for example Contains 1-page descriptions of each plant we carry.

5 In the **Create a version each time you edit a file in this document library?** section, select **Yes**.

Leave all other areas of the page on their default settings. You have entered all the information necessary to create a document library.

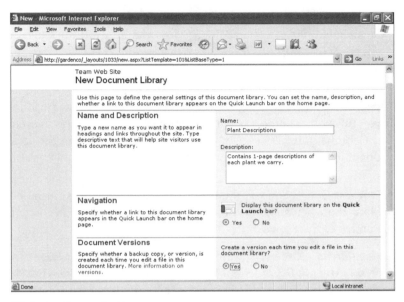

6 Click the **Create** button.

The new *Plant Descriptions* document library appears.

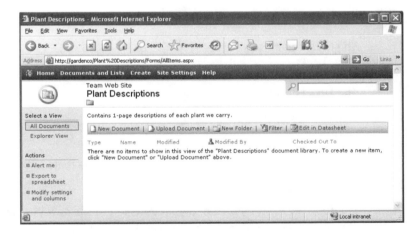

CLOSE Internet Explorer.

Creating Form Libraries

Form libraries function similarly to document libraries, but store specific types of documents—forms—and have enhanced integration with Microsoft InfoPath, such as allowing you to create form libraries from InfoPath. On the companion CD, see the

"Using Windows SharePoint Services with InfoPath 2003" document, which discusses in detail how Windows SharePoint Services and InfoPath work together.

Forms are a more structured type of information. They have a set of fields that are filled out in a uniform manner. Form libraries are excellent for structured documents, such as Purchase Orders or Vacation Requests. To get the full benefit from *form libraries*, you need to use InfoPath for designing and filling out forms. The following exercise walks you through creating a new form library by using Windows SharePoint Services. On the companion CD, see the "Using Windows SharePoint Services with InfoPath 2003" document to see how to create a new form library from within InfoPath.

In this exercise, you will open the SharePoint site and create a new form library called *Purchase Orders*. You will then associate a Purchase Order form template with that library so when someone fills out the form, they will be presented with the standard Purchase Order form.

USE the practice file *Purchase Order Template.xsn* in the practice file folder for this chapter. The practice file folder is located in the *My Documents\Microsoft Press\SharePoint Services SBS\Chapter 05* folder.
OPEN the SharePoint site in which you'd like to create a form library. If prompted, type your user name and password, and then click OK.
BE SURE TO verify that you have sufficient rights to create a form library. If in doubt, see the Appendix on page 260.

1   On the top link bar, click **Create**.

     The Create Page page appears.

2   In the **Document Libraries** section, click **Form Library**.

     The New Form Library page appears.

3   In the **Name** box, type Purchase Orders.

4   In the **Description** box, type Contains purchase orders..

     You have entered all the information necessary to create a form library.

5   Click the **Create** button.

     The form library is created and you are taken to the new Purchase Orders form library. However, at this point, if you click Fill Out This Form, you will be presented with a blank form. You still need to associate a necessary form template with the newly created library.

6   In the **Select a View:** section on the left side of the page, click **Explorer View**.

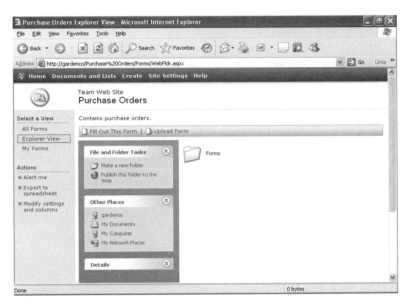

7 Double-click the **Forms** folder.

8 Copy Purchase Order Template.xsn from the practice file folder to the **Forms** folder by dragging the file into the **Purchase Orders** window.

9 In the **Actions** section on the left side of the page, click **Modify Settings and Columns**.

The Customize Purchase Orders page appears.

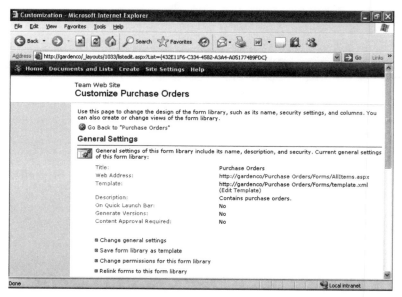

10 In the **General Settings** section, click the **Change General Settings** link.

11 In the **Form Template** section at the bottom of the page, replace *Purchase Orders /Forms/template.xml* with Purchase Orders/Forms/Purchase Order Template.xsn.

12 Click **OK**, and then click **Go Back to "Purchase Orders"**.

You are taken back to the Purchase Orders library. The form library is now ready to be used. If you click on Fill Out This Form and have InfoPath installed, you can fill out a new Purchase Order.

CLOSE Internet Explorer.

Tip   If you have InfoPath, you can also create a new Forms Library directly from InfoPath by going to the File menu and selecting Publish. From there, follow the wizard. Refer to the "Using Windows SharePoint Services with InfoPath 2003" document on the companion CD for detailed instructions.

Creating Picture Libraries

Picture libraries work the same way as document libraries, except they are optimized for storing the picture file type. The picture library provides special views for looking at all of the pictures in the library as a slideshow. It also provides enhanced features for editing and downloading pictures using integration with Microsoft Office Picture Manager.

In this exercise, you will open the SharePoint site and create a Picture Library for storing photographs of each employee.

OPEN the SharePoint site in which you'd like to create a Picture Library. If prompted, type your user name and password, and then click OK.

BE SURE TO verify that you have sufficient rights to create a Picture Library. If in doubt, see the Appendix on page 260.

1 On the top link bar, click **Create**.

The Create Page page appears.

2 In the **Picture Libraries** section, click **Picture Library**.

The New Picture Library page appears.

3 In the **Name** box, type Employee Photos.

4 In the **Description** box, type Contains photographs of each employee.

You have entered all the information necessary to create a picture library.

5 Click the **Create** button.

The picture library is created and you are taken to the new Employee Photos picture library.

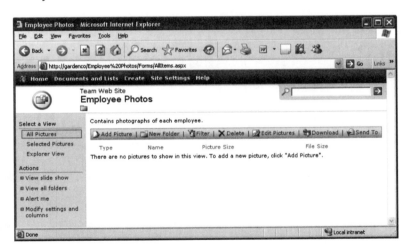

CLOSE Internet Explorer.

Adding Documents

Document libraries without any content in them are not very useful. After a library has been created, you can populate it with content. Once documents are in the library, you can search for and filter them to make it easier to find what you are looking for. Document libraries also give you the ability to track changes that happen in a document and revert to older versions if necessary. These topics will be covered in the next chapter, but first, you need to make sure your documents are available in the SharePoint library.

In this exercise you will make two new plant descriptions available to employees by uploading them to the Plant Descriptions library.

USE the practice files *WaterOak.doc* and *NeedlepointHolly.doc* in the practice file folder for this chapter. The practice file folder is located in the *My Documents\Microsoft Press\SharePoint Services SBS \Chapter 05 folder.*
OPEN the SharePoint site to which you'd like to upload a file to a document library. If prompted, type your user name and password and click OK.

1   On the top link bar, click **Documents and Lists**.

2   In the **Document Libraries** section, click the name of the document library you would like to upload a document to, for example **Plant Descriptions**.

The Plant Descriptions document library appears.

3   Click **Upload Document**.

> ⬆ Upload Document

The Plant Descriptions: Upload Document page appears.

4   Click the **Browse** button.

5   In the **Choose File** dialog box, browse to the file you would like to upload, for example *WaterOak.doc*, and then click **Open**.

6   Click **Save and Close**.

> 💾 Save and Close

You are taken back to the Plant Descriptions library.

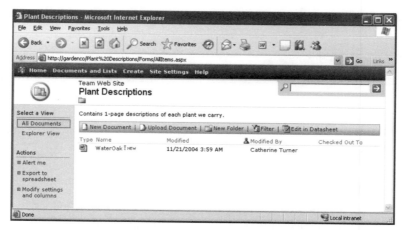

7   Repeat Steps 3–6 for the *NeedlepointHolly.doc* file.

CLOSE Internet Explorer.

> **Tip** You can also upload a document by copying and pasting using Windows Explorer and using the Explorer View in Windows SharePoint Services (on the left side of the document library page).

Adding Pictures

Adding pictures to a picture library is much like adding documents to a document library. In this exercise, you will add an employee picture to the Employee Photos document library.

USE the practice file *pjcov.jpg* in the practice file folder for this chapter. The practice file folder is located in the *My Documents\Microsoft Press\SharePoint Services SBS\Chapter 05* folder.
OPEN the SharePoint site that you'd like to use to upload a picture to a picture library. If prompted, type your user name and password, and then click OK.

1 On the top link bar, click **Documents and Lists**.

2 In the **Picture Libraries** section, click the picture library you would like to store a photo in, for example **Employee Photos**.

The Employee Photos document library appears.

 3 Click **Add Picture**.

The Employee Photos: Add Picture page appears.

4 Click the **Browse** button.

5 In the **Choose File** dialog box, browse to the file you would like to upload, for example *pjcov.jpg*, and then click **Open**.

6 Click **Save and Close**.

You are taken back to the Employee Photos library.

CLOSE Internet Explorer.

Creating a New Folder in a Library

When there are numerous documents in a library, you might want to create a new folder for documents to help organize the documents in a better way.

> **Tip** SharePoint Services provides other mechanisms for organization as well, such as Views and Filters, but people are often familiar with folders and it is easiest to create a folder structure. These will be discussed in Chapter 6, "Managing Libraries."

In this exercise, you will create a folder for documents that are classified as In-Progress so they can be differentiated from complete documents.

OPEN the SharePoint site that you'd like to use to add a folder to a document library. If prompted, type your user name and password, and then click OK.

1 On the top link bar, click **Documents and Lists**.

2 In the **Document Libraries** section, click **Plant Descriptions**.

The Plant Descriptions document library appears.

3 Click **New Folder**.

The **Plant Descriptions: New Folder** page appears.

4 In the **Name** Box, type the name of the folder you would like to create, for example In Progress.

5 Click **Save and Close**.

The updated Plant Descriptions page appears with the In Progress folder added to the page.

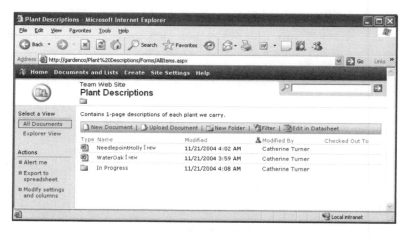

CLOSE Internet Explorer.

Checking Documents In and Out from the Document Library

One of the features that Windows SharePoint Services provides is basic document management. *Checking out* and *checking in* documents lets others know what documents you are working on so they don't work on them at the same time. Check-in also enables you to enter comments about what you've changed, which others can then view.

In this exercise, you will change the comments of a document to reflect that this is the final version of the document.

OPEN the SharePoint site from which you'd like to check a document in or out. If prompted, type your user name and password, and then click OK.

1   On the top link bar, click **Documents and Lists**.

2   In the **Document Libraries** section, click **Plant Descriptions**.

The Plant Descriptions document library appears.

3   Move your mouse over the document you would like to check out, for example *WaterOak.doc*.

An arrow appears to the right of the document name.

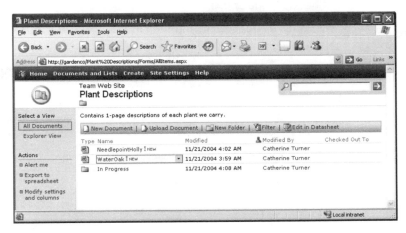

4   Click on the arrow.

A menu of options for working with the document appears.

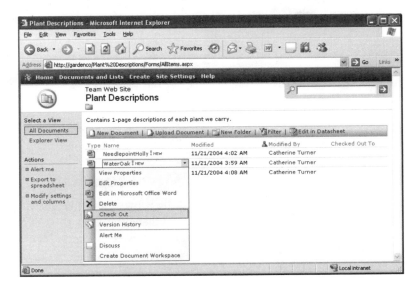

5   Click **Check Out**.

> **Note**   Notice that under the Checked Out To column, your name (*Catherine Turner* in the example) will appear. The document is now checked out to you and, if you want, you can make changes to the document. For this exercise you are just going to check it back in and add the comments.

6   Move your mouse over **WaterOak.doc** and, when the arrow appears to the right of it, click on the arrow.

7   Click **Check In**.

The Check In page appears.

8   Select **Check In Document**, and then in the **Check In comments** box, type This is the final version of this document.

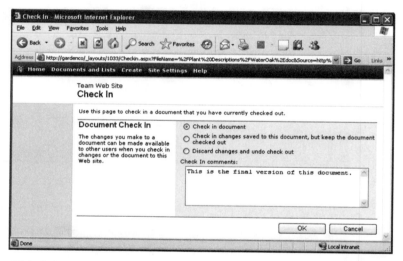

9   Click **OK**.

You are taken back to the Plant Description document library. Notice that under the Checked Out To column, your name (*Catherine Turner* in this exercise) is no longer listed.

CLOSE Internet Explorer.

Checking Documents In and Out from Office 2003

Checking documents in or out using the browser is a nice feature, but not nearly as useful as checking documents in and out using the Microsoft Office System. Office 2003 has built-in SharePoint integration and you can easily check documents in and out using any of the Microsoft Office applications.

In this exercise, you will open a document from a SharePoint library in Word and check it out. You will make minor modifications to the document, save it, and then check it back in to the document library.

OPEN the SharePoint site from which you'd like to check a document in or out. If prompted, type your user name and password, and then click OK.

1 On the top link bar, click **Documents and Lists**.

2 In the **Document Libraries** section, click **Plant Descriptions**.

The Plant Descriptions document library appears.

3 Move your mouse over the document that you would like to edit, for example *WaterOak.doc*, and when the arrow appears to the right of the document name, click the arrow.

4 Select **Edit in Microsoft Office Word**.

5 To open the file, in the dialog box that displays a warning, click **OK**.

The file opens in Microsoft Office Word. You might be presented with a User Name dialog box to enter your name and initials. If so, enter your name and initials.

6 Click **File**, and then click **Check Out**.

B
Bold

7 Select the first instance of *Water Oak* and then by using the Bold button on the Formatting toolbar, change it to bold.

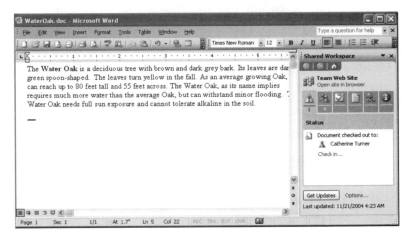

8 Click **File**, and then click **Save**.

9 Click **File**, and then click **Check In**.

10 In the **Check In Comments** dialog box, type This is the copy edited with Microsoft Office Word..

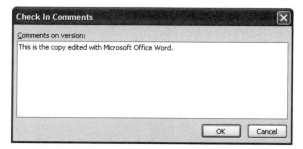

11 Click **OK**, and then close Microsoft Office Word.

CLOSE Internet Explorer.

Working with Version History

When versioning is enabled, Windows SharePoint Services creates a separate copy of the document each time it is edited. While this takes up extra space on the server, it makes it easy to go back to an older version of the document if necessary. A more in-depth discussion of versioning will be covered in Chapter 6, "Managing Libraries."

When you view a document's Version History, you will see a list of times this document was edited and saved as well as the author's comments on those changes. In this exercise, you will see what changes have been made to the WaterOak.doc document, and then revert back to the final copy of the document.

OPEN the SharePoint site for which you'd like to see the version history for a document. If prompted, type your user name and password, and then click OK.

1 On the top link bar, click **Documents and Lists**.

2 In the **Document Libraries** section, click **Plant Descriptions**.

The Plant Descriptions document library appears.

3 Move your mouse over the document for which you want to see the version history, for example *WaterOak.doc*, and when an arrow appears to the right of the document name, click the arrow.

A drop-down menu appears.

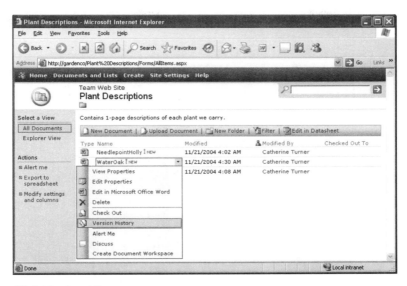

4   Click **Version History**.

You are taken to the Versions saved for WaterOak.doc page. Each version of the document you saved, the date and time that version was created, and any comments for it appears.

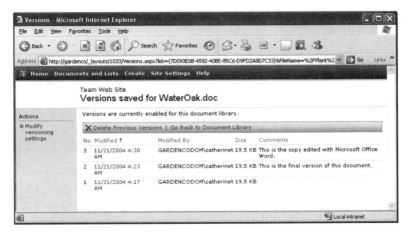

5   Move the mouse over the date of the document where the comments read *This is the final version of this document.*, and then click the arrow that appears.

6   On the drop-down menu, click **Restore**.

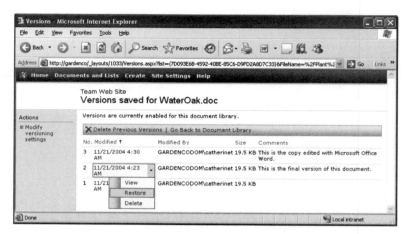

7 In the dialog box indicating that you are about to replace the current version with the selected version, click **OK**.

You will see that there is now an additional version. Windows SharePoint Services actually copies the version you want to restore and makes it the newest version.

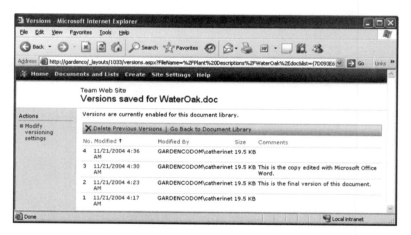

CLOSE Internet Explorer.

Deleting Documents

Over time, documents accumulate and you eventually need to delete those that are no longer needed.

In this exercise, you will delete a document that is no longer in use.

OPEN the SharePoint site from which you'd like to delete a document. If prompted, type your user name and password, and then click OK.

1 On the top link bar, click **Documents and Lists**.

2 In the **Document Libraries** section, click **Plant Descriptions**.

The Plant Descriptions document library appears.

3 Move your mouse over the document you would like to delete, for example *WaterOak.doc*, and when an arrow appears to the right of the document name, click the arrow.

4 On the drop-down menu, click **Delete**.

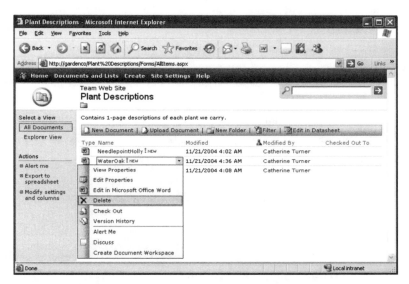

5 In the dialog box that asks if you are sure, click **OK**.

The document is deleted from the Plant Descriptions document library.

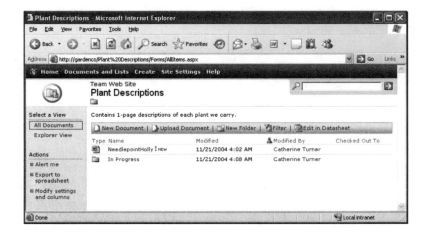

CLOSE Internet Explorer.

Using Alerts

One of the most difficult things in business is knowing when information changes. Windows SharePoint Services helps with this problem by enabling you to subscribe to an *alert*. When a document you subscribe to changes, you will get an e-mail message stating that the document has changed.

For example, you (*Catherine Turner* in the example) may want to know when the document *NeedlepointHolly.doc* is updated. In this exercise, you will set up an alert for this document, and then receive an alert that it has been changed.

OPEN the SharePoint site on which you'd like to have an alert on a document set up. If prompted, type your user name and password, and then click OK.

1 On the top link bar, click **Documents and Lists**.

2 In the **Document Libraries** section, click **Plant Descriptions**.

The Plant Descriptions document library appears.

3 Move your mouse over the document for which you would like an alert, for example *NeedlepointHolly.doc*, and when an arrow appears to the right of the document name, click the arrow.

4 Click **Alert Me**.

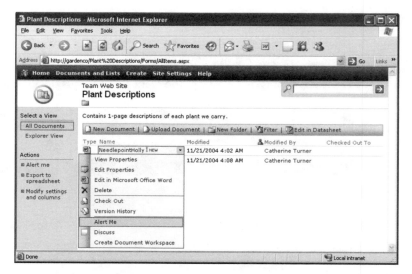

The New Alert: Plant Descriptions: NeedlepointHolly.doc page appears. You are given several options on the frequency of alerts as well as when to be alerted. The default values are fine for this exercise. If the "My e-mail address is" box is blank, type in an e-mail address.

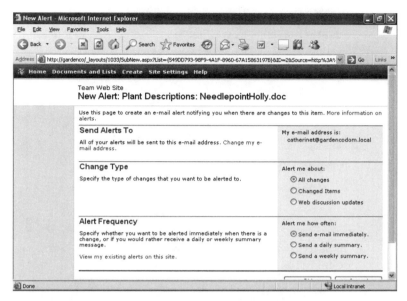

5   Click **OK**.

Important   If your server is not configured to send e-mail message, an Error page will appear. If this page appears, you will not be able to complete the rest of the steps in this section.

You are taken back to the Plant Descriptions document library.

6   Move your mouse over **NeedlepointHolly.doc**, and when an arrow appears to the right of the document name, click the arrow.

7   Select **Edit in Microsoft Office Word**.

8   In the dialog box that appears displaying a warning, click **OK** to open the file.

The file will open in Microsoft Office Word.

9   Click **File**, and then click **Check Out**.

10   Select the first instance of *Needlepoint Holly*, and then by using the Bold button on the Formatting toolbar, change it to bold.

11   Click **File**, and then click **Save**.

12   Click **File**, and then click **Check In**.

13   In the **Check In Comments** dialog box, click **OK**.

14   Close **Microsoft Office Word**.

After a few minutes, you should receive two e-mail messages. The first message indicates that an alert was successfully created and looks like the following:

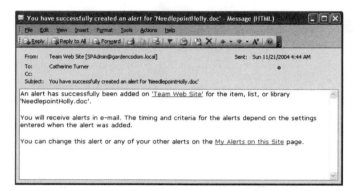

The second message indicates that NeedlepointHolly.doc has been modified and looks like the following:

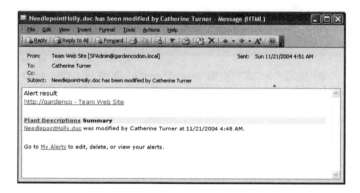

CLOSE Internet Explorer.

Key Points

- Libraries provide a central location to store documents, forms, and pictures so they can be easily shared.

- You can create Document Libraries for very specific topics and give them a descriptive name.

- Remember to check out a document before you edit it.

- You can check documents in and out using Microsoft Office applications.

- Set up alerts on the documents when you want to know that a document has been changed.

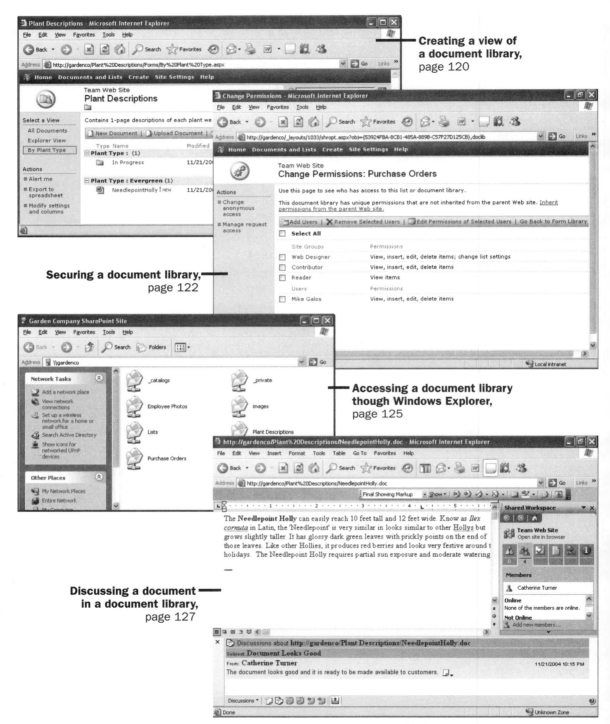

Creating a view of a document library, page 120

Securing a document library, page 122

Accessing a document library though Windows Explorer, page 125

Discussing a document in a document library, page 127

Chapter 6 at a Glance

6 Working with Library Settings

In this chapter you will learn to:
- ✔ Configure a library.
- ✔ Work with library columns.
- ✔ Work with document metadata.
- ✔ Create a view of a document library.
- ✔ Secure a library.
- ✔ Use Web folders to access a Document Library.
- ✔ Use the document discussions functionality.
- ✔ Delete a library.

As we discussed in the last chapter, document libraries are one of the most powerful features of Microsoft Windows SharePoint Services. The additional features available in Windows SharePoint Services—such as versioning, approval, and navigation settings—are what make SharePoint document libraries more compelling than using networked shared folders. You can use SharePoint libraries to store multiple versions of your documents, require approval for documents to be published, and sort and filter content easily.

In this chapter, you will learn how to manage document libraries and enable additional library features. You will learn how to work with a library's columns and document metadata. You will also learn how to create a view of a document library, secure the library, use Web folders to access it, use the document discussions functionality, and delete a library. You will use the document library Plant Descriptions and the form library Purchase Orders created in Chapter 5, "Creating and Managing Libraries," for the exercises in this chapter.

See Also Do you need only a quick refresher on the topics in this chapter? See the Quick Reference entries on pages xxiv–xxvi.

Important Before you can use the practice files and sites provided for this chapter, you need to install them from the book's companion CD to their default locations. See "Using the Book's CD-ROM" on page vii for more information.

Important Remember to use your SharePoint site location in place of *http://gardenco* in the exercises.

Configuring a Library

Each document library has settings you can change from the General Settings page. You can change the library's name and description along with navigation, versioning, and approval settings.

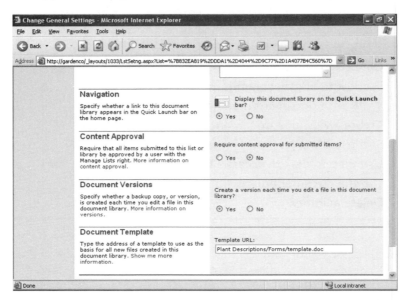

With the Navigation settings, you can specify whether to show a link to your library on the Quick Launch bar on the left side of the home page of the site. Libraries that are not shown on the Quick Launch bar can be accessed using the Documents and Lists link at the top of the home page, but using the Quick Launch bar makes it easier to find your libraries.

With the Document Versions settings, you can turn on or turn off versioning of documents that are stored in the library. If you turn on versioning, each time a document is changed, Windows SharePoint Services saves a copy of each edited version of the document. This enables you to have multiple versions of the same document, so that you can easily see what the document contained before modifications were made and revert to any previous version if need be.

With the Content Approval settings, you can specify whether documents require approval in the library. If you enable Content Approval, you must approve new and modified documents before they appear for other users. The Content Approval setting is useful in situations in which you don't want content showing up for everyone right away. For example, you might want to review vacation requests and approve them before they show up in the library on your site for all employees to see.

In General Settings, you also have the option to specify a default template for the library. If you apply a template, when a user clicks New Document in the library, Windows SharePoint Services opens a document based on this document template for the user.

In this exercise you will make changes to the settings of the Purchase Orders form library you created in Chapter 5, "Creating and Managing Libraries." You have heard from your employees that they have a hard time finding the Purchase Orders library on the site, so you want the link to the library to show up in the Quick Launch bar on the front page of the site. Also, because you are making changes to the library, you decide that you want to approve purchase orders in this library before they appear in the library for other employees to see them.

OPEN the SharePoint site in which you'd like to edit library settings. If prompted, type your user name and password, and then click OK.
BE SURE TO verify that you have sufficient rights to configure a library. If in doubt, see the Appendix on page 260.
BE SURE TO complete the form library creation exercise in Chapter 5 on page 94.
Alternatively, you can create a practice site for this chapter based on site template *Chapter 6 Starter.stp* in the practice file folder for this chapter. The practice file folder is located in the *My Documents \Microsoft Press\SharePoint Services SBS\Chapter 06* folder. See "Using the Book's CD-ROM" on page vii for instructions on how to create a practice site.

1   On the top link bar, click **Documents and Lists**.

2   In the **Document Libraries** section, click **Purchase Orders**.

You are taken to the Purchase Orders form library.

3   Under **Actions**, click **Modify Settings and Columns**.

You are taken to the Customize Purchase Orders page.

4   In the **General Settings** section, click the **Change General Settings** link

5   In the **Navigation** section, select **Yes** to the question *Display this form library on the Quick Launch bar?*.

6   In the **Content Approval** section, select **Yes** to the question *Require content approval for submitted items?*.

7   Click **OK**, and then in the top link bar, click **Home**.

Purchase Orders now is displayed on the Quick Launch bar.

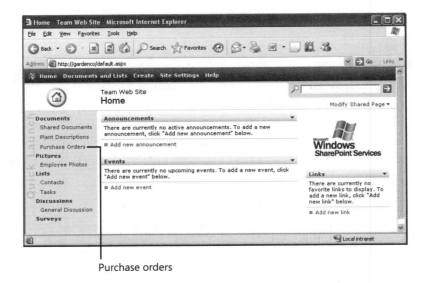

Purchase orders

CLOSE Internet Explorer.

Working with Library Columns

Like lists, library *columns* enable you to enter *metadata* for documents. This metadata can then be used by Document Library views to filter and sort documents. Metadata can also make it easier to find documents and know what type of information a document contains without having to open the document. You need to make sure you have a sufficient number of columns to effectively describe the documents you are working with. For instance, in the *Plant Descriptions* document library you might want columns for Plant Color, Plant Family, and Plant Type. That way, you could quickly find, for example, all *Red* plants in order to narrow down the plants you are looking for.

In this exercise, you will add a column to the Plant Descriptions document library for Plant Type (Deciduous and Evergreen).

OPEN the SharePoint site in which you'd like to add columns to a document library. If prompted, type your user name and password, and then click OK.

BE SURE TO verify that you have sufficient rights to edit document library columns. If in doubt, see the Appendix on page 260.

BE SURE TO complete the document library creation exercise in Chapter 5 on page 92.

Alternatively, you can create a practice site for this chapter based on site template *Chapter 6 Starter.stp* in the practice file folder for this chapter. The practice file folder is located in the *My Documents \Microsoft Press\SharePoint Services SBS\Chapter 06* folder. See "Using the Book's CD-ROM" on page vii for instructions on how to create a practice site.

1 On the top link bar, click **Documents and Lists**.

2   In the **Document Libraries** section, click **Plant Descriptions**.

The Plant Descriptions document library appears.

3   Under **Actions**, click **Modify Settings and Columns**.

The Customize Plant Descriptions page appears.

4   Under **Columns**, click **Add a New Column**.

The Plant Description: Add Column page appears.

5   In the **Column Name** box, type the name of the new column, for example Plant Type.

6   In **The type of information in this column is:** list, select **Choice**.

7   Under **Require that this column contains information:**, select **Yes**.

8   In the **Type each choice on a separate line:** box, delete the text shown.

9   In the **Type each choice on a separate line:** box, type the name for your column, such as Deciduous, and then press Enter.

10   On the next line, type Evergreen.

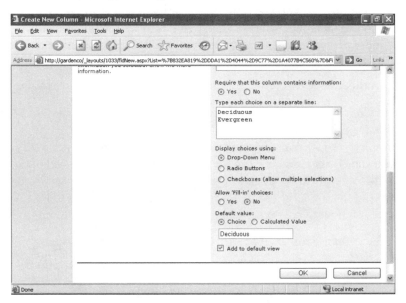

11   Click **OK**, and then click **Go Back to "Plant Description"**.

The new column named *Plant Type* is displayed on the far right.

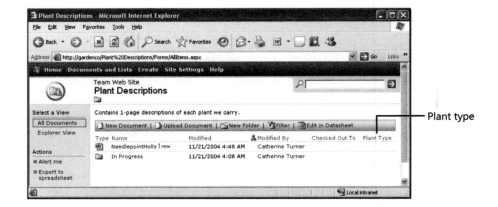

Plant type

CLOSE Internet Explorer.

Working with Document Metadata

When viewing documents in a SharePoint document library, often just seeing the title is not enough to know exactly what the document is about. With SharePoint libraries you can use metadata, which is data that describes the document. Using metadata, you can more easily find a specific document or a document about a specific topic. You can filter and sort documents based on specific metadata.

In this exercise, you will add metadata to the *NeedlepointHolly.doc* document.

OPEN the SharePoint site in which you'd like to apply metadata to a document. If prompted, type your user name and password, and then click OK.
BE SURE TO complete the adding documents exercise in Chapter 5 on page 98.
Alternatively, you can create a practice site for this chapter based on site template *Chapter 6 Starter.stp* in the practice file folder for this chapter. The practice file folder is located in the *My Documents \Microsoft Press\SharePoint Services SBS\Chapter 06* folder. See "Using the Book's CD-ROM" on page vii for instructions on how to create a practice site.

1   On the top link bar, click **Documents and Lists**.

2   In the **Document Libraries** section, click **Plant Descriptions**.

    The Plant Descriptions document library appears.

3   Move your mouse over **NeedlepointHolly.doc**, and then when an arrow appears to the right of the document name, click the arrow.

4   Click **Edit Properties**.

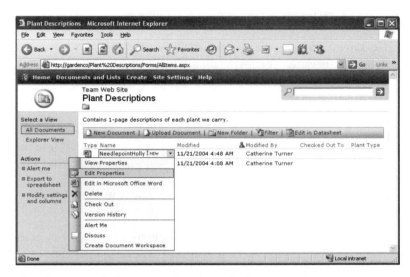

The Plant Descriptions: NeedlepointHolly Page appears.

5 In the **Plant Type** field, select **Evergreen**.

6 Click **Save and Close**.

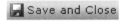

The Plant Descriptions document library appears. Evergreen now shows up under Plant Type for NeedlepointHolly.doc.

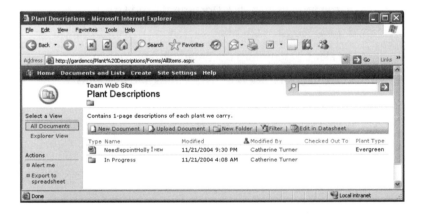

CLOSE Internet Explorer

Creating a View of a Document Library

Document Library *views* are very similar to the list views you learned about in the previous chapter. Views use the metadata on documents to filter, sort, or group documents together, thus making them easier to find. For example, the Plant Descriptions library could have two different views: one that shows only documents pertaining to plants in a particular family, and another that shows the documents sorted by how long the Garden Company has been carrying a specific type of plant. If you are familiar with Microsoft Office Excel, you may think of views like PivotTables that enable you to see different sets of data pivoting on document metadata. Numerous possibilities exist for the views you can have. Bear in mind though these views are based on the document metadata, so make sure you have all the columns you would like to filter, sort, and group documents by.

In this exercise, you will open the SharePoint site and create a view of the Plant Description document library. This view will group plants by their Plant Type field (Evergreen or Deciduous).

OPEN the SharePoint site in which you'd like to create a view of a document library. If prompted, type your user name and password, and then click OK.

BE SURE TO complete the adding documents exercise in Chapter 5 on page 98.

Alternatively, you can create a practice site for this chapter based on site template *Chapter 6 Starter.stp* in the practice file folder for this chapter. The practice file folder is located in the *My Documents \Microsoft Press\SharePoint Services SBS\Chapter 06* folder. See "Using the Book's CD-ROM" on page vii for instructions on how to create a practice site.

1   On the top link bar, click **Documents and Lists**.

2   In the **Document Libraries** section, click **Plant Descriptions**.

    The Plant Descriptions document library appears.

3   Under **Actions**, click **Modify Settings and Columns**.

    The Customize Plant Descriptions page appears.

4   Under **Views**, click **Create a New View**.

    The Plant Description: Create View page appears.

5   Click **Standard View**, and then in the **View Name** box, type a name for the view, such as By Plant Type.

6   Scroll down and expand **Group By**.

    A list of options is displayed to the left of Group By.

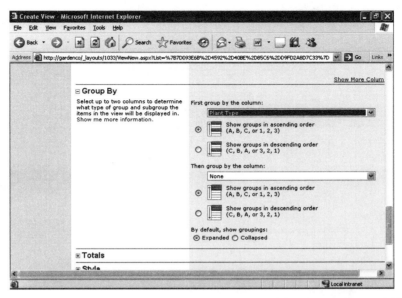

7 From the **First group by the column:** box, select the column you would like to group by, for example **Plant Type**.

8 Click the **OK** button.

The Customize Plant Description page appears.

9 Click **Go Back to "Plant Descriptions"**.

The Plant Descriptions document library appears and in the left pane, a new view called By Plant Type is displayed.

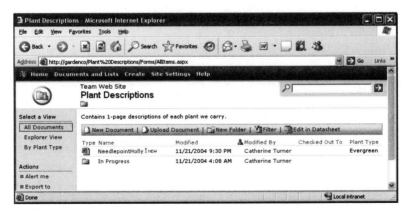

10 Under **Select a View**, click **By Plant Type**.

The Plant Descriptions document library appears, but the view is different. Documents are grouped by the Plant Type property.

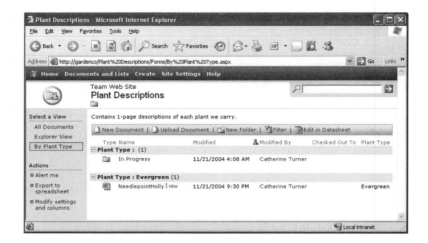

CLOSE Internet Explorer.

Securing a Library

After you have created a library, you might want to grant people more privileges or restrict their privileges. More often than not, you will want to give some people more access rights to a particular library. For instance, Catherine Turner might have given Mike Galos reader permission to the overall site when it was created. However, later she might decide that she wants him to be able to create purchase orders in the Purchase Orders library. Mike currently has only Reader access to this library because that is his overall permissions level on the site. Catherine Turner can give Mike additional access to the Purchase Orders library so that Mike can add new documents. However, Mike isn't required to create documents on the rest of the site, only to read documents.

In this exercise, you will open the SharePoint site, navigate to the *Purchase Orders* form library, and grant a user, such as Mike, access to add and modify Purchase Orders.

OPEN the SharePoint site in which you'd like to secure a document library. If prompted, type your user name and password, and then click OK.
BE SURE TO verify that you have sufficient rights to change document library security. If in doubt, see the Appendix on page 260.
BE SURE TO complete the form library creation exercise in Chapter 5 on page 92.
Alternatively, you can create a practice site for this chapter based on site template *Chapter 6 Starter.stp* in the practice file folder for this chapter. The practice file folder is located in the *My Documents \Microsoft Press\SharePoint Services SBS\Chapter 06* folder. See "Using the Book's CD-ROM" on page vii for instructions on how to create a practice site.

1 On the top link bar, click **Documents and Lists**.

2 In the **Document Libraries** section, click **Purchase Orders**.

The Purchase Orders document library appears.

3 Under Actions, click **Modify Settings and Columns**.

The Customize Purchase Orders page appears.

4 Under **General Settings**, click **Change permissions for this Form Library**.

The Change Permissions: Purchase Orders page appears.

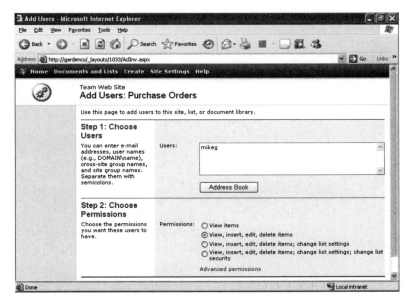

5 Click **Add Users**.

The Add Users: Purchase Orders page appears.

6 In the **Users:** box, type the user name or email address of the user you'd like to grant permissions to, for example, mikeg.

7 Under **Permissions**, select **View, insert, edit, delete items**.

8 Click the **Next** button.

The contents of the Add Users: Purchase Orders page changes.

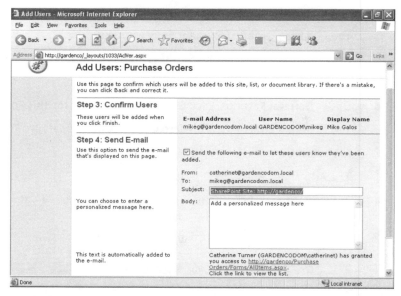

9 Click **Finish**.

Mike is now added as a user and can create and modify Purchase Orders. You are then taken back to the Change Permissions: Purchase Orders page where you can see Mike listed.

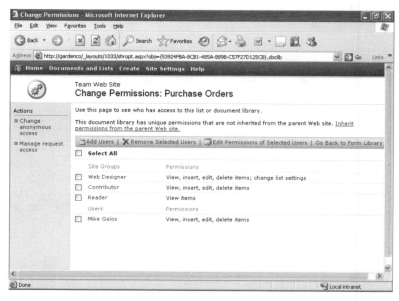

Windows SharePoint Services also sends an e-mail message to Mike to let him know he has been granted the permissions.

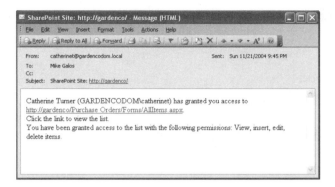

CLOSE Internet Explorer

Using Web Folders to Access a Document Library

Long-time computer users are often more comfortable accessing files and folders in the standard Windows Explorer interface rather than using a Web-based interface. In addition to the Web-based interface, SharePoint document libraries can be connected to using *Web folders*, which are a feature of Windows 2003, Windows XP, and Windows 2000.

In this exercise, you will use Windows Explorer to create a Web folder that points to your SharePoint site. You can then use that Web folder to open a library on the site in the familiar Windows Explorer interface environment.

1   Click **Start**, click **My Computer**, and then on the left side of the screen click **My Network Places**.

The My Network Places window appears.

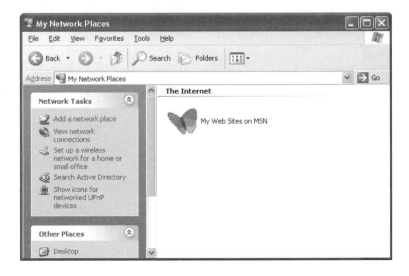

2   If the **Network Tasks** pane appears on the left, click **Add a network place**; otherwise, double-click the **Add Network Place** icon.

The Add Network Place Wizard appears.

3   Click **Next**.

4   Click **Choose another network location**, and then click **Next**.

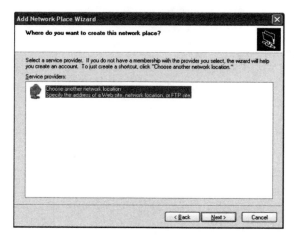

5   In the **Internet or Network Address** box, type the name of your SharePoint site, for example http://gardenco, and then click **Next**.

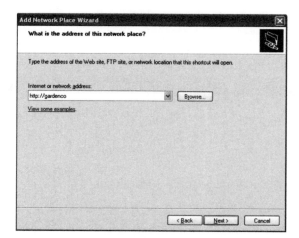

6   In the **Type a name for this network place** box, type the name of your SharePoint site, for example Garden Company SharePoint Site, and then click **Next**.

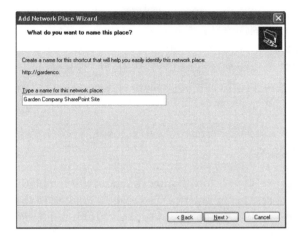

7 Click **Finish**.

The SharePoint site that includes your document libraries appears.

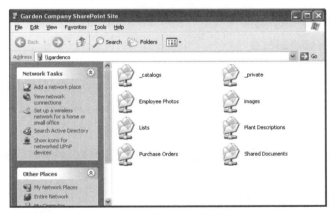

8 Anytime you open My Network Places, you will see the link to Garden Company SharePoint Site.

CLOSE the Garden Company SharePoint Site window.

Tip If you are having a problem accessing the document library using Web folder, make sure the WebClient service is started. If you do not know how to do this, ask your System Administrator.

Using the Document Discussions Functionality

With Windows SharePoint Services, along will Microsoft Office 2003, you can store comments from a document or about a document on your SharePoint server. This is an expansion of Office Server Extensions from previous Office releases, so if you have used Office Server Extensions, you already will be familiar with SharePoint document discussions.

Document discussions functionality enables you to leave comments in a document, or about a document, much like the Comment command in Microsoft Office Word, but stores the discussions on the server rather than in the document itself. This enables multiple users to comment on a document at the same time.

In this exercise, you will add a comment on document, *NeedlepointHolly.doc*, stating that the document is ready for customers.

OPEN the SharePoint site in which you'd like to discuss a document. If prompted, type your user name and password, and then click OK.

BE SURE TO complete the document addition exercise in Chapter 5 on page 98.

Alternatively, you can create a practice site for this chapter based on site template *Chapter 6 Starter.stp* in the practice file folder for this chapter. The practice file folder is located in the *My Documents \Microsoft Press\SharePoint Services SBS\Chapter 06* folder. See "Using the Book's CD-ROM" on page vii for instructions on how to create a practice site.

1 On the top link bar, click **Documents and Lists**.

2 In the **Document Libraries** section, click **Plant Descriptions**.

The Plant Descriptions document library appears.

3 Move your mouse over **NeedlepointHolly.doc** and when an arrow appears to the right of the document name, click the arrow.

4 Click **Discuss**, and then in the File Download dialog box, click **Open**.

The file opens in Word inside the Internet Explorer shell and the Discussions bar appears at the bottom of the window.

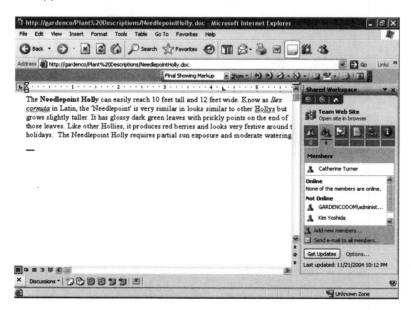

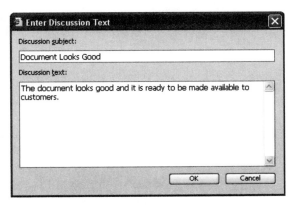

5 In the lower-left corner, click **Discussions**, and then select **Insert about the Document**.

6 In the **Discussion subject:** box, type a subject for the discussion, for example Document Looks Good.

7 In the **Discussion text:** box, type the body of the discussion, for example The document looks good and it is ready to be made available to customers.

8 Click **OK**.

The text appears in the Discussions pane.

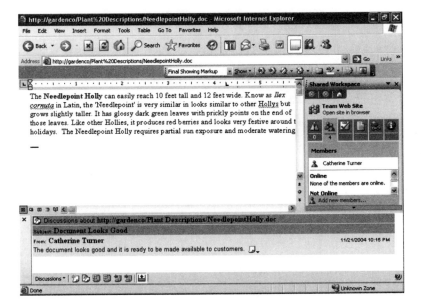

> **Tip** The next time you open Internet Explorer, the Discussions bar will appear at the bottom of the window. To turn the Discussions bar on or off, click the View menu, click Explorer Bar, and then click Discuss.

CLOSE Internet Explorer.

Deleting a Library

Over time, you might accumulate libraries that are no longer needed. You might want to delete them to create space or because corporate policy dictates that communications are only kept for a set period of time.

In this exercise you will delete a library that is no longer in use.

OPEN the SharePoint site in which you'd like to delete a library. If prompted, type your user name and password, and then click OK.

BE SURE TO verify that you have sufficient rights to delete a library. If in doubt, see the Appendix on page 260.

BE SURE TO complete the form library creation exercise in Chapter 5 on page 94.

Alternatively, you can create a practice site for this chapter based on site template *Chapter 6 Starter.stp* in the practice file folder for this chapter. The practice file folder is located in the *My Documents \Microsoft Press\SharePoint Services SBS\Chapter 06* folder. See "Using the Book's CD-ROM" on page vii for instructions on how to create a practice site.

1. On the top link bar, click **Documents and Lists**.

2. In the **Document Libraries** section, click the library you would like to delete, for example **Purchase Orders**.

   The Purchase Orders form library appears.

3. Under **Actions**, click **Modify Settings and Columns**.

   The Customize Purchase Orders page appears.

4. Under **General Settings**, click **Delete this form library**.

5. When the warning that the library will be permanently deleted appears, click the **OK** button.

   You are taken back to the Documents and Lists page.

CLOSE Internet Explorer

Key Points

- You can use General Settings to make libraries appear on the Quick Launch bar.

- You can configure a library to save all versions of a document when changes are made.

- You can require approval before documents in the library appear to other users.

- Views use document metadata to sort, filter, or group, so make sure you have the right columns on your library to sort, filter, and group effectively.

- You can secure a document library by giving people additional permissions or restricting permissions.

- Web folders can be used to access files in a document library instead of using a Web interface.

- Document discussions are stored on the server and enable multiple users to comment on a document at the same time.

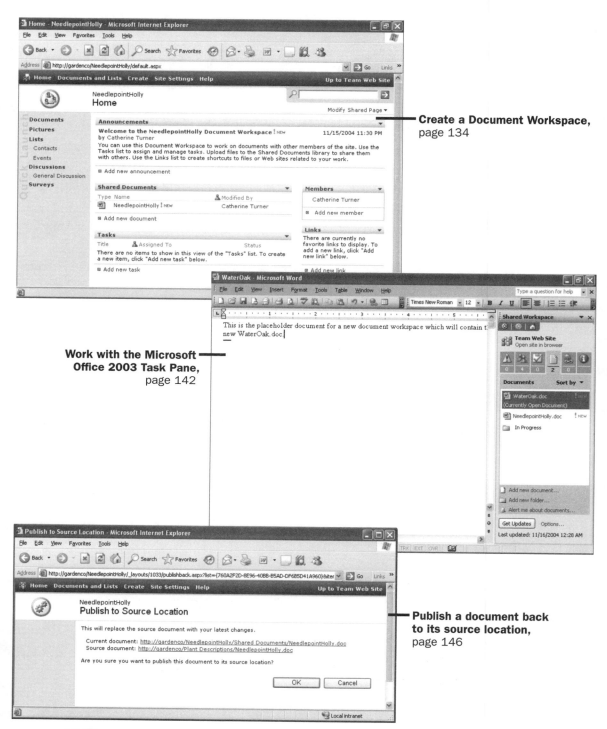

Create a Document Workspace,
page 134

Work with the Microsoft Office 2003 Task Pane,
page 142

Publish a document back to its source location,
page 146

Chapter 7 at a Glance

7 Working with Document Workspaces

In this chapter you will learn to:

✔ Create a Document Workspace.

✔ Create a Document Workspace within Microsoft Office 2003.

✔ Access an existing Document Workspace.

✔ Work with the Office 2003 Shared Workspace task pane.

✔ Publish a document back to a document library.

✔ Delete a Document Workspace.

Document Workspaces have many features that enable you to work on a particular document more easily. You can collaborate with others on a single document in a convenient environment where you can create or store a document, and associate links with that document. Additionally, Microsoft Office 2003 has tight integration between the products in the Office System and Document Workspaces.

You can think of a Document Workspace as a temporary SharePoint site. It is a collaborative environment for discussing, editing, and writing a single document, and enhances content creation. The Document Workspace usually has a short life—several months at most—because its main purpose is to help with content creation. Once the document is finished, it should be stored in a regular document library, as discussed in the previous chapters, for other people to find and read. Then the Document Workspace for that document can be deleted. Because the lifecycle for a Document Workspace is short, you can expect to be creating and deleting Document Workspaces fairly often.

In this chapter, you will learn how to efficiently work with Document Workspaces. You will learn how to create them and access existing ones. You will also learn how to work with the Office 2003 Shared Workspace task pane, publish a document back to a document library, and delete a Document Workspace.

See Also   Do you need only a quick refresher on the topics in this chapter? See the Quick Reference entries on pages xxvi–xxix.

Important   Before you can use the practice files and sites provided for this chapter, you need to install them from the book's companion CD to their default locations. See "Using the Book's CD-ROM" on page vii for more information.

Important Remember to use your SharePoint site location in place of *http://gardenco* in the exercises.

Creating a Document Workspace

There are two ways to create a document library. The first way is to create it through the SharePoint Web interface, and the second way is to create it using a Microsoft Office 2003 application. Both methods will be covered in this chapter. With either method, the resulting Document Workspace will be the same, only the procedure you use to create it will be different.

A Document Workspace centers around one particular document. It is important to stress that fact. You only want one document per Document Workspace because Document Workspaces are linked back to their original document—enabling you to easily copy the document from the Document Workspace back to its original source location. This is a unique feature of Document Workspaces, which are not found in any other type of SharePoint site. This way, you and your team members can work on the document without interfering with the main site or having people read the document before it is complete.

In this exercise, you will create a Document Workspace from an existing document using the SharePoint Web interface.

OPEN the SharePoint site where you'd like to create a Document Workspace. If prompted, type your user name and password, and then click OK.
BE SURE TO complete the "Adding Documents" exercise in Chapter 5 on page 98.
Alternatively, you can create a practice site for this chapter based on site template *Chapter 7 Starter.stp* in the practice file folder for this chapter. The practice file folder is located in the *My Documents \Microsoft Press\SharePoint Services SBS\Chapter 07* folder. See "Using the Book's CD-ROM" on page vii for instructions on how to create a practice site.

1   On the top link bar, click **Documents and Lists**.

2   In the **Document Libraries** section, click **Plant Descriptions**.

    You are taken to the Plant Descriptions document library.

3   Move your mouse over **NeedlepointHolly.doc**, and when an arrow appears to the right of the document name, click the arrow.

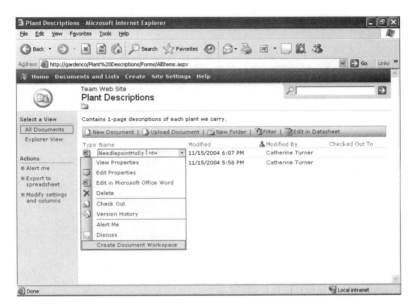

4   Click **Create Document Workspace**.

The Create Document Workspace page appears.

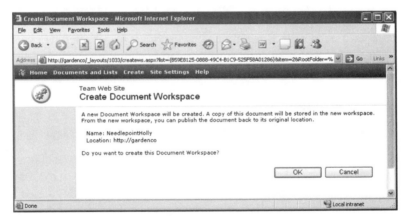

5   Click **OK**.

A new Document Workspace is created for you and populates with information from the NeedlepointHolly.doc document.

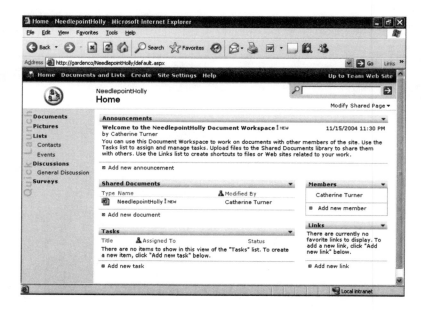

CLOSE Internet Explorer.

Tip You can also create a Document Workspace manually by using the Create link on the home page of the site. However, this will not provide the same integration with an existing document as the above process does. To get the full benefits of a Document Workspace, you should create it from an existing document as described above or create it from an Office 2003 application, which is explained in the next section.

Creating a Document Workspace within Microsoft Office 2003

Office 2003 provides tools that enable you to work with a Document Workspace through a task pane. In this section you will use the Microsoft Office 2003 task pane to create a Document Workspace. The Document Workspace that is created is very similar to the one you created in the last exercise; the only difference is that the Document Workspace is created from within a Microsoft Office 2003 application.

In this exercise, you will create a new document and use Microsoft Office Word 2003 to generate a new Document Workspace for that document.

OPEN the SharePoint site where you'd like to create a Document Workspace for a document in Office 2003. If prompted, type your user name and password, and then click OK.
BE SURE TO complete the "Working with Library Columns" exercise in Chapter 6 on page 116. Alternatively, you can create a practice site for this chapter based on site template *Chapter 7 Starter.stp* in the practice file folder for this chapter. The practice file folder is located in the *My Documents \Microsoft Press\SharePoint Services SBS\Chapter 07* folder. See "Using the Book's CD-ROM" on page vii for instructions on how to create a practice site.

1 On the top link bar, click **Documents and Lists**.

2 In the **Document Libraries** section, click **Plant Descriptions**.

The Plant Descriptions document library appears.

3 Click **New Document**, and then when a dialog box appears indicating that some files can harm your computer, click **OK**.

New Document

A new document is opened in Microsoft Office Word.

4 Type some information into the document, for example, This is the placeholder document for a new document workspace which will contain the new WaterOak.doc.

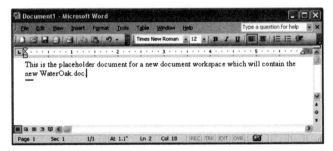

5 Click **File**, and then click **Save**.

6 In the **File name** box, type the name of the document, for example WaterOak.doc.

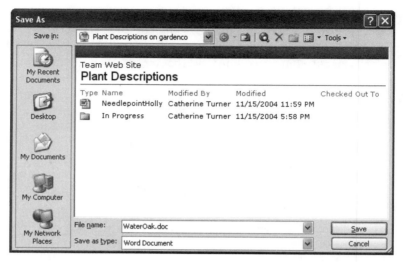

7 Click the **Save** button.

8 In the **Web File Properties Dialog** box, select **Deciduous**.

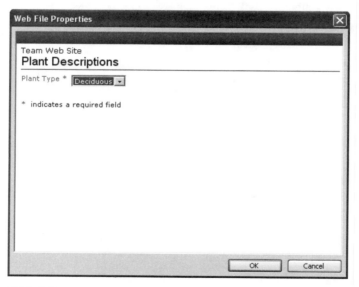

9 Click **OK**.

The file is saved to the Plant Descriptions Document Library.

10 Click **View**, and then click **Task Pane**.

The Microsoft Office task pane appears on the right side of the application.

11 At the top part of the task pane, click **Getting Started**.

A drop-down list of selections appears.

12 Select **Shared Workspace**.

13 Click the **Documents** tab.

Documents tab

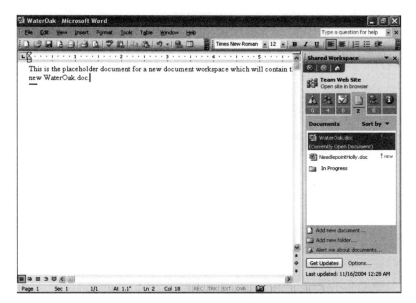

14 Move your mouse over **WaterOak.doc**, and when an arrow appears to the right of the document name, click the arrow.

15 Click **Create Document Workspace**.

A dialog box appears asking if you are sure you want to create the Document Workspace.

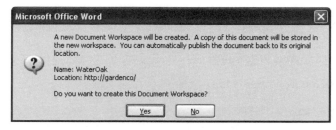

16 Click **Yes**.

Microsoft Office Word displays the progress and creates a Document Workspace for this document.

17 Close Microsoft Office Word.

A dialog box appears asking you if you would like to save a local copy of the document.

18 Click **Skip**.

You can choose to save a local copy if you want, but it is not necessary.

CLOSE Internet Explorer.

Accessing an Existing Document Workspace

After you create a Document Workspace, you have to access it in order to work on the document. Unless you know where to look, it can be difficult finding the Document Workspace again after you first create it.

In this exercise, you will browse to the Document Workspace for NeedlepointHolly.doc, which you created in the first exercise.

OPEN the SharePoint site where you'd like to access an existing Document Workspace. If prompted, type your user name and password, and then click OK.

1 On the top link bar, click **Documents and Lists**.

2 Under **See Also** on the left-hand side of the screen, click **Document Workspaces**.

The Sites And Workspaces page appears.

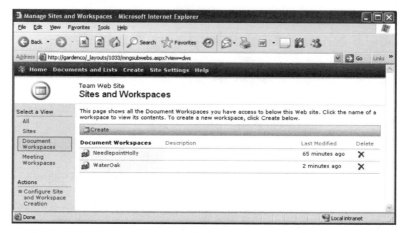

3 Under **Document Workspaces**, click the Document Workspace you would like to access, for example **NeedlepointHolly**.

The NeedlepointHolly Document Workspace appears, which you can work with as you would any SharePoint site.

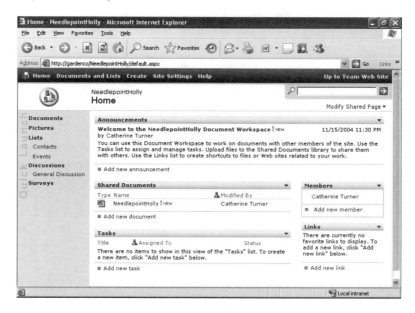

CLOSE Internet Explorer.

Working with the Office 2003 Shared Workspace Task Pane

The Office 2003 Shared Workspace task pane has six tabs that present different information. Following is a description of each tab:

Status tab

- **The Status tab.** This is the first tab from the left on the task pane and is used to give you information about the status of the document, such as who the document is checked out to.

Member tab

- **The Member tab.** This is the second tab from the left on the task pane and is used to show you a list of people who have access to the Document Workspace. It also shows you who is online if you have a presence client installed, such as Windows Messenger.

Tasks tab

- **The Tasks tab.** This is the third tab from the left on the task pane and shows the list of tasks from the Task list of the Document Workspace.

Documents tab

- **The Documents tab** This is the fourth tab from the left on the task pane and shows a list of documents in the SharePoint site.

Links tab

- **The Links tab** This is the fifth tab from the left on the task pane and shows links from the Links list of the Document Workspace.

Info tab

- **The Info tab** This is the last tab from the left on the task pane and shows general information about the document, such as who created the document, who last modified the document and when the document was last modified.

In this exercise, you will work with some of the features of the Shared Workspace task pane in Microsoft Office Word 2003. You will add a task to the Document Workspace, add a user to the Document Workspace, and check the document information all from within Word.

OPEN the SharePoint site in which you'd like to work with a document in a Document Workspace. If prompted, type your user name and password, and then click OK.

1   On the top link bar, click **Documents and Lists**.

2   In the **See Also** section on the left-hand side of the page, click **Documents Workspaces**.

The Sites And Workspaces page appears.

3 Click **WaterOak**.

The Water Oak Document Workspace appears.

4 Move your mouse over **WaterOak.doc** and when an arrow appears to the right of the document name, click the arrow.

5 Click **Edit in Microsoft Office Word**.

A dialog box appears indicating that some files can harm your computer.

6 Click **OK**.

The document is opened in Word.

7 If the Shared Workspace task pane does not show up on the right side of the screen, click **View**, and then click **Task Pane**.

8 Click the **Members** tab.

Your name appears (Catherine Turner in this example) listed as the only member of this Document Workspace.

9 Toward the bottom of the task pane, click the **Add New Members** link.

The Add New Members dialog box displays.

10 In the **Enter e-mail addresses or user names, separated by semicolons** box, type the e-mail address or user name of a user you want to add, for example mikeg.

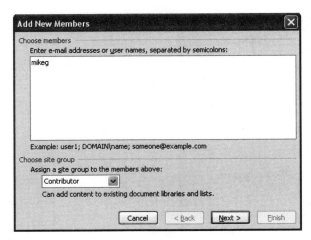

11 Click the **Next**, and then click **Finish**.

If your server is configured for e-mail, the Add New Members dialog box will appear.

12 Clear the check box to send an e-mail invitation to the new members, and then click **OK**.

The user (Mike Galos in this example) is listed as one of the members of the Shared Workspace and he now has permissions to edit the document.

13 Click on the **Tasks** tab.

14 In the bottom section of the pane, click the **Add New Task** link.

The Task dialog box appears.

15 In the **Title** box, type a name for the task, for example Write description of the Water Oak in the Water Oak document.

Leave the Status and Priority boxes set to their defaults.

16 In the **Assigned To** box, select a user to assign the task to, for example Mike Galos.

17 In the **Description** box, type a description for the task, for example, Right now, the Water Oak document is just a placeholder and we need to add actual content to the document.

18 In the **Due Date** box, select the due date for the task, for example 12/15/2005.

Leave the hours and minutes boxes set to their default settings.

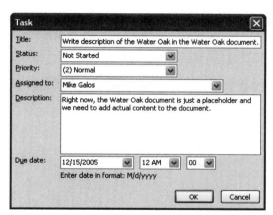

19 Click **OK**.

The new task you just entered appears in the task pane.

20 Click on the **Info** tab.

The date and time the document was modified as well as the user who created the document and the user who most recently modified it is displayed.

CLOSE Microsoft Word and Internet Explorer.

Publishing a Document Back to a Document Library

The ability to publish a document back to its original source document library is one of the unique features of Document Workspaces. Essentially, what this feature does is copy the document back into the source library. It keeps you from having to remember where the document originally came from, while still being able to keep it up to date.

In this exercise, you will publish a document from the Document Workspace back to the document library.

OPEN the SharePoint site in which you'd like to publish a document from a document library back to the main site. If prompted, type your user name and password, and then click OK.

1   On the top link bar, click **Documents and Lists**.

2   In the **See Also** section on the left-hand side of the page, click **Document Workspaces**.

    The Sites And Workspaces page appears.

3   Click **NeedlepointHolly**.

    The **NeedlepointHolly** Document Workspace is displayed.

4   Move your mouse over **NeedlepointHolly.doc** and when an arrow appears to the right of the document name, click the arrow.

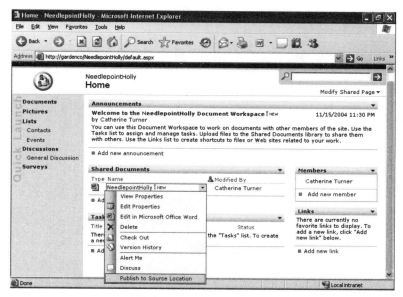

5 Click **Publish to Source Location**.

The Publish To Source Location page appears.

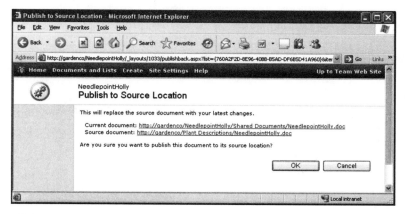

6 Click **OK**.

This copies the latest version of NeedlepointHolly.doc from the Document Workspace to the original document library NeedlepointHolly.doc came from (in this case, Plant Descriptions) and a confirmation that the operation completed successfully appears.

CLOSE Internet Explorer.

Deleting a Document Workspace

When you are finished with a Document Workspace, you will want to delete it in order to save space on your SharePoint server. Deleting it also reduces the clutter when people are trying to find other Document Workspaces.

In this exercise, you will delete the NeedlepointHolly.doc Document Workspace.

OPEN the SharePoint site from which you'd like to delete a Document Workspace. If prompted, type your user name and password, and then click OK.

1 On the top link bar, click **Documents and Lists**.

2 In the **See Also** section on the left side of the page, click **Document Workspaces**.

The Sites And Workspaces page appears.

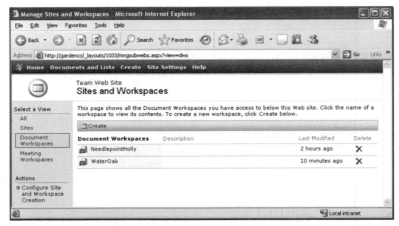

Delete

3 Under the **Delete** column, click the **X** that corresponds to **NeedlepointHolly**.

The Delete Web Site page appears and warns you that all the information contained in the site will be destroyed.

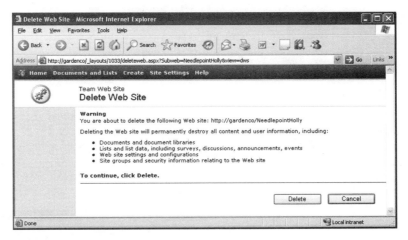

4   Click the **Delete** button.

The Sites And Workspaces page appears. Notice that the NeedlepointHolly Document Workspace is no longer listed.

CLOSE Internet Explorer.

Key Points

- ■   You can create Document Workspaces for documents that are in progress.

- ■   Using Document Workspaces, you can more easily communicate and collaborate about a particular document.

- ■   With the Microsoft Office 2003 Shared Workspace task pane, you have access to information directly from a SharePoint site and you are able to update that information directly within Office.

- ■   You can create a document library from an existing document in a document library so you can use the Publish To Source Location feature to update the original document with the latest version.

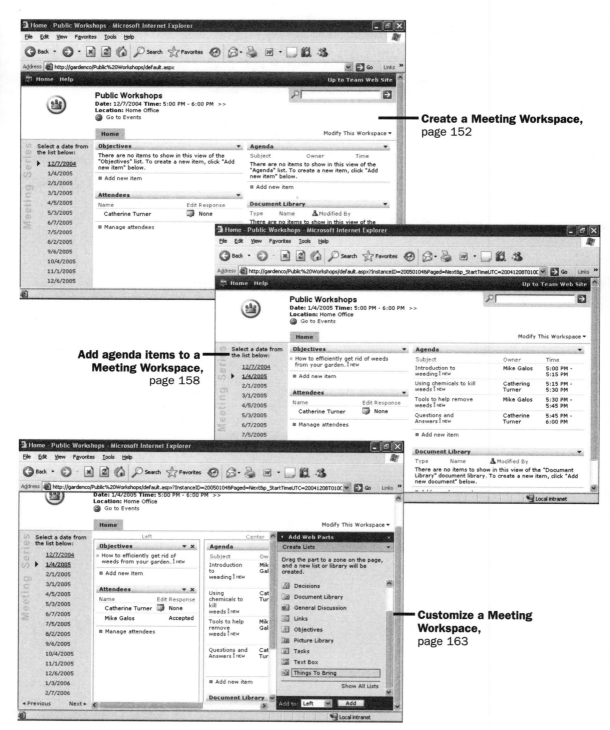

Create a Meeting Workspace,
page 152

Add agenda items to a Meeting Workspace,
page 158

Customize a Meeting Workspace,
page 163

Chapter 8 at a Glance

8 Working with Meeting Workspaces

In this chapter you will learn to:

✔ Create a Meeting Workspace.

✔ Understand the home page of a Meeting Workspace.

✔ Add items to a Meeting Workspace.

✔ Customize a Meeting Workspace.

Every company holds meetings. Usually those meetings have a specific agenda. Sometimes participants need to prepare for the meeting by completing some task prior to it, whether it is reading a document, putting together a list of questions, or perhaps bringing a prototype with them. Often, a meeting becomes inefficient because the preparation tasks that participants are expected to do are not communicated effectively. In addition, after the meeting is over, sometimes meeting notes or follow-up steps are not given to the participants.

Microsoft Windows SharePoint Services provides a feature called Meeting Workspace, which helps to improve communication before and after a meeting by supplying a common place to store information that is relevant for the meeting. By providing a single point of communication, Meeting Workspaces can help make meetings more efficient—something every organization, large and small, can use.

In this chapter, you will learn to create a Meeting Workspace by using a template for a SharePoint event. After the Meeting Workspace is created, you will learn to add items to it, such as objectives, agendas, and attendees. You will also learn to customize the Meeting Workspace by adding a Web Part and then adding items to the Web Part.

See Also Do you need only a quick refresher on the topics in this chapter? See the Quick Reference entries on pages xxix–xxx.

Important   Before you can use the practice files provided for this chapter, you need to install them from the book's companion CD to their default locations. See "Using the Book's CD-ROM" on page vii for more information.

Important   Remember to use your SharePoint site location in place of *http://gardenco* in the exercises.

Creating a Meeting Workspace

There are two different ways to create a Meeting Workspace. The first is to create a new SharePoint subsite manually and then apply the Basic Meeting Workspace template to it. The second way is to use one of the default SharePoint events to generate the Meeting Workspace associated with this event. Both will be covered in this section.

Creating a Meeting Workspace Using a Template

When you create a Meeting Workspace by using the Basic Meeting Workspace template, some default content is added automatically. Three lists—Objectives, Agenda, and Attendees—and a document library are created, which function just like any list or library, as discussed in Chapters 4 and 6, respectively. Each of these lists has a Web Part on the front page of the Meeting Workspace, making it easy to convey information in any of them. Additionally, the Attendees list displays the name of the user who created the Meeting Workspace as the meeting organizer.

In this exercise, you will create a Meeting Workspace by using the Basic Meeting Workspace template to use for storing notes from the weekly status meeting.

OPEN the SharePoint site in which you'd like to create a Meeting Workspace. If prompted, type your user name and password, and then click OK.
BE SURE TO verify that you have sufficient rights to create a site. If in doubt, see the Appendix on page 260.

1   On the top link bar, click **Create**.

The Create Page page appears.

2   Under the **Web Pages** section, click **Sites and Workspaces**.

You are taken to the New SharePoint Site page.

3   In the **Title** box, type the name of the workspace you would like to create, for example Weekly Status Meeting.

4   In the **Description** box, type a description for the Meeting Workspaces, for example This site contains information about the weekly status meeting.

5   In the **URL Name:** box, type the URL for the Meeting Workspace, for example weeklystatus.

Leave the default settings for the Permissions section. You have now entered everything you need to create the new site.

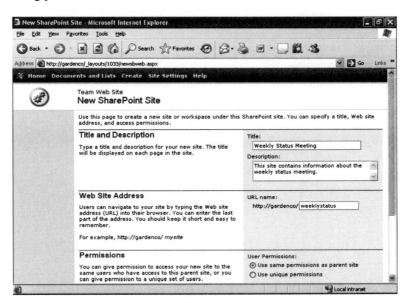

6   Click the **Create** button.

A new site is created at *http://gardenco/weeklystatus* and you are taken to the Template Selection page.

7   In the **Template** box, select **Basic Meeting Workspace**.

Note   You can also create a Multipage Meeting Workspace by selecting the Multipage Meeting Workspace template. A multipage Meeting Workspace is very similar to a basic Meeting Workspace, except the multipage one creates additional blank pages so that you can add your own content.

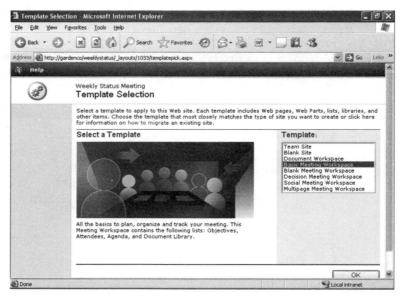

8 Click **OK**.

You are taken to the newly created Weekly Status Meeting page.

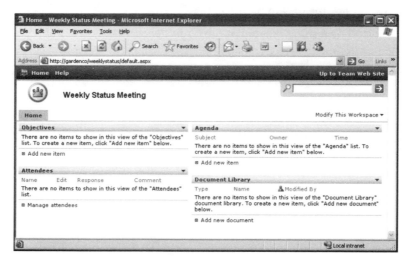

CLOSE Internet Explorer.

Creating a Meeting Workspace for a SharePoint Event

You might want to create a Meeting Workspace for an event that is already in a SharePoint events list, which is even easier to create because Windows SharePoint Services performs most of the work for you.

In this exercise, you will create a Meeting Workspace for recurring Public Workshops events. There are many people involved with the Public Workshops and having details in a Meeting Workspace on the SharePoint site makes it much easier to communicate information, including changes, to everyone involved. You will be adding information to this workspace in the next several sections.

OPEN the SharePoint site in which you'd like to create a Meeting Workspace. If prompted, type your user name and password, and then click OK.

BE SURE TO verify that you have sufficient rights to create a site. If in doubt, see the Appendix on page 260.

BE SURE TO complete the steps to create recurring Public Workshops events in the "Add, Edit, and Delete List Items" exercise in Chapter 4 on page 65.

Alternatively, you can create a practice site for this chapter based on site template Chapter 8 Starter.stp in the practice file folder for this chapter. The practice file folder is located in the *My Documents \Microsoft Press\SharePoint Services SBS\Chapter 08* folder. See 'Using the Book's CD-ROM' on page vii for instructions on how to create a practice site.

1 Under the **Events** Web Part, click one of the **Public Workshops** events.

The Events: Public Workshops page appears.

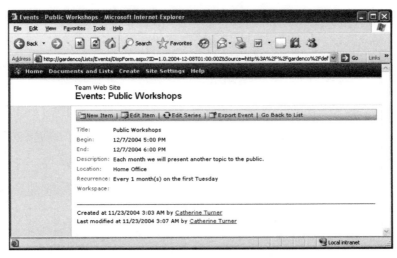

2 Click **Edit Item**.

3 Click **Edit Series**.

4 Select the **Use a Meeting Workspace to organize attendees, agendas, documents, minutes, and other details for this event.** checkbox.

5 Click **Save and Close**.

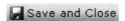

You will be taken to the New or Existing Meeting Workspace page. Because a Meeting Workspace was not created for this event yet, you will create one. All of the information is already filled out for you.

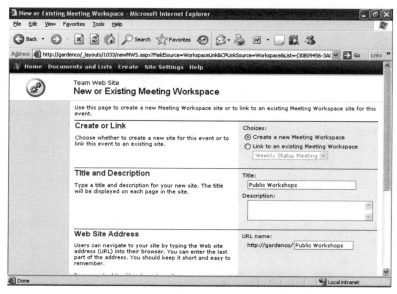

6   Click **OK**.

A new site is created at *http://gardenco/Public%20Workshops* and you are taken to the Template Selection page.

7   In the **Template** box, select **Basic Meeting Workspace**.

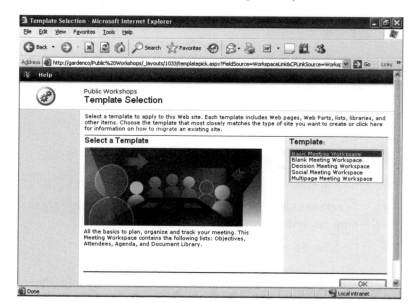

8 Click **OK**.

You are taken to the newly created Public Workshops page. In the left pane, notice the links for each recurrence of the event.

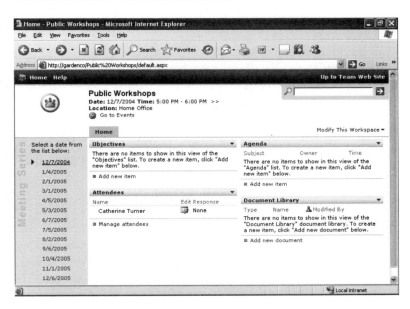

CLOSE Internet Explorer.

Understanding the Home Page of a Meeting Workspace

Once you have created a Meeting Workspace, you should familiarize yourself with the home page layout. On the home page of a generic workspace are Web Parts for Objectives, Attendees, Agenda, and document library. These are the items that apply to every meeting. A meeting should always have at least one objective as well as an agenda, to let people know what the meeting is about. The meeting workspace is organized in a way that makes it easy for the organizer to communicate why they are holding the meeting. Also, there must always be a list of meeting attendees. The document library does not necessarily have to be used, but it is convenient to have one created as a place to store documents that attendees might need to read before the meeting, a Microsoft PowerPoint file containing the presentations, or meeting minutes after the meeting concludes.

If you create a Meeting Workspace from a recurring event, additional information is provided on the Meeting Workspace page. At the top of the page is the Date and Time of the meeting as well as the Location of the meeting, if specified. This is useful information to have in case someone needs it. Additionally, on the left side of the page is a list of dates that represent each instance of a recurring meeting. Each of these dates has its own Meeting Workspace page associated with it, enabling you to have different objectives, agendas, attendees, and documents for each specific instance of the meeting. For example, the Public Workshops meeting presents a different topic each month, so it makes sense to have different objectives, agendas, attendees, and documents for every monthly event.

Adding Items to a Meeting Workspace

To get the most use out of a Meeting Workspace, you need to add information and relevant details to it so people are motivated to visit your Meeting Workspace. In this section you will add information to each of the default Web Parts in the Public Workshops Meeting Workspace.

Adding an Objective to a Meeting Workspace

First, the topic for the next Public Workshop focuses on dealing with weeds in the garden. Catherine Turner wants to communicate this focus to anyone who visits the Meeting Workspace page.

In this exercise you will add this topic as an objective to the Meeting Workspace.

OPEN the Meeting Workspace that you created in the previous exercise (*http://gardenco /Public%20Workshops* in the example). If prompted, type your user name and password, and then click OK.

You can also get to the Meeting Workspace by opening the base SharePoint site (*http://gardenco*), clicking one of the Public Workshops under the Events Web Part, and then clicking the Workspace link.

1 On the left side of the page under **Select a date from the list below:**, click the date of the next meeting (1/4/2005 in this example; your date will vary based on the date you perform this exercise.).

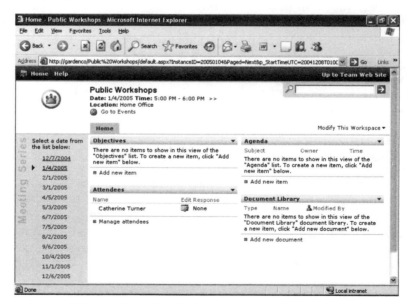

2 Under the **Objectives** Web Part, click **Add new item**.

You are taken to the Objectives: New Item page.

3 In the **Objective** box, type the meeting objective, for example How to efficiently get rid of weeds from your garden..

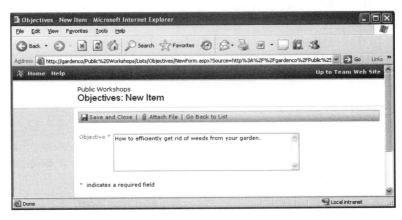

4 Click **Save and Close**.

You have created the objective for this Public Workshop and are taken back to the home page of the Meeting Workspace. The new objective appears in the Objectives Web Part.

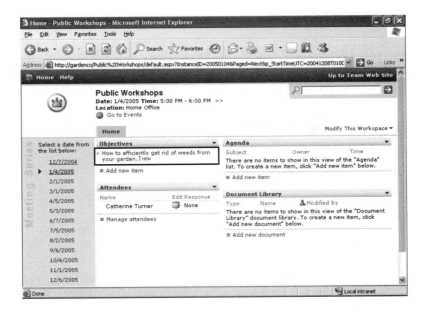

CLOSE Internet Explorer.

Adding an Agenda to a Meeting Workspace

Next, Catherine Turner wants to communicate the agenda for the next Public Workshop. This includes assigning an owner to each agenda item and scheduling a time for the Public Workshop. Catherine has decided that Mike Galos will present the Introduction session and the Weeding Tools session. She will present the pros and cons of weeding with chemicals as well as answer questions. Each session will last for 15 minutes.

In this exercise, you will create an agenda for the Meeting Workspace based on this scenario.

OPEN the Meeting Workspace that you created in the previous exercise (*http://gardenco /Public%20Workshops* in the example). If prompted, type your user name and password, and then click OK.

1 On the left side of the page, under **Select a date from the list below:**, click the date of the next meeting (1/2/2005 in this example; your date will vary based on the date you perform this exercise.).

2 Under the **Agenda** Web Part, click **Add new item**.

The Agenda: New Item page appears.

3 In the **Subject** box, type a subject for the agenda, for example Introduction to weeding.

4 In the **Owner** box, type the name of a person who is responsible for this agenda item, for example Mike Galos.

5 In the **Time** box, type the time for this agenda item, for example 5:00 PM – 5:15 PM.

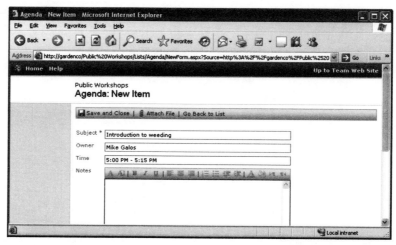

6 Click **Save and Close**.

You have created the first agenda item for this Public Workshop and are taken back to the home page of the Meeting Workspace. The new agenda appears in the Agenda Web Part. Using steps 2–6 as a guide, create another three items for the workshop agenda. The information for each agenda item is provided in the following table:

Subject	Owner	Time
Using chemicals to kill weeds	Catherine Turner	5:15 PM – 5:30 PM
Tools to help remove weeds	Mike Galos	5:30 PM – 5:45 PM
Questions and Answers	Catherine Turner	5:45 PM – 6:00 PM

You have created the final agenda item for this Public Workshop and are taken back to the home page of the Meeting Workspace.

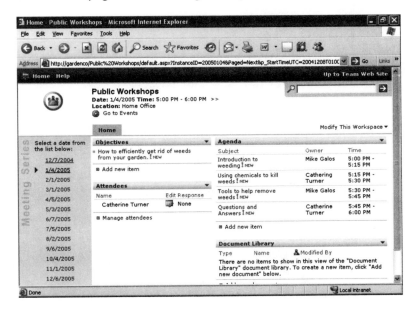

CLOSE Internet Explorer.

Adding an Attendee to a Meeting Workspace

Finally, since you specified that Mike Galos will be presenting two topics in the meeting, you need to add him to the Attendees list. Listing Mike as an attendee ensures that the visitors to the workspace know that Mike will attend the meeting and they'll be able to contact him by e-mail if necessary.

In this exercise, you will add a user, Mike Galos, to the attendees list.

OPEN the Meeting Workspace that you created in the previous exercise (*http://gardenco /Public%20Workshops* in the example).

1   On the left side of the page, under **Select a date from the list below:**, click the date of the next meeting (1/4/2005 in this example; your date will vary based on the date you perform this exercise.).

2   Under the **Attendees** Web Part, click **Manage Attendees**.

The Attendees page appears.

3   Click **Add Attendee**.

       Add Attendee

You are taken to the Attendees: New Item page.

4   In the **Name** box, type the e-mail address or user name of the attendee, for example gardencodom\mikeg.

Note   You can also use the Microsoft Outlook Address Book to import users if you have Outlook 2003 installed.

5   In the **Response** drop-down list, select Accepted.

6   In the **Attendance** drop-down list, select Required.

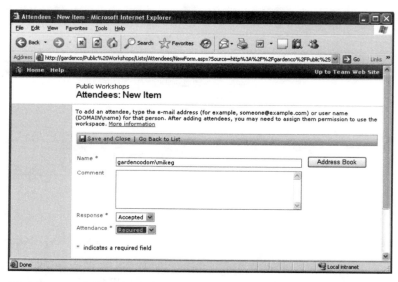

7   Click **Save and Close**.

You have added Mike as an Attendee for this Public Workshop and are taken back to the Attendees list. You may add additional attendees if you want by using the same procedure.

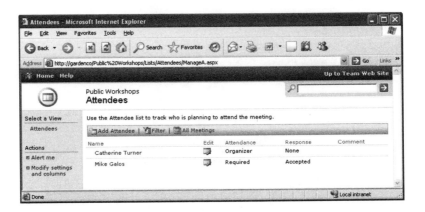

CLOSE Internet Explorer.

Customizing a Meeting Workspace

Now that you have added all the information to the default Meeting Workspace, you might want to customize the Meeting Workspace home page to present more information. You can do this by adding Web Parts and lists.

Note   If you add a Web Part to any page in a Meeting Workspace that has multiple dates listed on the left-side of the page, the Web Part is added to all pages.

Adding a Web Part

In this exercise you will add a Web Part to the Meeting Workspace. Catherine wants to ensure that all attendees know what they are expected to bring with them to the meeting; therefore, the Web Part you will be adding is Things To Bring.

See Also   We will look into customizing a SharePoint site using Web Parts in detail in Chapter 12, "Working with Web Parts."

OPEN the Meeting Workspace to which you would like to add a Web Part. If prompted, type your user name and password, and then click OK.
BE SURE TO verify that you have sufficient rights to add Web Parts. If in doubt, see the Appendix on page 260.

1   On the left side of the page, under **Select a date from the list below:**, click the date of the next meeting (1/4/2005 in this example; your date will vary based on the date you perform this exercise.).

2 On the right side of the page, near the top, click **Modify this Workspace** and then click **Add Web Parts**.

The Add Web Parts tool pane appears on the right side of the page.

3 In the Add Web Parts tool pane, click **Things To Bring**.

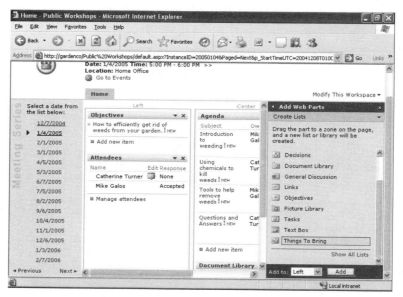

4 Click the **Add** button.

The Things To Bring list is now added to the home page of the Meeting Workspace.

Close

5 In the upper right corner of the Add Web Parts tool pane, click the **Close** button to close the tool pane.

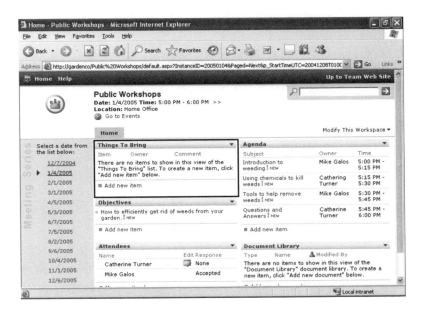

CLOSE Internet Explorer.

Adding Items to a Web Part

Now that there is a Things To Bring Web Part, you need to add items to this Web Part. In our scenario, Catherine Turner wants to make sure the attendees bring chemical weeding samples to the Public Workshop.

In this exercise, you will add that item to the Things To Bring Web Part.

OPEN the Meeting Workspace to which you added the Things To Bring Web Part in the previous exercise. If prompted, type your user name and password, and then click OK.

1 On the left side of the page, under **Select a date from the list below:** click the date of the next meeting (1/4/2005 in this example; your date will vary based on the date you perform this exercise.).

2 Under the **Things To Bring** Web Part, click **Add new item**.

You are taken to the Things To Bring: New Item page.

3 In the **Item** box, type the name of the item, for example Weed removal chemical samples.

4 In the **Comment** box, type a reason for bringing the item, for example Please bring samples to aid our presentation as well as promote sales.

5 In the **Owner** box, type the name of the person responsible for bringing the item, for example Catherine Turner.

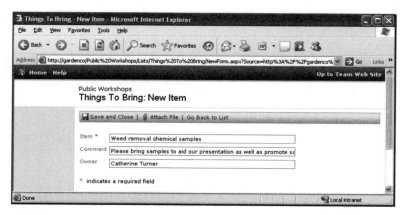

6   Click **Save and Close**.

You have added an item to the Things To Bring list for this Public Workshop and are taken back to the home page of the Meeting Workspace. You may add additional items to the Things To Bring list using the same procedure.

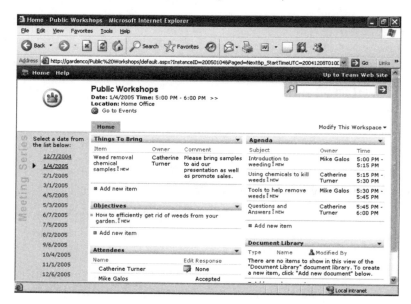

CLOSE Internet Explorer.

Key Points

■ Meeting Workspaces communicate key information about a meeting.

■ You can create a Meeting Workspace from recurring events if you want to have different information each time the meeting occurs.

■ After the Meeting Workspace is created, add relevant information to the Objectives, Agenda, and Attendees Web Parts.

■ Use the Document Library in a Meeting Workspace to store presentations, documents, pictures, meeting minutes, or other material relevant to the meeting.

■ You can customize a Meeting Workspace by adding Web Parts.

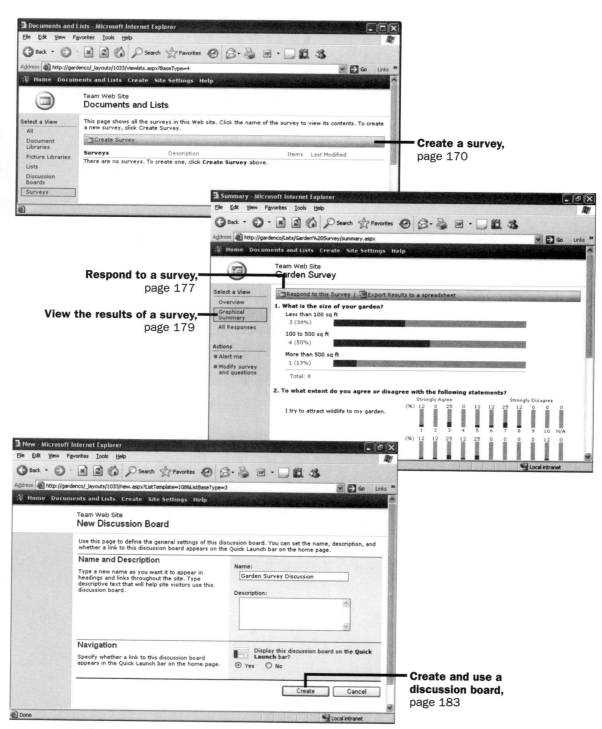

Create a survey,
page 170

Respond to a survey,
page 177

View the results of a survey,
page 179

**Create and use a
discussion board,**
page 183

Chapter 9 at a Glance

9 Working with Surveys and Discussion Boards

In this chapter you will learn to:

✔ Create a survey.

✔ Respond to a survey.

✔ View the results of a survey.

✔ Create and use a discussion board.

Chapter 4 introduced you to Microsoft Windows SharePoint Services lists. With two specialized SharePoint lists, *surveys* and *discussion boards*, you can gather feedback and information from users of your site.

By creating a survey, you can determine the format of the user's feedback. You can configure also whether respondents' names appear in the survey results. If names are configured to appear, you can see how each user responded; if names are configured not to appear, the survey is anonymous. Windows SharePoint Services tallies the results and can compile a graphical summary of the responses.

By creating a discussion board, you can allow users to determine the type of response they give. A discussion board invites users to discuss issues with one another by starting topics and posting replies.

Tip   Discussion boards are also known as *message boards*, or on the Internet, as *Internet forums*.

In this chapter you will learn how to create and respond to a survey, and then view the survey results. You will also learn how to create and use a discussion board.

See Also   Do you need only a quick refresher on the topics in this chapter? See the Quick Reference entries on pages xxx–xxxii.

Important   Before you can use the practice files provided for this chapter, you need to install them from the book's companion CD to their default locations. See "Using the Book's CD-ROM" on page vii for more information.

Important   Remember to use your SharePoint site location in place of *http://gardenco* in the exercises.

Creating a Survey

Surveys are created for a number of reasons. For example, you might need to create a survey to ask for a user's opinions, or you might need to collect factual information for marketing purposes. No matter what their purpose, all surveys involve the creation of a survey "container," and then the creation and administration of questions.

These questions can be one of two basic types:

- **Open-ended questions** have no definitive answer. Open-ended questions give users the opportunity to answer in their own words, rather than just checking one of a limited list of alternatives. An example of an open-ended question is, "Are there any other comments you would like to add about the services or products that The Garden Company supplies?" The advantage of open-ended questions is that responses can be very useful, often yielding quotable material and an insight into the issues that are of most concern to the respondents of the survey. The disadvantage is that the responses are more difficult to catalog and interpret.

- **Closed-ended questions** have a finite set of answers from which the user chooses. One of the choices might be "Other" or "N/A" to allow users to specify that their answer is not one of those supplied or that the question is not applicable to them. The advantage of closed-ended questions is that they are easy to gather data from and that they lend themselves to statistical analysis. The disadvantage is that they are more difficult to write than open-ended questions, because the choices must include all the possible answers a user could give for each question.

Users can respond to a survey in a number of ways, such as by typing in text, by selecting items from a menu, by clicking yes or no, or by entering a numeric or currency value. When you use Windows SharePoint Services to create a question, you can specify the type of answer, as summarized in the following table.

Answer	Question Type	Description
Single line of text	Open	Use this answer type when you want users to enter just a few words. You can specify the maximum number of characters a user can type.
Multiple lines of text	Open	Use this answer type when you want users to type one or more sentences. You can specify the maximum number of lines users can type and whether users can format their responses, such as by changing the font or text color.

Answer	Question Type	Description
Choice	Closed and Open	Use this answer type when you want users to choose from a set of selections that you provide. You can create a multiple-choice question, in which users pick the best answer or answers from among the possible choices, represented as a drop-down list, a set of option buttons, or a set of check boxes. You can make the question open-ended by allowing users to type their own choice.
Rating Scale	Closed	This answer type is often called a *Likert scale*. Use this answer type when you want users to choose their preference on a numeric scale. Questions with this type of answer are often used to obtain feedback on the services you have provided. Users indicate how closely their feelings match the question or statement on a rating scale. The number at one end of the scale represents most agreement, or "Strongly Agree," and the number at the other end of the scale represents least agreement, or "Strongly Disagree."
Number	Open	Use this answer type when you want users to enter a numeric value. You can specify a lower and upper limit for the value and the number of decimal places users can enter.
Currency	Open	Use this answer type when you want users to enter a monetary value. You can select the currency format based on a geographic region, a lower and upper limit for the value, and the number of decimal places users can enter.
Date and Time	Open	Use this answer type when you want users to enter a date or a date and time.
Lookup	Closed	This answer type is very similar to the Choice answer type, in that the responses are predetermined. Use this answer type to point users to an existing list on your site that contains the available choices.
Yes/No	Closed	This answer type presents the user with a check box and can be used when you want users to respond with Yes or No (True or False). Questions that require this answer type are sometimes known as *categorical questions*.

With each of these answer types, you can specify whether an answer is required or optional, and you can provide a default answer for each question.

In this exercise, you will create a survey on a SharePoint Web site.

OPEN the SharePoint site in which you would like to create your survey. The exercise will use the *http://gardenco* **site, but you can use whatever site you want. If prompted, type your user name and password, and then click OK.**
BE SURE TO verify that you have sufficient rights to create a list. If in doubt, see the Appendix on page 260.

1 On the Quick Launch bar, click **Surveys**.

The Documents and Lists page is displayed.

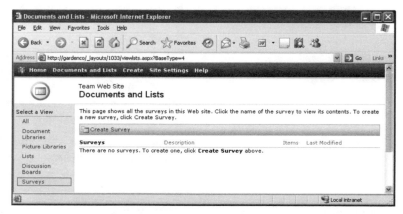

2 Click **Create Survey**.

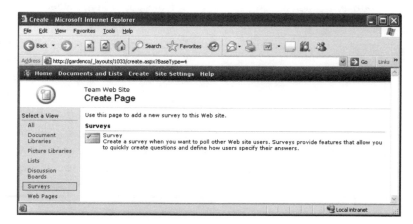

The Create Page page is displayed.

3 Under **Surveys**, click **Survey**.

The New Survey form is displayed.

4 In the **Name** box, type Garden Survey.

5 In the **Navigation** section, leave the **Yes** option selected.

6 In the **Survey Options** section, for the **Store user names in survey results?** and **Allow multiple responses?** options, select **Yes**.

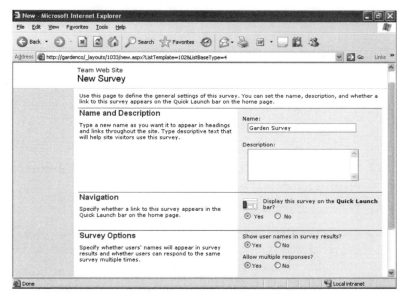

7 At the bottom of the page, click the **Next** button.

The Garden Survey: Add Question page is displayed.

8 In the **Question and Type** section, in the **Question** box, type What is the size of your garden?, and then select the **Choice (menu to choose from)** option.

9 In the **Optional settings for your question** section, for the **Require a response to this question** option, select **Yes**.

10 In the **Type each choice on a separate line** box, replace the existing text with the following three lines:

Less than 100 sq ft
100 to 500 sq ft
More than 500 sq ft

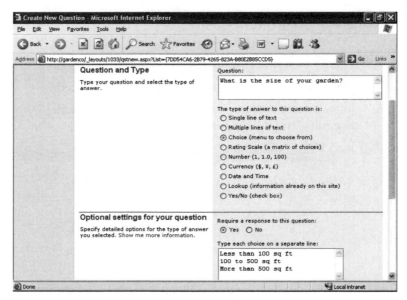

11 Under **Display choices using**, make sure the **Radio Buttons** option is selected. (This is the default setting.)

12 At the bottom of the page, click the **Next Question** button.

13 In the **Question and Type** section, in the **Question** box, type To what extent do you agree or disagree with the following statements?, and then select the **Rating Scale (a matrix of choices)** option.

14 In the **Optional settings for your question** section, for the **Require a response to this question** option, select **Yes**.

15 In the **Type each choice on a separate line** section, replace the existing text with the following three lines:

I try to attract wildlife to my garden.
Wildlife can damage my garden.
People should consider wildlife when making or maintaining their garden.

16 Click the down arrow to the right of **Number Range** box, and then click **10**.

17 In the first **Range Text** box, type Strongly Agree, replace the text in the middle box with a space, and then in the last box, type Strongly Disagree.

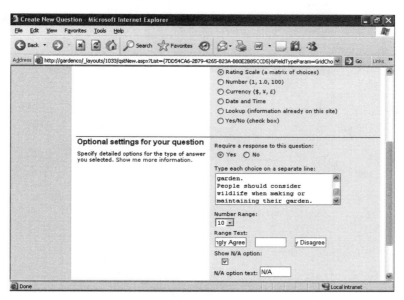

18 At the bottom of the page, click the **Next Question** button.

Tip If a Microsoft Internet Explorer dialog box is displayed stating that the Rating Scale Range Text contains invalid characters, then it is likely you deleted the text in the middle Range Text box and did not enter a space character. To correct this, click OK in the dialog box, and then enter a space in the middle Range Text box.

19 In the **Question and Type** section, in the **Question** box, type How much money, in total, did you spend on your garden over the last year?, and then select the **Currency ($, ¥, £)** option.

20 In the **Optional settings for your question** section, for the **Require a response to this question:** option, select **Yes**.

21 To the right of the **Number of decimal places** box, click the down arrow, and then click **2**.

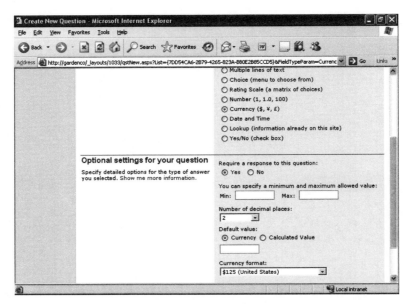

22 At the bottom of the page, click the **Finish** button.

The Customize Garden Survey page is displayed.

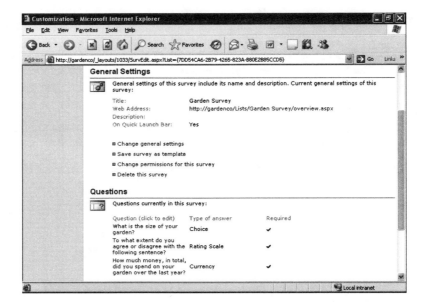

Tip   In the Questions section of the Customize Garden Survey page, you can add, modify, delete, or change the order of your survey questions. To modify or delete an existing survey question, click the appropriate question in the "Question (click to edit)" column. When the Edit Question page is displayed, either modify the question and click OK, or click the Delete button to delete the survey question.

CLOSE Internet Explorer.

Responding to a Survey

As surveys are created on a SharePoint Web site, you might find that you need to respond to them. Surveys are created to gather information, and it is important that you know how to respond to surveys. As a survey creator, users must respond to your survey so you can analysis their responses. It is good practice that once you have created a survey that you see the survey from an user's perspective, by completing at least one test response.

In this exercise, you will respond to a survey.

OPEN the SharePoint site in which the survey is located. If prompted, type your user name and password, and then click OK. The exercise will use the Garden Survey created in the previous exercise, but you can use whatever survey you want.
BE SURE TO verify that you have sufficient rights to contribute to the list. If in doubt, see the Appendix on page 260.

1   On the Quick Launch bar, under **Surveys**, click **Garden Survey**.

The Garden Survey page is displayed.

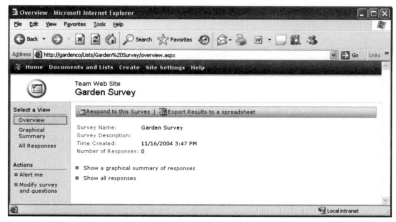

2   Click **Respond to this Survey**.

The Garden Survey: New Item page is displayed.

3 Select the **Less than 100 sq ft** option, then for the ranking questions options, select **1**, **2**, and **8**, and for the money question enter **20**.

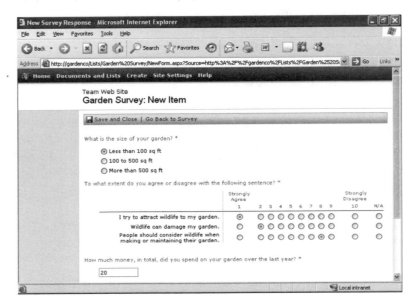

4 Click **Save and Close**.

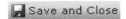

The Garden Survey page is displayed.

5 Repeat steps 2 through 4 several times, entering different responses each time.

CLOSE Internet Explorer.

Note If you do not allow multiple responses when you create a survey and you try to test it more than once, an Error page is displayed stating that you are not allowed to respond again to the survey. To correct this problem, display the Garden Survey page, and then in the left navigation column, under Actions, click "Modify survey and questions." On the Customize Garden Survey page, in the General Settings section, click "Change general settings." On the Survey Settings: Garden Survey page, in the Survey Options section, select Yes as the "Allow multiple responses" option, and then click OK. Then click Go Back to "Garden Survey" to enter additional responses.

Viewing the Results of a Survey

After users respond to your survey, you will need to examine and analyze the results. Windows SharePoint Services provides three ways to display a quick summary of the survey data:

- **Overview.** This view displays the survey's name, description, date and time of creation, and number of responses.

- **Graphical Summary.** This view displays the response data for each survey question in a graphical form. The number of responses is displayed as a value and a percentage of the total number of responses received.

- **All Responses.** This view displays a list of each survey response, the date and time the response was last modified, and, if applicable, the name of the user who created it. In this view, responses can be modified or deleted.

Important Surveys are created with item-level permissions set so that all responses can be read by all users, but users can only edit their own responses. If you want to prevent users from changing their responses, display the survey and in the left navigation column under Actions, click "Modify survey and questions." On the Customize Survey page, in the General Settings section, click "Change permissions for this survey." On the Change Permissions page, click "Modify item-level security," and in the Item-level Permissions section, in the "Edit Access: Specify which responses users can edit" list, click None. Setting survey permissions is similar to setting document library permissions.

See Also For more information about setting document library permissions, see Chapter 5, "Creating and Managing Libraries."

You can also export survey result data to a spreadsheet, where you can use the data analysis features available in Microsoft Office Excel 2003.

In this exercise, you will view the survey responses. After editing one of your responses to the survey, you will export the results of the survey to Excel, and then find the average amount spent on gardens by users who responded to your survey.

OPEN the SharePoint site in which the survey is located. If prompted, type your user name and password, and then click OK. The exercise will use the Garden Survey used in the previous two exercises, but you can use whatever survey you want.

BE SURE TO verify that you have sufficient rights to access the list. If in doubt, see the Appendix on page 260.

1 On the Quick Launch bar, under **Surveys**, click **Garden Survey**.

The Garden Survey page is displayed in Overview view.

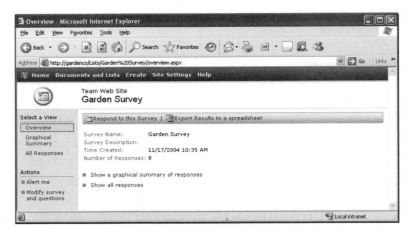

2   In the left navigation column, under **Select a View**, click **Graphical Summary**.

The Garden Survey page is displayed in Graphical Summary view.

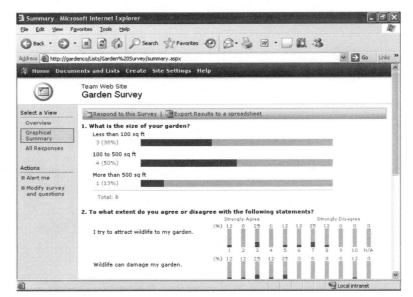

3   In the left navigation column, under **Select a View**, click **All Responses**.

The Garden Survey page is displayed in the All Responses view.

4   Point to the **View Response #1** survey item, click the down arrow, and then in the drop-down list, click **Edit Item**.

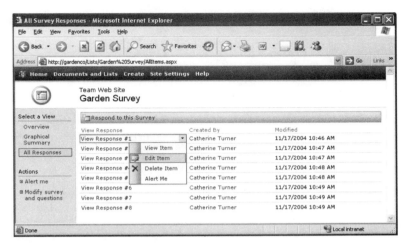

5   Select the 100 to 500 sq ft option, and then click **Save and Close**.

6   In the left navigation column, under **Select a View**, click **Overview**, and then click **Export Results to a spreadsheet**.

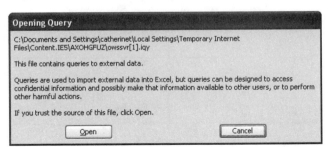

Export Results to a spreadsheet

Tip   Export Results to a Spreadsheet is available in both Overview and Graphical Summary views.

7   If the **File Download** dialog box appears with a warning that some files can harm your computer, click the **Open** button.

Excel opens.

8   In the **Opening Query** dialog box, click the **Open** button.

9   If a Microsoft Excel dialog box appears with a warning about hidden or read-only columns, click **OK**.

The survey responses are displayed as an Excel list surrounded by a dark blue border and with AutoFilter enabled in the header row of every column. If the List tool bar appears, close it.

181

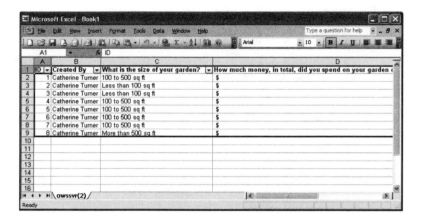

Note Rating Scale survey questions are not exported into the spreadsheet, but all other answer types are.

10 In column D, click the first empty cell below the Excel list, and then on the **Insert** menu, click **Function**.

11 In the **Insert Function** dialog box, in the **Select a function** list, click **AVERAGE**, click **OK**, and then in the **Function Arguments** dialog box, click **OK**.

Excel displays the average amount survey respondents spent on their gardens in the last year.

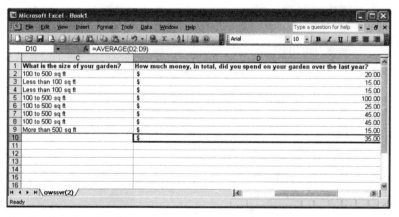

Save

12 On the Standard toolbar, click the **Save** button.

The Save As dialog box appears.

13 On the left side of the dialog box, click the **My Documents** icon. If you installed the practice files, open *Microsoft Press\SharePoint Services SBS\Chapter 09*. Then in the **File name** box, type MyGardenSurvey, and click the **Save** button.

CLOSE Excel and Internet Explorer.

See Also   For more information about how to use Excel lists to share data with other users, see "Importing Data from an Excel Spreadsheet to a List in SharePoint" in Chapter 11.

Creating and Using a Discussion Board

Discussion boards provide a forum on which visitors to your site can converse about topics that interest them. SharePoint sites that were created with the Team, Document Workspace, or Social Meeting site templates, include a discussion board called *General Discussion*. You can display the discussion board by using either the Quick Launch bar or the Documents and Lists page.

You can use a discussion board to start new discussions and sort and filter existing discussions. You can also change the design of the discussion board and create alerts that notify you of changes to the discussion board.

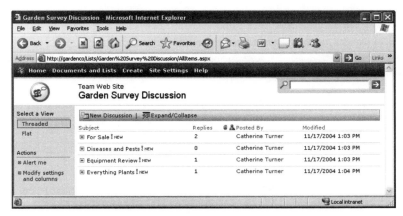

Windows SharePoint Services can display a discussion board in two views:

- **Flat view** lists replies in chronological order (the order in which they were created).

- **Threaded view** lets you view comments grouped by conversation, or *thread*. All messages that are part of the same thread appear together in the order in which they were created.

You can post new topics and replies to the General Discussion discussion board or you can create new discussion boards. You can configure discussion board security settings so that users can participate in one discussion board but not another.

Important   Discussion boards are created with the same item-level permissions as surveys; that is, all discussions and replies can be read by all users, but users can edit only their own discussions and replies.

In this exercise, you create a new discussion board, add a new topic, delete a topic, and then remove the discussion board.

OPEN the SharePoint site in which you would like to create a discussion board. If prompted, type your user name and password, and then click OK.
BE SURE TO verify that you have sufficient rights to create a list. If in doubt, see the Appendix on page 260.

1 On the Quick Launch bar, click **Discussions**.

The Documents and Lists page is displayed.

2 Click **Create Discussion Board**.

Create Discussion Board

The Create Page is displayed.

3 In the **Discussion Boards** section, click **Discussion Board**.

The New Discussion Board form is displayed.

4 In the **Name** box, type Garden Survey Discussion.

5 In the **Navigation** section, make sure the **Yes** option is selected.

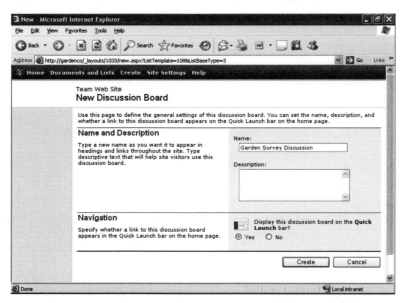

6 At the bottom of the page, click the **Create** button.

The Garden Survey Discussion page is displayed.

Note Because both Surveys and Discussion Boards are specialized lists, the name of the list needs to be unique within the site; hence, you cannot call the discussion board in this exercise *Garden Survey* because that would conflict with the Garden Survey survey you created in the first exercise.

7 Click **New Discussion**.

 New Discussion

8 In the **Subject** box, type Garden Survey – overall comments.

9 In the **Text** box, type What did you think of the range of questions on the Garden Survey?

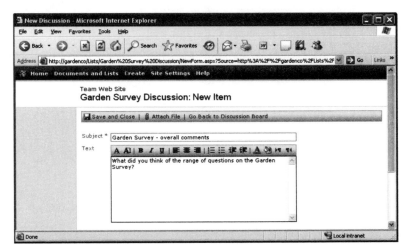

10 Click **Save and Close**.

11 Point to the **Garden Survey – overall comments** item, click the down arrow, and in the drop-down list, click **Reply**.

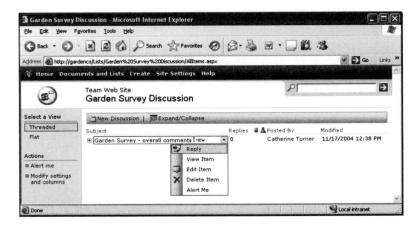

12 In the **Subject** box, replace the contents with Garden Survey – Additional Question.

13 In the **Text** box, type We could add an additional question that asks users whether they subscribe to The Garden Company's monthly newsletter. The answer type would be Yes/No.

14 Click **Save and Close**.

15 Click **Expand/Collapse**.

Expand/Collapse

All discussions and replies are displayed.

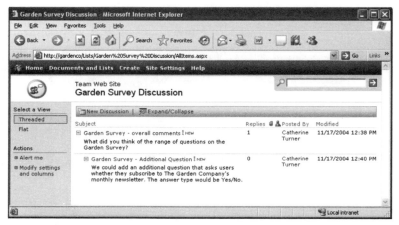

16 In the left navigation column, under **Select a View**, click **Flat**.

All discussion and reply items are displayed.

Tip In Flat view, you can sort and filter discussion items.

17 Point to the **Garden Survey – overall comments** item, click the down arrow, and then in the drop-down list, click **Delete Item**.

18 In the Microsoft Internet Explorer dialog box asking if you are sure you want to delete the item, click **OK**.

19 In the left navigation column, under **Actions**, click **Modify settings and columns**.

The Customize Garden Survey Discussion page is displayed.

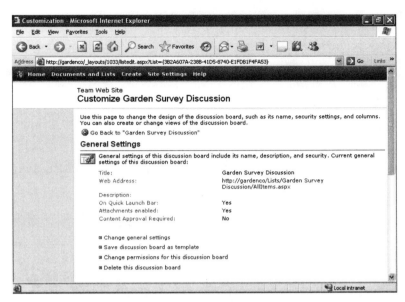

20 On the **Customize Garden Survey Discussion** page, click **Delete this discussion board**.

21 In the Microsoft Internet Explorer dialog box asking if you are sure you want to delete it, click **OK**.

The discussion board is deleted and the Documents and Lists page is displayed.

CLOSE Internet Explorer.

> **Tip** From the Customize page, you can enable content approval, create columns other than Subject and Text, or display views other than Threaded and Flat.

Key Points

- In a survey, you can create questions and control the response format.

- In a survey, you can create both open-ended and closed-ended questions.

- Windows SharePoint Services provides three views to summarize survey responses: Overview, Graphical Summary, and All Responses.

- You can export survey responses to a spreadsheet where you can perform more complex data analysis.

- With a discussion board, users can create and reply to discussion topics.

- You can view discussions in either Flat view or Threaded view.

- Surveys and discussion boards are specialized lists. Their permissions can be controlled independently of the site and of other lists. You can apply item-level permissions to prevent users from editing their survey responses or messages.

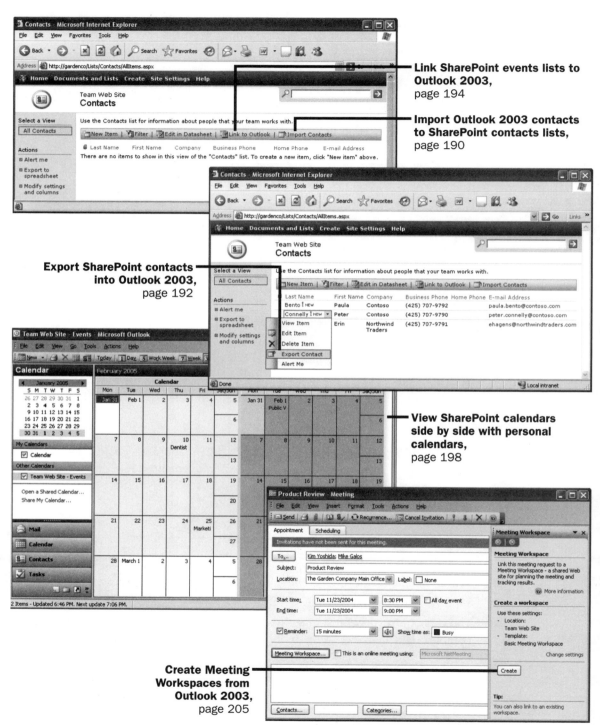

Link SharePoint events lists to Outlook 2003, page 194

Import Outlook 2003 contacts to SharePoint contacts lists, page 190

Export SharePoint contacts into Outlook 2003, page 192

View SharePoint calendars side by side with personal calendars, page 198

Create Meeting Workspaces from Outlook 2003, page 205

Chapter 10 at a Glance

10 Using Windows SharePoint Services with Outlook 2003

In this chapter you will learn to:

✔ Import Outlook 2003 contacts to SharePoint contacts lists.

✔ Export SharePoint Contacts into Outlook 2003.

✔ Link SharePoint Events lists to Outlook 2003.

✔ View SharePoint Calendars side by side with personal calendars.

✔ Copy appointments to personal calendars and set reminders.

✔ Manage SharePoint Alerts in Outlook 2003.

✔ Create Meeting Workspaces from Outlook 2003.

Microsoft Windows SharePoint Services integrates with Microsoft Office Outlook 2003, so you can keep a local read-only copy of your team's calendars and contacts lists. This local read-only copy is then available when you are not connected to the network and can be manually or automatically synchronized with the SharePoint site when you next connect. You can also import *contacts* from your Outlook *Address Book* into a contacts list on a SharePoint Web site and export individual contacts or events to your Outlook Contacts or *Calendar* folders. With other integration features, you can manage all of your SharePoint *alerts* from one Outlook dialog box, and by using Outlook *meeting requests* you can create Meeting Workspace sites.

In this chapter you will learn how to import Outlook Contacts to SharePoint Contacts lists, and then export SharePoint Contacts into Outlook 2003. You will also learn how to link SharePoint Events lists to Outlook; view SharePoint Calendars side by side with personal calendars; copy appointments to personal calendars and set reminders for those appointments; manage SharePoint Alerts in Outlook; and create meeting workspaces from Outlook.

See Also   Do you need only a quick refresher on the topics in this chapter? See the Quick Reference entries on pages xxxii–xxxiv.

Important   Remember to use your SharePoint site location in place of *http://gardenco* in the exercises.

BE SURE TO install and activate Microsoft Office 2003 before beginning any of the exercises in this chapter.

Importing Outlook 2003 Contacts to SharePoint Contacts Lists

If you have contact information in your Outlook Contacts folder, you can import them into a SharePoint contacts list. You can then share the contact information with users who visit your SharePoint site. The contacts imported in the SharePoint contacts list can be modified and deleted; however, these changes are not reflected in your Outlook Contacts folder, and changes made in your Outlook Contacts folder are not promoted to the SharePoint contacts list.

In this exercise, you will import the contact information from your Outlook Address Book to a contacts list on a SharePoint site.

OPEN the SharePoint site to which you would like to import the contact information. The exercise will use the *http://gardenco* site, but you can use whatever site you want. If prompted, type your user name and password, and then click OK.
BE SURE TO verify that you have sufficient rights to add contacts to a contacts list. If in doubt, see the Appendix on page 260.

> **Tip** This exercise works with Outlook 2002 as well as Outlook 2003.

1 On the **Quick Launch** bar, under the **Lists** section, click **Contacts**.

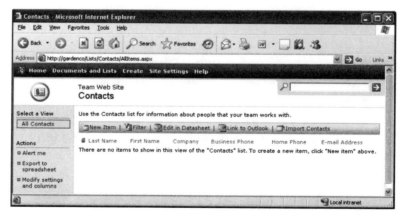

2 Click **Import Contacts**.

3 If the Choose Profile dialog box is displayed, select the profile that corresponds to your e-mail account, and then click **OK**.

The Select Users to Import dialog box is displayed.

4   From the **Show Names from the:** drop-down list, under **Outlook Address Book**, select **Contacts**.

Note   Users can be chosen from personal Contacts lists stored in Outlook, from contact information held in the Exchange Server *Global Address List* (GAL) or from other address lists that might be available in the Select Users to Import dialog box. Only those contacts with e-mail addresses are displayed. If you want to import a contact that does not have an e-mail address, you first need to edit the contact in Outlook, add a "dummy" address, such as, *someone@example.com*. Save the contact and then import the contact record into the SharePoint list.

5   Select the users you wish to import, and then click **OK**.

Tip   You can select multiple users by holding down the ⌈Ctrl⌋ or ⌈Shift⌋ key when you use the mouse to select the user.

6   If a **Microsoft Office Outlook** warning dialog box appears stating that a program is trying to access e-mail addresses you have stored in Outlook, click the **Allow access for:** check box, and then select **5 minutes** from the drop-down list.

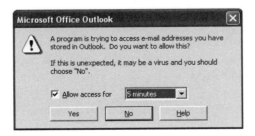

7 Click **Yes**.

The SharePoint Contacts list is redisplayed in the browser and now contains the new contact items.

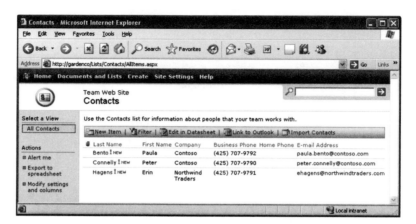

CLOSE Internet Explorer.

Exporting SharePoint Contacts into Outlook 2003

You can export any single contact or event item from a SharePoint list to Outlook. Once exported, the item in Outlook and the item on the SharePoint site can be edited independently. Use Outlook to edit the item that you exported to the Contacts or Calendar folder or use a browser to edit the original item in the SharePoint contacts or events list. There is no link between these two items, therefore amendments made to the item in Outlook are not reflected in the SharePoint list on your SharePoint Web site.

Although this section explains how to export a contact item into Outlook, you can export an event item using the same technique.

Warning   You cannot export a recurring series of events using this technique. You can export any individual occurrence from a recurring series by opening it from the Calendar view on your SharePoint site and then following the steps below.

In this exercise, you will export contacts from a contacts list on a SharePoint site into Outlook 2003.

OPEN the SharePoint site in which the contacts list is located. If prompted, type your user name and password, and then click OK. The exercise will use the Contacts list which was populated in the previous exercise, but you can use whatever contacts list you want. Ensure that there are contact items added to the list.
BE SURE TO verify that you have sufficient rights to read the contents of a contacts list. If in doubt, see the Appendix on page 260.

1   On the **Quick Launch** bar, under the **Lists** section, click **Contacts**.

2   In the **Contacts** list, move your mouse over the name of the user you want to export, so that a dark blue border appears around the user, and then click on the down arrow to the right of the user.

A drop-down menu appears.

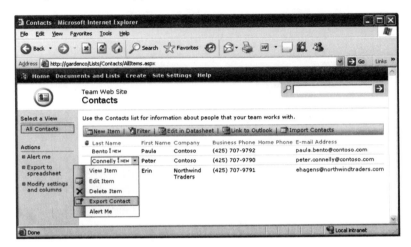

3   Click **Export Contact**.

The File Download dialog box opens.

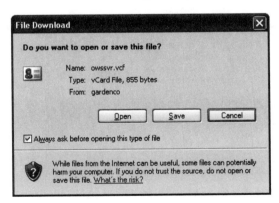

4   Click **Open** to open the owssvr.vcf file.

Note   The ability to add any single contact or event from a SharePoint list into your Outlook Contacts or Calendar is possible because Windows SharePoint Services supports the *vCard* and *iCalendar* standards for data interchange.

A new Contact form appears with information entered into the Outlook contact fields that correspond to the fields completed in the contact item in the SharePoint list.

5   If the **Full Name** field is blank, type the name of the contact. If the **File as:** field is blank, click the down arrow to the right of the field and select an appropriate value.

6   Click **Save and Close**.

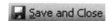

Note   If the name or e-mail address of the contact already exists in your Outlook Contacts folder, the Duplicate Contact Detected dialog box is displayed, so that you can resolve the conflict. Select the "Update new information from this contact to the existing one" option then click OK.

The contact is added to your Outlook Contacts folder.

CLOSE Internet Explorer.

Linking SharePoint Events Lists to Outlook 2003

With Outlook 2003, you can link any SharePoint contacts or events list to Outlook. This section explains how to link a SharePoint events list to Outlook. To link a SharePoint contacts list use the same technique.

By linking a SharePoint events list to Outlook, you are creating an Outlook Calendar folder in which a read-only copy of the data from the SharePoint list is stored locally. In this way, once you have created an event item in a SharePoint list, you can keep track of the event from the Outlook Calendar folder—even if you are not connected to the network. The advantage of this method over exporting event items, described in the previous section, is that you can copy a read-only version to the events in a SharePoint list—even recurring events—and when you are connected to the network and switch to the linked Outlook Calendar folder, Outlook synchronizes with the SharePoint list and approximately every 20 minutes thereafter.

Because the linked calendar folder is read-only, you cannot create, modify, or delete event items using Outlook. To create, edit, or delete event items, you must use the browser, navigate to the appropriate events list on your SharePoint site, and amend them.

In this exercise you will copy events locally to your machine. Using the method specified in this exercise, whenever you are connected to the network, the events in your Outlook calendar folder automatically refreshes with the events list on the SharePoint site.

OPEN the SharePoint site in which the events list is located. If prompted, type your user name and password, and then click OK.
BE SURE TO have an events list populated with at least one events item. If you do not have an events item, complete the relevant steps from the exercise in Chapter 4 that explains how to add, edit, and delete list items.

Note   Alternatively, you can create a practice site for this chapter based on site template *Chapter 10 Starter.stp* in the practice file folder for this chapter. The practice file folder is located in the *My Documents\Microsoft Press\SharePoint Services SBS\Chapter 10* folder. See "Using the Book's CD-ROM" on page vii for instructions on how to create a practice site.

1   Click **Events** on the Events bar to display the Events page.

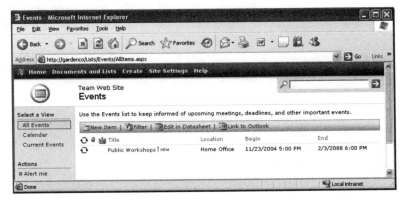

2   Click **Link to Outlook**.

Link to Outlook

A Microsoft Office Outlook warning dialog box appears asking if you want to add the folder to Outlook.

3 Click **Yes**.

Outlook opens and displays the Events Calendar in either Day, Work Week, Week, or Month Calendar view. In the navigation pane, under the Other Calendars, the new linked folder is selected automatically. The Outlook status bar contains the number of items in the current Calendar view, the time of the last update, and the next scheduled update.

4 On the Standard toolbar, click the **Month** button. If the current calendar view does not contain any event items, use the scroll bar until you can see them.

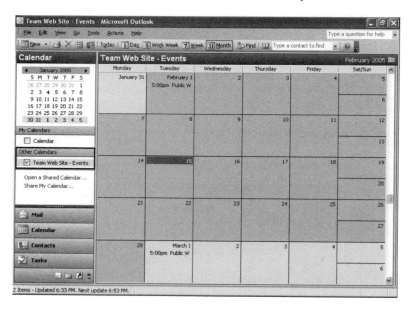

Warning You can't edit the appointments in the calendar directly from Outlook. If you try to edit an appointment and then click the Save and Close button, a Microsoft Office Outlook warning dialog box is displayed, asking whether you want to save a copy of the appointment in your default Calendar folder.

5 To update the Outlook copy, right-click the **Events** Calendar folder, and in the drop-down menu, click **Refresh**.

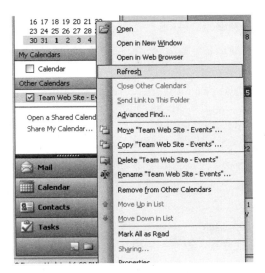

An Outlook Send/Receive Progress dialog box appears showing the progress of the update.

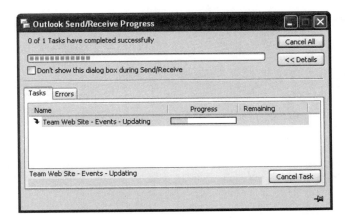

Tip To remove a linked SharePoint list from Outlook, right-click the name of the folder in the navigation pane under Other Calendars, and then select Delete *foldername* from the drop-down menu.

CLOSE Outlook and Internet Explorer.

Viewing SharePoint Calendars Side by Side with Personal Calendars

With Outlook you can work with multiple calendars, enabling you to create calendars for specific purposes, such as one for work and one for your home life. With Outlook 2003 you can view several calendars at the same time. When you view and scroll multiple calendars, they all display the same date or time period. This features is particularly useful if you have created a SharePoint linked Calendar folder.

In this exercise, you will view both your personal Outlook calendar and a linked SharePoint events list.

BE SURE TO start Microsoft Outlook before you begin this exercise.
BE SURE TO have a linked SharePoint events list or complete the third exercise in this chapter that explains how to link a SharePoint Events list to Outlook 2003.

1 In the Outlook navigation pane, under **My Calendars**, select the **Calendar** check box.

2 In the Outlook navigation pane, under **Other Calendars**, select the **Events** check box.

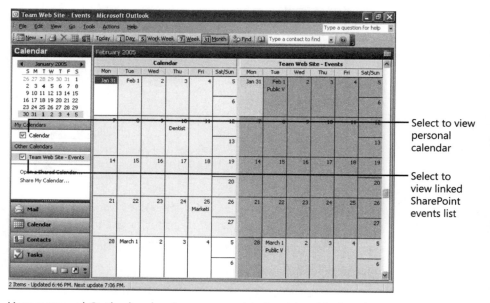

Select to view personal calendar

Select to view linked SharePoint events list

Your personal Outlook calendar appears side by side with the SharePoint events calendar you linked to in the previous exercise. The background color of the calendar folder name matches the color on the displayed calendar so that you can tell which is which.

CLOSE Outlook.

Copying Appointments to Personal Calendars and Setting Reminders

When you view several calendars, for example a calendar of a colleague who has shared their calendar, a calendar you have added for personal events, as well as your own My Calendar, at the same time, you can copy an appointment from one calendar to your own Outlook Calendar so that you can avoid double-booking appointments in your Outlook Calendar. You can also set reminders in your own Outlook Calendar; however, you can't set reminders from appointments in a linked SharePoint Events Calendar. When you copy an appointment from the SharePoint Calendar, you create a static copy of the appointment that is no longer linked to the SharePoint list and will not be refreshed when Outlook synchronizes the linked SharePoint Calendar to the SharePoint list.

In this exercise, you will copy an event from a linked calendar to your personal calendar.

BE SURE TO start Microsoft Outlook before you begin this exercise.
To complete this task, you must have a linked calendar or complete the fourth exercise in this chapter that explains how to view the SharePoint Calendar side by side with your personal calendar.

1 In Outlook, with your personal Calendar and linked SharePoint Events Calendar visible, double-click an appointment in the **Events** calendar that you want to copy to your own personal calendar.

An Appointment (Read-Only) dialog box is displayed.

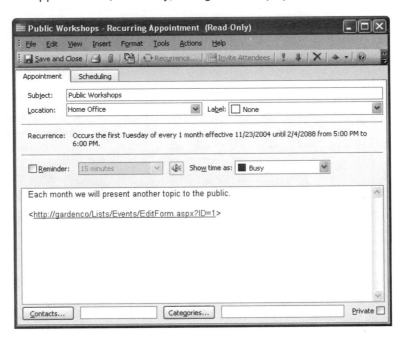

Copy to
Personal
Calendar

Close

2 On the Standard toolbar, click the **Copy to Personal Calendar** button once, and then close the **Appointment** dialog box by clicking the **Close** button in the top right hand corner.

Important If you click the Copy to Personal Calendar button multiple times, an appointment is added to your personal calendar for each click of the button.

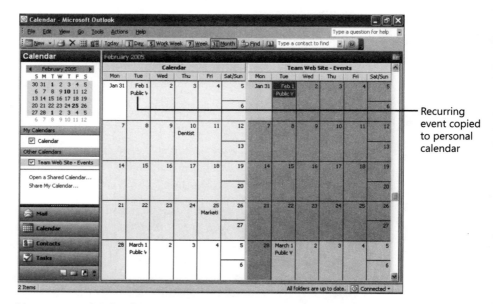

Recurring event copied to personal calendar

Your personal Calendar now contains a static copy of the event. If the event is a recurring event, then the copy in your personal Outlook calendar also functions as a recurring appointment.

Tip With your personal Calendar visible side by side with the SharePoint Calendar, you can drag the appointment from the SharePoint Calendar to your personal calendar. This creates a copy in your personal calendar, but be careful because if you drag it to a different date and time slot in your personal Calendar, then it will not match the SharePoint event.

3 Double-click the copy of the appointment in your personal calendar.

4 If this is a recurring item, the **Open Recurring Item** dialog box is displayed. Select **Open this occurrence**, and then click **OK**.

5 Select the **Reminder** check box and click **Save and Close**.

CLOSE Outlook and any Internet Explorer windows you might have open.

Managing SharePoint Alerts in Outlook 2003

When you create an alert for an item, such as a document, list item, document library, list, survey, or a search result, you immediately receive a confirmation e-mail message notifying you that the alert was successfully created. This message indicates that the alert process is working. The confirmation message also contains information about the alert and provides links to the SharePoint site where the item is located. When someone makes a change to the item, you receive an e-mail message alert that indicates what was changed, who made the change, and when the change was made.

By default, Windows SharePoint Services does not provide an alert aggregation capability for all of your alerts across all SharePoint sites. To manage your alerts using the browser you would have to visit each site that has an alert set. To help you manage your alerts, you could save the message notifying you that an alert was successfully created because it provides a link to the SharePoint site. You could then use the e-mail message alert to navigate to those sites where you have alerts set.

In an environment where there are many SharePoint sites, managing your alerts could be a daunting task if you only had the links in e-mail alert messages and your memory of which SharePoint sites you had alerts set up. With Outlook 2003, you can manage the e-mail alerts received from all SharePoint intranet and trusted Web sites from one dialog box.

In this exercise, you will use Outlook to create a new alert. In a previous exercise in this chapter you exported contact details from a SharePoint contacts list into your Outlook Contacts folder. As there is no automated way of ensuring exported contact items remain in synch with their counterpart in the SharePoint contacts list, by setting up an alert you will be notified if anyone changes the contact details on SharePoint contacts list.

BE SURE TO start Microsoft Outlook before you begin this exercise and open your inbox. The exercise will use the SharePoint Contacts list on the *http://gardenco* site, but you can use any list or library on whatever site you want.

1   On the Outlook menu, click **Tools**, and then click **Rules and Alerts**.

Warning   If you don't have the Rules and Alerts option on the Tools menu, you are probably viewing your Outlook Calendar. Click Mail to view your e-mail messages.

The Rules and Alerts dialog box is displayed.

2   Click the **Manage Alerts** tab.

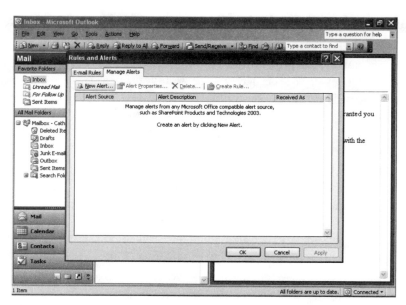

3   Click **New Alert**.

The New Alert dialog box is displayed.

4   In the **Web site Address** text box, type the URL of a SharePoint site that contains a contacts list, and then click **Open**.

An Internet Explorer window opens displaying the New Alert Web page.

5   Select the **Contacts** option.

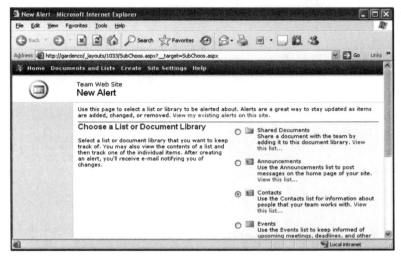

6   Scroll down to the end of the Web page, and then click the **Next** button.

The New Alert: Contacts: All items page is displayed.

7   In the **Send Alerts To** section, type your e-mail address if it doesn't already appear. Review the other settings.

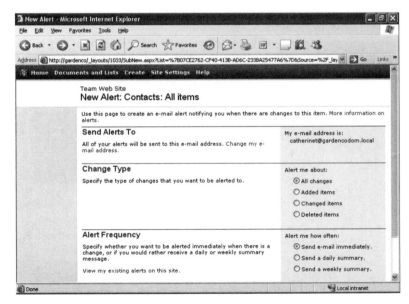

8   Scroll to the bottom of the page, and then click **OK**.

Note   If your SharePoint server has not configured to send e-mail, an Error page will display.

The "My Alerts on this Site" page is displayed. and, under the "Frequency: Immediate" section, the alert "Contacts: All items" is listed for "All changes."

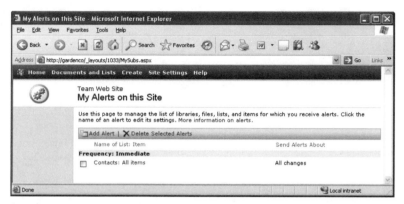

9 Close all the Internet Explorer windows.

10 Switch to Outlook where the **Rules and Alerts** dialog box should still be visible.

A new alert for Contacts: All items (All Changes) should be listed.

Note If the alert does not appear in the Rules and Alerts dialog box, click OK and then close Outlook. Restart Outlook and reopen the Rules and Alerts dialog box.

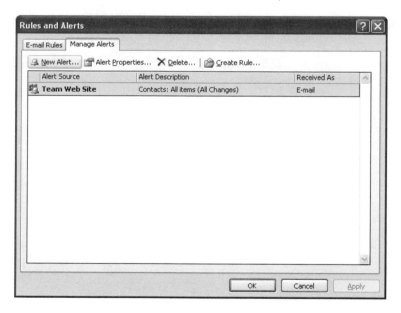

From the Rules and Alerts dialog box you can:

- Alter the properties of an alert. The Alert Properties dialog box provides links to: the SharePoint site, modify the alert, view the item on which the alert is set, and the "My Alerts on this Site" Web page.

- Select multiple Alerts by using the Ctrl or Shift key when you click an alert. You can then click the Delete button to delete all the alerts you selected. Click Yes to the Microsoft Office Outlook warning dialog box that appears and asks if you want to delete the selected rows.

- Use Outlook Rules to manage your alerts, so that a notification window pops up, a sound is played, the alert e-mail message is moved to a specified folder, or some other action is performed on the alert message.

CLOSE all Outlook dialog boxes, and then close Outlook.

See Also For more information about managing alerts on lists and documents using the browser, see in Chapter 4, "Working with Lists," and Chapter 5, "Creating and Managing Libraries."

Creating Meeting Workspaces from Outlook 2003

When you create an Outlook 2003 meeting request, you can also create a *Meeting Workspace* site, or link the meeting to an existing workspace site. In Chapter 8, you were introduced to Meeting Workspaces, which enable you to share your meeting agenda and objectives, publish documents and files, track tasks, and complete other collaborative activities through one central location. By centralizing this information, your meeting attendees have access to the latest information and you avoid sending files through your e-mail system.

In this exercise, you will create a Meeting Workspace from Outlook.

BE SURE TO start Microsoft Outlook before you begin this exercise.
BE SURE TO verify that you have sufficient rights to create a SharePoint site. If in doubt, see the Appendix on page 260.

1 In Outlook, on the Standard toolbar, click the down arrow to the right of **New**, and then click **Appointment**.

   A new, untitled appointment form opens.

2 On the Standard toolbar, click **Invite Attendees**.

   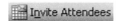

   The appointment form is converted into an untitled meeting request form and displays a To text box where you can invite others to the meeting.

3 In the **To** text box, type the e-mail addresses of people you want to invite to this meeting and, in the **Subject** text box, type **Product Review**.

Important SharePoint uses the Subject of the meeting request as the Meeting Workspace site name. If you create a Meeting Workspace site with a blank meeting request Subject line, Outlook will create a Meeting Workspace site with the name *UntitledXXX*, where *XXX* is a number based on the number of existing untitled named sites.

4 In the **Location** text box, type **The Garden Company Main Office**.

5 Click the **Meeting Workspace** button.

The Meeting Workspace task pane appears to the right of the form.

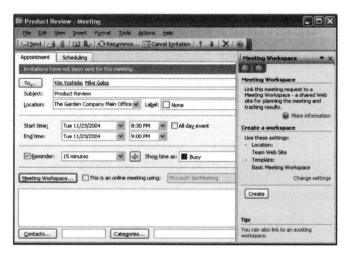

6 In the **Meeting Workspace** task pane, in the **Create a workspace** section, click **Change settings**.

The Meeting Workspace task pane displays the "Select a workspace" settings.

7 Click the down arrow next to **Select a location**, and then select **Other**.

The Other Workspace Server dialog box is displayed.

8 Type the URL of a SharePoint site.

The Meeting Workspace site will be a subsite of the SharePoint site you type here.

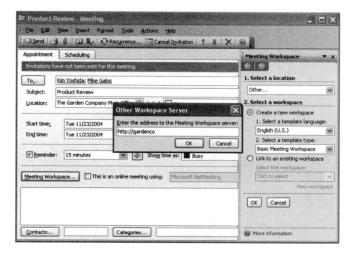

Note You can't create a new Meeting Workspace site under an existing Meeting Workspace site. You must also be a member of a site group with the Create Subsites right for the parent site.

9 Click **OK**.

Tip You can select a different language for your site if other language packs are installed on your SharePoint server. You can also choose a different Meeting Workspace template. By default, SharePoint installs five Meeting workspace templates: Basic Meeting Workspace, Blank Meeting Workspace, Decision Making Workspace, Social Meeting Workspace, and Multipage Meeting Workspace.

10 In the **Meeting Workspace** task pane, click **OK**, and then click **Create**.

Outlook connects to the SharePoint Web site and creates the workspace. The meeting request and Meeting Workspace task pane are updated.

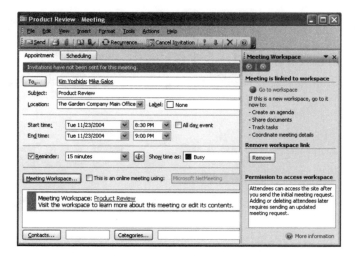

11 On the Standard toolbar, click **Send**.

Outlook attempts to add the attendees to the Meeting Workspace site in the Contributor site group. If Outlook was unable to include the attendees to the site, you will receive a notification.

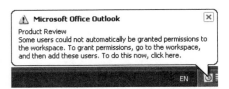

To add or remove attendees after creating the Meeting Workspace, add or remove them from the meeting request in Outlook. When you send the meeting request, Outlook will update the Meeting Workspace.

Important   If you change the meeting request and click Save and Close instead of clicking Send, the updates will not be sent to the Meeting Workspace site.

You can also add and remove attendees through the Meeting Workspace site by clicking Manage attendees in the Attendees area; however, this will not update the meeting request in Outlook, which you will need to do manually.

Attendees can access the Meeting Workspace site you created by clicking the link in the invitation e-mail they receive from you. Here is a sample of the invitation e-mail:

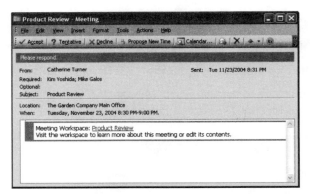

Clicking the Product Review link displays the Product Review Meeting Workspace site.

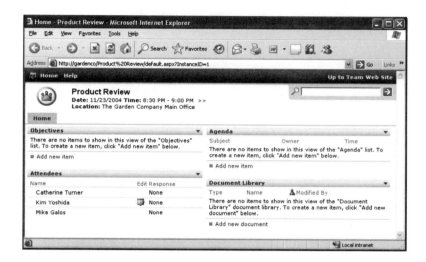

CLOSE Outlook and any Internet Explorer windows you might have open.

Key Points

- You can import personal contacts listed in your personal Outlook Contacts folder into a SharePoint contacts list.

- You can export any single contact or event item from a SharePoint list to Outlook 2003. There is no synchronization between SharePoint and Outlook for exported items.

- You can link any SharePoint contacts or events list to Outlook. This creates a read-only folder in Outlook that you can manually synchronize with the SharePoint list or that synchronizes automatically every 20 minutes.

- In Outlook 2003, you can view multiple calendars side by side. These calendars can be linked SharePoint events lists.

- You can manage all your SharePoint alerts from the Outlook 2003 Rules and Alerts dialog box.

- You can create a Meeting Workspace site from Outlook with a Meeting Request. Using this technique, you create a Meeting Workspace as a subsite to a SharePoint Web site.

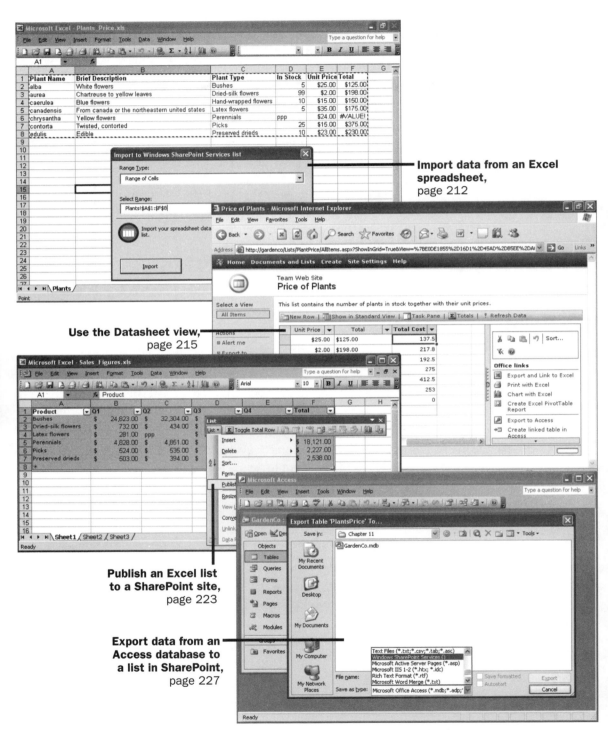

Import data from an Excel spreadsheet, page 212

Use the Datasheet view, page 215

Publish an Excel list to a SharePoint site, page 223

Export data from an Access database to a list in SharePoint, page 227

Chapter 11 at a Glance

11 Using Windows SharePoint Services with Excel 2003 and Access 2003

In this chapter you will learn to:

✔ Import data from an Excel spreadsheet to a list in SharePoint.

✔ Use the Datasheet view.

✔ Export a SharePoint list to an Excel spreadsheet.

✔ Publish an Excel list to a SharePoint site.

✔ Export data from an Access database to a list in SharePoint.

✔ Import a list to an Access Table.

✔ Link an Access table to a SharePoint list.

Microsoft Windows SharePoint Services provides the collaborative backbone to the Microsoft Office System. In previous chapters, you saw how, within Office 2003, you could share and manage documents stored in a SharePoint Web site. You also created SharePoint sites from your Office programs.

This chapter focuses on the integration of Windows SharePoint Services with Microsoft Office Excel 2003 and Microsoft Office Access 2003. With both these products you can export and import data to and from SharePoint lists. Excel 2003 also provides two-way synchronization between Excel spreadsheets and SharePoint lists, so you can work with lists when you are offline, and then synchronize the changes when you reconnect.

See Also Do you need only a quick refresher on the topics in this chapter? See the Quick Reference entries on pages xxxiv–xxxvii.

 Important Before you can use the practice files in this chapter, be sure you install them from the book's companion CD to their default location. See "Using the Book's CD-ROM" on page vii for more information.

Importing Data from an Excel Spreadsheet to a List in SharePoint

In many situations, you might already have data within a spreadsheet, but later find that you need to share the data with other members of your team. SharePoint has the ability to import data from an Excel spreadsheet into a SharePoint list. Users with appropriate permissions may read the SharePoint list, while others may even revise the list or enter additional data. You can choose to import all the spreadsheet data, a *range* of cells, a *named range*, or an *Excel list*.

In this exercise, you will use your browser to create a SharePoint custom list that contains data imported from an Excel spreadsheet.

OPEN the SharePoint site to which you would like to import data from the Excel spreadsheet. Remember to use your SharePoint site location in place of *http://gardenco* in the exercises. If prompted, type your user name and password, and then click OK.

USE the Plants_Price.xls document in the practice file folder for this topic. This practice file is located in the *My Documents\Microsoft Press\SharePoint Services SBS\Chapter 11* folder.

BE SURE TO install and activate Microsoft Office 2003 before beginning any of the exercises in this chapter, and that you have sufficient rights to create a new list. If in doubt, see the Appendix on page 260.

1   On the top link bar, click **Create**.

The Create page is displayed.

2   In the **Custom Lists** section, click **Import Spreadsheet**.

The New List page is displayed.

3   In the **Name** text box, type PlantPrice.

Tip   Any URL in SharePoint is limited to 260 characters. The name you type here is used to create the URL and title of the list. Later in this exercise you will alter the title with a user-friendly name.

4   In the **Description** text box, type This list contains the number of plants in stock together with their unit prices.

Note   If you import a spreadsheet into a site based on the Meeting Workspace template, an option button appears on the New List page enabling you to share the same items for all meetings. If you choose not to share the same items for all meetings, then each meeting displays the list with just the items added for that date.

5   Click the **Browse** button.

The Choose file dialog box appears showing either your My Documents folder or the last folder you accessed.

6   If the My Documents folder is not displayed in the **Choose file** dialog box, click the **My Documents** icon.

7   Double-click the folder names **Microsoft Press**, **SharePoint Services SBS**, and **Chapter 11**, and then double click the file **Plants_Price.xls**.

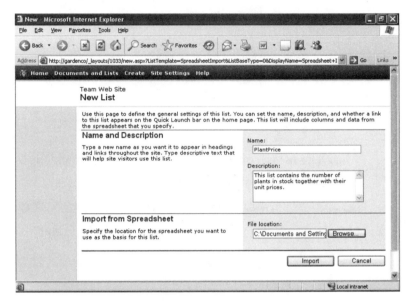

8   On the **New List** page, click the **Import** button.

Excel opens Plants_Price.xls and displays the Import to Windows SharePoint Services List dialog box.

9   From the **Range Type** drop-down list, select **Range of Cells**, then press Tab.

10   In the spreadsheet, select the range of cells A1 to F8, and then on the dialog box, click the **Import** button.

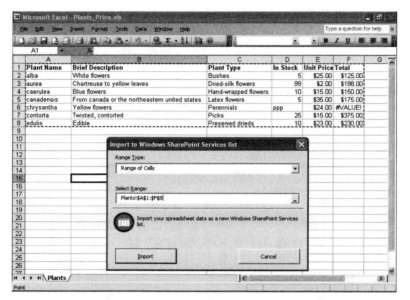

The All Items view of the PlantPrice list is displayed, and the URL in the Address box is *http://gardenco/Lists/PlantPrice/AllItems.aspx*.

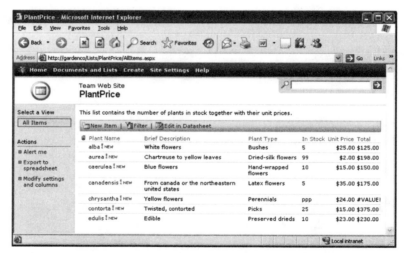

11 In the left navigation bar under **Actions**, click **Modify settings and columns** to change the title of the list.

The Customize PlantPrice page appears.

12 Under **General Settings**, click **Change general settings**.

The List Settings: PlantPrice page appears.

13 Under the **Name and Description** section, in the **Name** text box, type a user-friendly name, such as Price of Plants.

14 Under the **Navigation** section, select the **Yes** option to display this list on the Quick Launch bar.

15 Click **OK** at the bottom of the page.

The Customize: Price of Plants page appears.

16 Click the **Go Back to "Price of Plants"** link.

The All Items view of the Price of Plants list appears. The title of the list has changed to Price of Plants, and this name change can be seen on the page, but the URL remains set as *http://gardenco/Lists/PlantPrice/AllItems.aspx*.

CLOSE Internet Explorer.

Using the Datasheet View

If you have created a list by importing an Excel spreadsheet, you might find it convenient to use a spreadsheet-like environment when editing, formatting, or entering data into your newly created list. This spreadsheet-like environment is called the *Datasheet view*, which was introduced in Chapter 4.

Using the Datasheet view of a list or library can be a huge productivity boost, but to make use of this view you must have Office 2003 installed on your computer and make sure your browser supports Microsoft ActiveX controls. If these requirements are not met, a message indicating that the list will be displayed in Standard view appears. Along with the Explorer view of a document library, the following list types do not support the datasheet view:

- Discussion board
- Survey
- Image gallery
- Web template library
- Web Part catalog
- Data sources
- Inbox

The Datasheet view presents all the list items of a list in a grid and facilitates editing across the entire table. A *task pane* on the right edge of the Datasheet view enables powerful integration between Windows SharePoint Services, Excel 2003, and Access 2003.

In the following exercise, you will add a new list item, edit an existing list item, remove an existing list item, add a list field, and briefly explore the task pane.

OPEN the SharePoint site where you imported data from the Excel spreadsheet. Remember to use your SharePoint site location in place of *http://gardenco* in the exercises. If prompted, type your user name and password and click OK.

BE SURE TO complete the first exercise in this chapter, "Importing Data from an Excel Spreadsheet to a List in SharePoint" before beginning this exercise.

BE SURE TO verify that you have sufficient rights to contribute to the list. If in doubt, see the Appendix on page 260.

1 On the **Quick Launch** bar under **Lists**, click **Price of Plants.**

2 Click **Edit in Datasheet** to change the display from Standard view.

Edit in Datasheet

The Standard view changes to the Datasheet view.

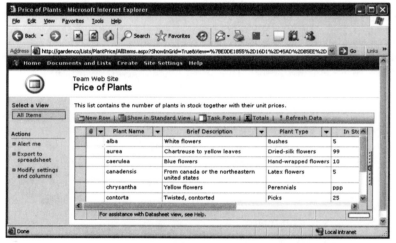

Edit

Saving

New Item

Note A Datasheet view consists of rows, each row corresponding to a list item. A column corresponds to a list field. The down arrow in the column headings is used to filter and sort the data. Using the Datasheet view is like editing a table in Access; when you type a value in a cell or choose a value from a drop-down list, an Edit icon appears to the far left indicating that changes have been made to the row. You can use the arrow keys or mouse to move from cell to cell to make changes to any row in the list. When you leave a row that was changed or you navigate away from the Web page, a Saving icon indicates that Windows SharePoint Services is updating the database with your changes. You can continue making changes to different rows, and Windows SharePoint Services saves your changes in the background. If your changes result in a conflict or error, the Datasheet view updates with information necessary to resolve the conflict or error. The last row in the Datasheet view is always empty and the New Item icon is displayed in the left hand column. This empty row can be used to add additional list items to the list. The Datasheet view does not display the star (*) row for a document library.

Tip All list items in the list are displayed on one page in the Datasheet view regardless of how large the list is. Therefore, it isn't practical to edit extremely large lists using the Datasheet view. To improve performance of a Datasheet view, apply one or more filters to hide unnecessary columns, but do not remove those columns that are marked as Required.

3 In the last row of the list, in the **Plant Name** column, type nana, press Tab, type Dwarf, press Tab, and then type P.

Just like in Excel, the IntelliSense feature displays other values that occur in this column.

4 Press the ↓ to choose Picks, and then press Enter.

The new item row changes to the currently edited row and another new item row is added to the bottom of the list.

Tip Just like in other Microsoft Office programs, you can use Ctrl+X to cut, Ctrl+C to copy, Ctrl+V to paste, Ctrl+Z to undo any changes, and Esc to cancel edit on the current list item.

Horizontal Resize pointer

5 Position the pointer on the boundary between the column headings **Brief Description** and **Plant type** until the horizontal resize pointer appears.

6 Drag the column boundary to the right until the all the descriptions are on one line.

Vertical Resize pointer

Tip Rows can be resized in much the same way by using the vertical resize pointer between the rows. You can resize both rows and columns based upon content by double-clicking. You can also reorder columns; just drag them to the desired location.

7 Click on the far left cell to select the entire Blue flowers list item.

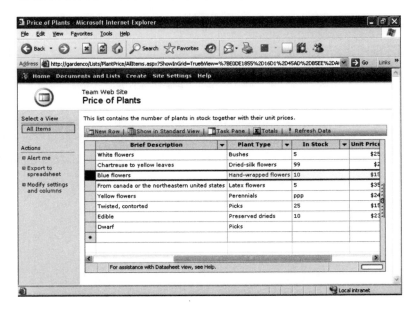

➡
Row Select
pointer

⬇
Column Select
pointer

↘
List Select
pointer

Tip It is possible to select and then delete multiple list items. Alternatively, while selected, you can copy and paste the list items into Office programs. You can select the entire list with a single click in the top left corner cell.

Holding down the [Shift] key while selecting list items selects all rows or columns between the first click and the second click. However, holding down the [Ctrl] key while selecting does not select and deselect list items regardless of adjacency like you might expect. Instead, it exclusively selects the clicked row, abandoning all other selection in the same way as clicking without holding down the [Ctrl] key.

8 Press the [Del] key to permanently remove the list item from the list.

A delete confirmation dialog box appears.

9 Click **Yes** to finish deleting the list item and redisplay the Datasheet view of the list.

10 Click the fourth cell in the **In Stock** column and replace ppp with 10, and then press [Tab].

11 Replace $24.00 with 25 and then press [Tab].

The list item is saved to the database and a dollar sign ($) is placed before the number 25. This is because the Unit Price column is a *Currency* type.

12 Replace #VALUE! with 250, and then press [Enter].

The list item is saved to the database, but no dollar ($) sign is placed before the number 250. When you imported the spreadsheet in the previous exercise, the In Stock and Total columns were created as a *Single line of text* type because they did not contain data of one particular type, whereas the Unit Price column contained only currency values. In the Excel spreadsheet, the Total column was a calculated column. To provide the same functionality in the SharePoint list, the column needs to be a calculated data type. You cannot change the data type of an existing column to a calculated data type. You have to create a new column of calculated data type.

13 Right-click on the **Total** column, and then click **Add Column** in the context menu.

The Price of Plants: Add Column page appears.

14 In the **Name and Type** section, in the **Column Name** text box, type Total Cost, and then select the **Calculated (calculation based on other columns)** option.

15 In the **Optional Settings for Column** section under the **Insert Column**, double-click **In Stock**.

16 Scroll to the bottom of the page and click **OK**.

17 Click the first cell in the **Total Cost** column, type =[In Stock]*[Unit Price]*1.1, and then press ⌷Enter⌷.

A dialog box appears warning you that the results of your calculation change could take some time.

18 Click **Continue**.

The Datasheet View status bar displays the formula you typed.

Note *Formulas* are equations that perform calculations on values in the list and are very similar to the formulas you would use in Excel, that is, they can contain *functions, column references, operators,* and *constants.* For example a formula could be =PI()*[In Stock]^2, where PI() is a function, * and ^ are operators, [In Stock] is a column reference and 2 is a constant.

19 Click on the vertical bar on the far right side of the Datasheet View page to expose the task pane, which enables you to quickly integrate the SharePoint site with Excel and Access 2003.

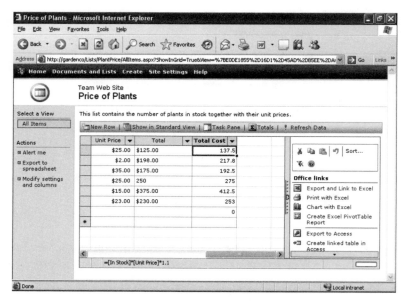

At the top of the task pane are a series of buttons for common commands, such as Cut, Copy, Paste, Undo, Custom Sort, Remove Filter/Sort and Help.

See Also More information on the Datasheet view can be found by clicking the Help icon in the task pane, by clicking the Help link on the Datasheet view status bar, by clicking a cell in the Datasheet view and then pressing F1, or by right-clicking any cell inside the Datasheet view and then clicking Help.

CLOSE Internet Explorer.

Exporting a SharePoint List to an Excel Spreadsheet

You can export the contents of SharePoint lists, results of a survey, or document libraries to an Excel spreadsheet. The exported list or library is a Web Query that stays updated with changes to the original list in your SharePoint site. The Excel spreadsheet maintains a connection to the SharePoint list, that is, the Excel spreadsheet is a *linked object*.

In this exercise, you will export a list from a SharePoint site to an Excel spreadsheet. You will add data to the spreadsheet and then synchronize the data in the spreadsheet with the contents of the list on the SharePoint site.

OPEN the SharePoint site where you have a list from which you can export data to an Excel spreadsheet. This exercise uses the list you created in the first exercise of this chapter. Remember to use your SharePoint site location and list in place of *http://gardenco* and *Price of Plants* in the exercises. If prompted, type your user name and password, and then click OK.

1 On the Quick Launch bar under the **Lists** section, click **Price of Plants**, and then click the **All Items** view.

Tip   The export process only exports the columns and rows contained in the list's current view, which in this exercise is the All Items view. If none of the views contain the data you want to export, then you will have to create a new view to meet your needs. Alternatively, you can choose one of the existing views, export the list to a spreadsheet, and then delete the unwanted data.

2   In the left navigation area under **Actions**, click **Export to spreadsheet**.

Tip   If this list was a survey, you would click Export Results to a spreadsheet.

3   If the **File Download** box is displayed, click the **Open** button.

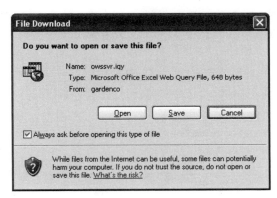

Excel opens a new workbook that contains one worksheet, named *owssvr(1)* and an Opening Query dialog box is displayed warning you of the risk of opening queries.

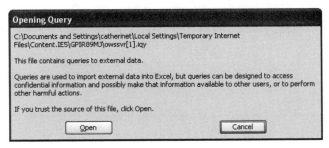

4   Click the **Open** button.

The owssvr(1) worksheet now contains an Excel List; each column in the list has an AutoFilter arrow in the header row and there is a dark blue border around the list. The List toolbar appears.

Tip   If the List toolbar does not appear, on the View menu point to Toolbars, and then click List.

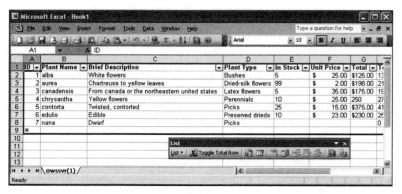

5 Click cell B9, type Carophyllus, press Tab, type To give strength and energy, press Tab type Pi, and then press Tab again.

IntelliSense completes the word *Picks* for you.

6 Type 5, press Tab, type 10, and then press Enter.

Excel places a dollar ($) sign before the number 10 and the Total Cost column calculates the data in that column. The columns in Excel have retained the data types from the exported SharePoint list.

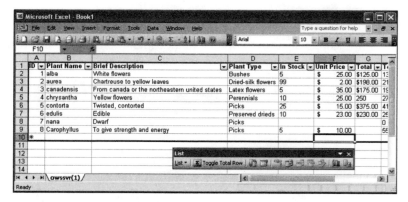

Synchronize List

7 On the **Lists** toolbar, click the **Synchronize List** button.

Discard Changes and Refresh

Tip If you wish to discard all the changes you have made to the spreadsheet, you can click the "Discard Changes and Refresh" button on the Lists toolbar.

Refresh

8 Switch back to the **Price of Plants** page, click the Internet Explorer **Refresh** button, and then verify that the Carophyllus item has been added to the bottom of the list.

9 Click **New Item**.

The Price of Plants: New Item page is displayed.

10 In the **Plant Name** text box, type Pumila and then click **Save and Close**.

The Pumila item is added to the Price of Plants list.

11 Switch back to Excel, on the **List** toolbar, click the **Synchronize List** button and verify that the Pumila item has been added to the bottom of the spreadsheet.

Tip You can also initiate exporting and linking a SharePoint list to Excel by using the Datasheet View task pane.

CLOSE Internet Explorer and Excel. You do not have to save the spreadsheet.

Publishing an Excel List to a SharePoint Site

Creating a SharePoint list from within Excel 2003 is known as *publishing* an Excel list. Once the list is on the SharePoint site, users can see the Excel data without opening Excel.

In this exercise, you will publish a spreadsheet to a SharePoint list by using Excel 2003 and a two-step wizard.

BE SURE TO start Excel before beginning this exercise.
USE the Sales_Figures.xls document in the practice file folder for this topic. This practice file is located in the *My Documents\Microsoft Press\SharePoint Services SBS\Chapter 11* folder. Remember to use your SharePoint site location in place of *http://gardenco* in the exercises.
OPEN the Sales_Figures.xls document.

1 In Excel, click any cell within the data.

2 On the **Data** menu, point to **List**, and then click **Create List**.

Note The Create List dialog box appears and the data is automatically selected. By selecting one cell in the data, Excel will automatically selects the range of cells that contain data. You can select a different range of cells to use for creating a list. In addition, if your data does not have headers, Excel creates them for you, and labels them Column1, Column2, and so on. If the data you want to export is already in an Excel list, you do not have to complete the first three tasks of this exercise.

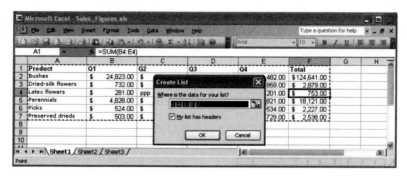

3   Click **OK**.

Excel converts the data in the workbook into a list. Each column header has an AutoFilter arrow and a dark blue border surrounds the data, that is, the list is active on the worksheet.

The List toolbar appears.

Note   If the list is not active on the worksheet, then the List toolbar disappears and the list border color changes to a light blue. To publish a list, it must be active on the worksheet. To make a list active click any cell in the list.

4   On the **List** toolbar, click the **List** button and from the menu, click **Publish List**.

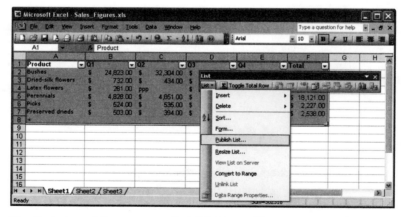

The first step of the two-step Publish List to SharePoint Site Wizard is displayed.

5   In the **Address** box, type http://gardenco.

6   Select the **Link to the new SharePoint list** check box.

Important   If "Link to the new SharePoint list" check box is selected, the spreadsheet is linked to the SharePoint list and you then can synchronize updates between the spreadsheet and the SharePoint list. However, once the SharePoint list is created, you cannot link the spreadsheet to the SharePoint list. Therefore, if you wish to synchronize updates between the list and the spreadsheet, be sure to select this check box now.

7   In the **Name** box, type SalesFigures, and in the **Description** box type, This list contains the number of plants in stock together with their prices.

8   Click the **Next** button.

Excel checks the data in each column to ensure that the data belongs to one of the data types supported by Windows SharePoint Services. If it doesn't, Excel usually applies the text data type to each column. Excel also checks whether each column contains only one type of data. If a column contains a mix of data type, for instance, numbers and text, then Excel would choose text as the data type. Once Excel has completed its check, the second step of the Publish List to SharePoint Site Wizard is displayed.

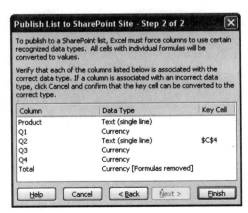

Look at the Key Cell column and notice that in Column Q2, cell *C4* contains a different data type from the rest of the cells in this column. In addition, the formulas for the Total column are removed.

Tip You could click the Cancel button, correct the erroneous data, and then restart the publishing process. Also, during the publishing process, because Excel removes formulas, once you have completed the publishing process and the data is on your SharePoint site, you might consider deleting the Total column and creating a calculated column.

9 Click the **Finish** button.

A Windows SharePoint Services dialog box is displayed with the URL of your new SharePoint List.

10 Click the **http://gardenco/Lists/SalesFigures/Allitemsg.aspx** link.

A new Internet Explorer window opens displaying the new SharePoint list.

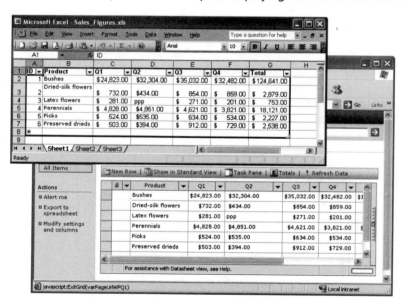

Note Before you close Excel, notice that the spreadsheet contains an extra column. When you publish a spreadsheet that is linked to a SharePoint list, an ID column is added as column A to your spreadsheet. The ID column contains a unique identifier for each record in the list. This is needed by the SharePoint site for updating purposes. This column is read-only and cannot be removed from the list unless you unlink the list from the SharePoint site. To unlink a spreadsheet from it's SharePoint site, on the Data menu, point to List, and then click Unlink List. To view the SharePoint list to which a spreadsheet is linked, on the Data menu, point to List, and then click "View List on Server."

CLOSE all Internet Explorer windows, close the Windows SharePoint Services dialog box by clicking OK, then close Excel after saving changes to the spreadsheet.

Exporting Data from an Access Database to a List in SharePoint

Access enables you to export a table or other database objects to a number of formats such as an external file, Lotus 1-2-3, Paradox, or dBase databases to an Excel workbook, to an XML document, or to an ODBC data source. With Access 2003, you can now export a table to a SharePoint site where a new list is created.

In this exercise, from within an Access database, you will export a table into a SharePoint site by creating a new SharePoint list.

USE the GardenCo.mdb database in the practice folder for the next three sections. This practice file is located in the *My Documents\Microsoft Press\SharePoint Services SBS\Chapter 11* folder. Remember to use your SharePoint site location in place of *http://gardenco* in the exercises.
BE SURE TO start Access before beginning this exercise.
OPEN the GardenCo.mdb database. If asked to block unsafe expressions, click Yes. Restart Access, open GardenCo.mdb, and then acknowledge the security warning.

1   In the **GardenCo: Database** window, click **Tables**.

2   Right-click the **PlantsPrice** table and from the context menu click **Export**.

The Export Table 'PlantsPrice' To dialog box is displayed.

3   From the **Save as type** drop-down list, select **Windows SharePoint Services()**.

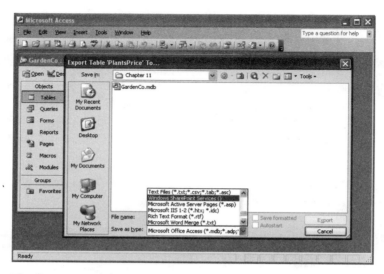

The first page of the Export to Windows SharePoint Services Wizard appears.

4 In the **Site** drop-down list, select **http://gardenco**.

Note If the URL for The Garden Company Web site does not appear in the drop-down list, type the URL in the Site text box.

5 In the **List Name** text box, type **accPlantsPrice**.

6 Leave the **Open the list when finished** check box selected.

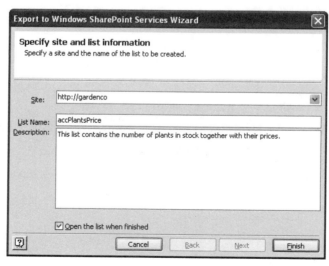

7 Click the **Finish** button.

The Microsoft Office Access dialog box is displayed with the message that Access has finished exporting the table to the Web site.

8   Click **OK**.

Internet Explorer displays the newly created accPlantsPrice list in Datasheet view.

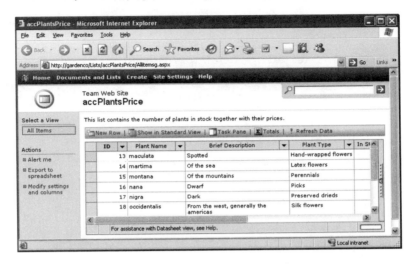

Tip   If you mistype the Web site name in the Site text box, Access displays a warning dialog box that it can't find the Web site. If this occurs, verify the address of the Web site and try again.

CLOSE Access and Internet Explorer.

Importing a List to an Access Table

With Access you can create a new table by importing data from an external data source, such as Lotus 1-2-3, Paradox or dBase databases, from an Excel workbook; from a Microsoft Outlook or Microsoft Exchange folder; from an XML document; or to an ODBC data source—and with Access 2003, from a SharePoint Web site. The data in the new table is not updated when subsequent changes are made to the data source after it is imported.

In this exercise, you will import data from a SharePoint list into an Access table.

USE the GardenCo.mdb database in the practice folder. This practice file is located in the *My Documents \Microsoft Press\SharePoint Services SBS\Chapter 11* folder. Remember to use your SharePoint site location in place of *http://gardenco* in the exercises. This exercise uses the SharePoint list, Price of Plants, you created in the first exercise of this chapter. You can use your own list if you want.
BE SURE TO start Access before beginning this exercise.
OPEN the GardenCo.mdb database and acknowledge the security warning, if necessary.

1   On the **File** menu, point to **Get External Data**, and then click **Import**.

The Import dialog box appears.

2 From the **Files of type** drop-down list, select **Windows SharePoint Services()**.

The "Select a site" page of the Import from Windows SharePoint Services Wizard appears.

3 In the **Sites** text box, type http://gardenco.

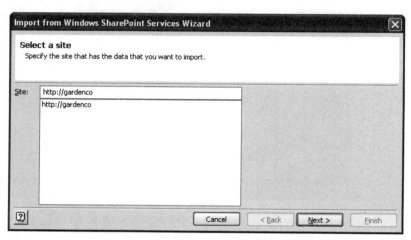

4 Click the **Next** button.

The "Select lists" page of the Import from Windows SharePoint Services Wizard appears.

5 In the **Lists** text box, select **Price of Plants**, and then select the **Import one or more lists** option.

Tip   If you choose to import one or more lists, then on the "Select lists" page you can select more than one list by holding down the ⌨ key at the same time as you select the list. If any of the columns in the SharePoint list were lookup columns, you can choose to maintain that *relationship* by selecting the "Retrieve IDs for lookup columns" check box. If you deselect this check box, the corresponding column in the Access database is not a lookup column, but contains values and not IDs.

6 Click the **Next** button.

The "Select related lists" page of the Import from Windows SharePoint Services Wizard appears. You will only see this page if the "Retrieve IDs for lookup columns" check box is selected.

7 Select the **Create linked tables to selected lists** option.

Note   The Price of Plants list contains a column named *Created By* and *Modified By*. These columns are lookup columns pointing to the UserInfo SharePoint list. By selecting this option, Access creates a linked table pointing to the UserInfo SharePoint list. Alternatively, you could choose for Access to import the UserInfo list at the same time as the Plants list.

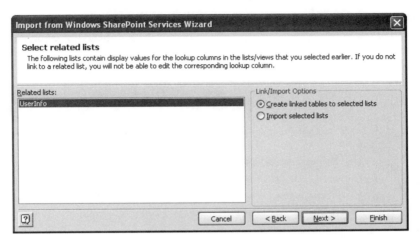

8   Click the **Next** button.

The Finish page of the Import from Windows SharePoint Services Wizard appears, detailing the options you have chosen.

9   Click the **Finish** button.

The Microsoft Office Access dialog box is displayed with the message that Access has finished importing from the SharePoint Web site.

10   Click **OK**.

Access now has two additional tables, Price of Plants and a linked table called *UserInfo*.

11   Double-click the **Price of Plants** table.

Access opens the Price of Plants table in Datasheet view.

12   If the **Enter Parameter Value** dialog box opens, click **Cancel**.

13   Click the first cell in the **Modified By** column and from the down arrow, select a name from the list. In this example, **Kim Yoshida** is selected.

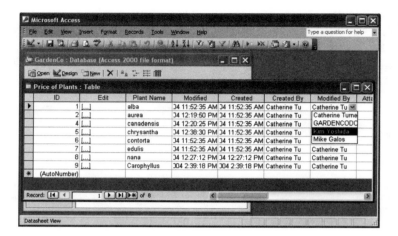

Tip Access obtained the list of users from the SharePoint site through the UserInfo linked table. To see the query used to access UserInfo, open the Price of Plants table in Design view, click on the Modified By field, and then click on the Lookup tab. In the Row Source field property, you will see a *SELECT query* connecting to the UserInfo linked table.

You could now edit the values in the other cells in the table. Such changes will not be reflected back in the Plants list on the SharePoint site. If you want to change the contents of the SharePoint list, the Access table provides a quick way of opening the SharePoint list in a browser. Click the [...] characters in the row you want to edit. Internet Explorer then displays the list item that relates to that row.

Warning Changes to the SharePoint list are not copied back to the Access table. Nor are changes to the Access table reflected back in the SharePoint list, that is, a linked object is not created as part of this process.

CLOSE Access and any Internet Explorer windows that are open.

Linking an Access Table to a SharePoint List

The previous two sections copied data so that the same data could be stored in both an Access database and in a list on a SharePoint site. However, there was no data synchronization between these two data locations. If you do not want to maintain two copies of that data, but you need to refer to the data within Access, then Access provides methods of accessing external data that is physically located outside an Access database. The easiest way to reference a SharePoint list externally is to use linked tables, which were known as *attached* tables prior to Access 95. A linked table stores only a connection to the SharePoint list. You should use linking rather than importing if the data is maintained by users or a separate program on the SharePoint Web site.

In this exercise, you will link a table to a SharePoint list.

USE the GardenCo.mdb database in the practice folder. This practice file is located in the *My Documents* *Microsoft Press\SharePoint Services SBS\Chapter 11* folder. Remember to use your SharePoint site location in place of *http://gardenco* in the exercises. This exercise uses the SharePoint list, SalesFigures, you created in a previous exercise of this chapter. You can use your own list if you want.
BE SURE TO start Access before beginning this exercise.
OPEN the GardenCo.mdb database and acknowledge the security warning if necessary.

1　On the **File** menu, point to **Get External Data**, and then click **Link Tables**.

　　The Link dialog box appears.

2　From the **Files of type** drop-down list, select **Windows SharePoint Services()**.

　　The Select a Site page of the Link to Windows SharePoint Services Wizard appears.

3　In the **Sites** text box, type http://gardenco, and then click the **Next** button.

　　The "Select lists" page of the Link to Windows SharePoint Services Wizard appears.

4　In the **Lists** text box, select **SalesFigures**, and then select the **Link to one or more views of a list** option.

　　Tip　When you import a view, only those columns shown on the view are imported.

5　Clear the **Retrieve IDs for lookup columns** check box.

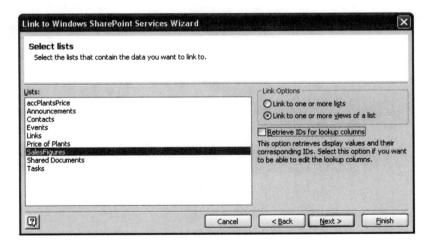

6 Click the **Next** button.

The "Select views" page of the Link to Windows SharePoint Services Wizard appears.

7 In the **Views** text box, click **All Items**.

Tip You can select multiple views on this page by holding down the [Ctrl] or [Shift] keys.

8 Click the **Next** button.

The Finish page of the Import from Windows SharePoint Services Wizard appears detailing the options you have chosen.

9 Click the **Finish** button.

The Microsoft Office Access dialog box is displayed with the message that Access has finished linking to the SharePoint Web site.

10 Click **OK**.

Access now has a linked table named SalesFigures: All Items.

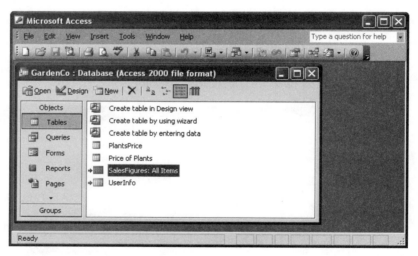

If changes are made to the linked table in Access or the SalesFigures list in SharePoint, the data will be synchronized.

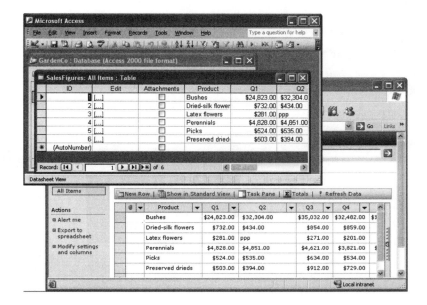

CLOSE Access.

Key Points

- From the browser you can create a Custom list, importing the data from an Excel spreadsheet.

- From the browser you can create an Excel spreadsheet and export data from a SharePoint list into it.

- From within Excel 2003 you can publish the data held within an Excel List into a newly created SharePoint list.

- You can synchronize changes between an Excel spreadsheet and a SharePoint list through a two-way synchronization process.

- With Access 2003, you can export and import data to and from SharePoint lists. The data in the Access table is not updated when subsequent changes are made to the SharePoint list, that is, there is no synchronization process between Access and a SharePoint site.

- In Access, you should create a new table that is linked to a SharePoint list when the data is maintained by users on the SharePoint Web site and you want Access to use the current data.

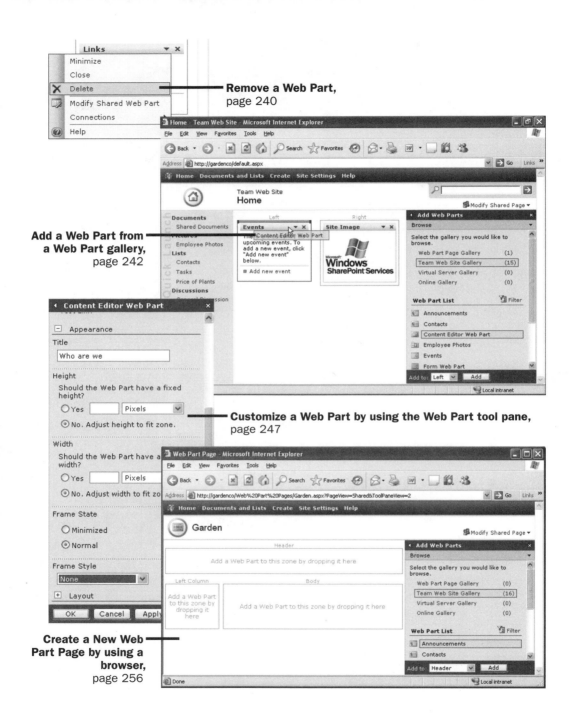

Remove a Web Part, page 240

Add a Web Part from a Web Part gallery, page 242

Customize a Web Part by using the Web Part tool pane, page 247

Create a New Web Part Page by using a browser, page 256

Chapter 12 at a Glance

12 Working with Web Parts

In this chapter you will learn to:

✔ Understand Web Parts and Web Part pages.

✔ Remove a Web Part.

✔ Add a Web Part from a Web Part gallery.

✔ Customize a Web Part by using the Web Part tool pane.

✔ Customize a home page by using Web Parts.

✔ Create a new Web Part Page by using a browser.

Web sites based on Microsoft Windows SharePoint Services use a technology known as *Web Part Pages*, which are special Web pages that contain one or more *Web Parts*. Web Parts are reusable components that can contain any kind of Web-based information, including analytical, collaborative, and database information. This technology enables Web sites to be flexible and highly customizable. To customize these sites you can use three types of tools: a browser, a Windows SharePoint Services-compatible Web page editing tool, such as Microsoft Office FrontPage 2003, or a programming tool, such as Microsoft Visual Studio .NET 2003. No one tool can do everything, and therefore it is likely that in any deployment of Windows SharePoint Services, all three tools will be used at some time or other.

This chapter introduces the basic concepts of Web Part Pages and Web Parts. Using the browser, you will learn how to view Web Part Pages in different ways, change the appearance of Web Part Pages by adding and removing Web Parts, and tailor a site by adding Web Part Pages.

See Also   Do you need only a quick refresher on the topics in this chapter? See the Quick Reference entries on pages xxxvii–xl.

Important   Remember to use your SharePoint site location in place of *http://gardenco* in the exercises.

Understanding Web Parts and Web Part Pages

Before we can talk about customizing any of the portal sites, we must cover certain basic concepts. A SharePoint site contains one or more Web Part Pages. Web Part Pages contain Web Parts that can display the contents held in the site's lists or document libraries as well as Web Parts that display other content. To customize Web sites, you must have the following rights, all of which are included in the Web Designer and Administrator site groups by default:

- Manage Lists
- Add and Customize Pages
- Apply Themes and Borders
- Apply Style Sheets

In this exercise, you will familiarize yourself with the customizing capabilities of Windows SharePoint Services.

OPEN the SharePoint site. The exercise will use the *http://gardenco* site, but you can use whatever SharePoint team site you want. If prompted, type your user name and password, and then click OK. BE SURE TO verify that you have sufficient rights to add contacts to a contacts list. If in doubt, see the Appendix on page 260.

1 In the upper-right corner of the Home page, click **Modify Shared Page**.

The Web Part Page menu displays these options:

- Add Web Parts
- Design this Page
- Modify Shared Web Parts
- Shared View
- Personal View

Shared View

Personal View

Tip The shared view icon is in a small orange box indicating that you are viewing this Web Part Page by using the *shared view*. Any changes you make to the Web Part Page are visible to all site users. As an administrator or a Web designer, when you first display a Web Part Page, the page is in the shared view and the Modify Shared Page link is shown in the upper-right corner beneath the Search box. You can make changes to a Web Part Page that only affect your view of the Web page, which is when you would use the *personal view*. You can switch between these two views by clicking Personal View on the Web Part Page menu. The link beneath the Search box is replaced by Modify My Page, and the personal view icon in the Web Part Page menu is placed in a small orange box to indicate that this is your current view. As an administrator or a Web designer, you cannot change the personal views of specific users, only the shared view and your own personal view. You will be shown Web Part Pages in shared view until you personalize them, then the personal view becomes your default view for that Web Part Page. You can reset the personal view to the shared view values by clicking Reset Page Content from the Web Part Page menu.

2 Click **Design this Page**.

The Web Part Page is displayed in design mode in a grid-like manner, with two *Web Part Page zones* denoted by two gray borders labeled at the top as *Left* and *Right*.

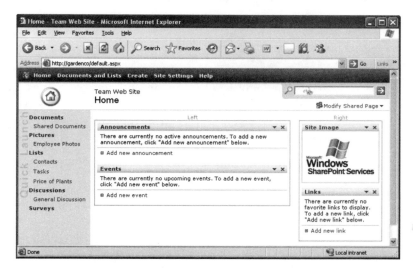

Web Part
Menu down
arrow

Close

Tip Web Part Page zones are containers for Web Parts, so on a SharePoint team site the *Left* zone contains the Web Parts *Announcements* and *Events*, whereas the *Right* zone contains the Web Parts *Site Image* and *Links*. In design mode, these Web Parts have a down arrow on their title bar and a Close button. The *Announcements*, *Events*, and *Links* Web Parts display information held within the *Announcements*, *Events* and *Links* lists, whereas the *Site Image* Web Part is a built-in Web Part that displays the Windows SharePoint Services image.

Other Web Part Pages may have more or less than two zones, depending on the Web Part Page template used when creating the Web Part Page. You can also add or remove zones from a Web Part Page by using a tool, such as FrontPage 2003.

3   In the upper-right corner of the page, click **Modify Shared Page**.

On the drop down menu, a check mark to the left of the "Design this Page" menu item appears denoting that the page is in design mode.

4   Click **Design this Page**.

The Web Part Page is displayed in normal mode, in which the zones are no longer visible. In addition, the Close buttons in the title bar of the Web Parts and the title bar of the Site Image Web Part are no longer visible.

CLOSE Internet Explorer.

Removing a Web Part

When created, SharePoint sites can contain a number of libraries, lists, one or more Web Part Pages, and on the Web Part Pages, one or more Web Parts. As you customize your site, you might decide that you do not require all the Web Parts on these Web Part Pages and want to remove them.

In this exercise, you will delete and close Web Parts to remove them from a Web site's Home page.

OPEN a SharePoint team site. The exercise will use the *http://gardenco* site, but you can use whatever site you want. If prompted, type your user name and password, and then click OK.

1   Verify that the link in the upper-right corner of the page is **Modify Shared Page**, indicating that you have the Web Part in Shared View.

Troubleshooting   If the link is Modify My Page, you have the page in Personal View. To switch to Shared View, click Modify My Page and on the menu, click Shared View. If the menu does not contain the Shared View option then you are not a member of the Administrator or Web Designer site group on this Web site.

2 Click the down arrow on the **Announcements** Web Part title bar, and from the Web Part menu, click **Close**, temporarily removing the Announcements Web Part from the Web page.

Tip You can also close Web Parts when you have a Web Page displayed in design mode by clicking Close from the Web Part menu or by clicking the Close button in the Web Part title bar.

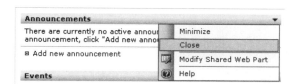

The Web Part Page is displayed with only three Web Parts.

3 In the upper-right corner of the page, click **Modify Shared Page** and from the Web Part Page menu, click **Design this Page**.

The Web Page is displayed in design mode with the zones clearly visible.

4 Click the down arrow on the **Links** Web Part title bar, and from the Web Part menu, click **Delete**.

5 When a Microsoft Internet Explorer dialog box appears asking if you want to delete this Web Part, click **OK**.

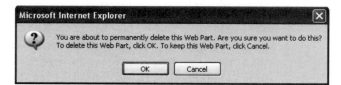

6 In the upper-right corner of the page, click **Modify Shared Page**, and then click **Design this Page** from the Web Part Page menu.

The Web Part Page is displayed in normal mode.

CLOSE Internet Explorer.

Adding a Web Part from a Web Part Gallery

As you customize your site, you might decide to add other information, as well as remove some of the Web Parts on the Web Part Pages. You can do this by adding additional Web Parts. Windows SharePoint Services provides built-in Web Parts for each Web site created. The two types of Web Parts you will most commonly use with the browser are:

■ **List View Web Parts (LVWP).** Web Parts that display the contents of libraries and lists.

■ **Built-in Web Parts.** Web Parts that display other content. There are six built-in Web Parts, which are described in the following table.

The six built-in Web Parts available on Web sites created from the Team site, Blank site or Document Workspace templates are summarized in the following table.

Web Part	Description
Content Editor Web Part	Use this Web Part to add content to a Web Part Page, such as formatted text, tables, and images. This Web Part enables you to add content by using a Rich Text Editor or a *HTML* source editor. The HTML <FORM> element is not allowed in the Content Editor Web Part. If you need to add a Web Part that uses the <FORM> element, consider using the Page Viewer Web Part or the Form Web Part.
Form Web Part	Use this Web Part if you want to send data to another Web Part through a *Web Part connection*. The content displayed in the other Web Part will be dependant on the data it receives.
Image Web Part	Use this Web Part to display pictures and photos. This Web Part is included by default on many sites' home Web Part Pages to display a logo.
Members	Use this Web Part to see a list of the site members and their online status.
Page Viewer Web Part	Use this Web Part to display content of a linked resource, such as a Web site, Web pages, files, or folders. In this way you can display a whole Web page within a Web Part. The linked content is isolated from other content on the Web Part Page and hence the content is displayed asynchronously from the rest of the page. This means that you can view and use other content in the other Web Parts on the page even if the link in this Web Part happens to take a long time to return its content. Also use this Web Part if you want to retrieve data from a server that requires authentication.
XML Web Part	Use this Web Part for *Extensible Markup Language* (XML) with *Extensible Stylesheet Language* (XSL) to define how the XML is displayed. You might use the XML Web Part to display structured data from database tables or queries, or XML-based documents.

Tip In addition to the built-in Web Parts, you can create your own Web Parts by using tools, such as FrontPage 2003 and Visual Studio .NET 2003, or import custom Web Parts. With FrontPage 2003, you can add a *Data View Web Part (DWVP)*, which can retrieve data from a variety of data sources, such as SQL databases, XML files, and Web Services, as well as data held in SharePoint lists and libraries. FrontPage 2003 provides a WYSIWYG *Extensible Stylesheet Language Transformation* (XSLT) editor that the developer uses to format the Data View Web Part.

In this exercise, you will customize the home page of a SharePoint site. You will add a Content Editor Web Part, a List View Web Part, and restore a Web Part from the Web Part Page Gallery.

OPEN a SharePoint site. The exercise will use the *http://gardenco* site, but you can use whatever site you want. If prompted, type your user name and password, and then click OK.
BE SURE TO complete the second exercise in this chapter, "Removing a Web Part" before beginning this exercise. Also, you must have a list that contains data, such as the *Price of Plants* list created in the "Importing Data from an Excel Spreadsheet to a List in SharePoint" exercise in Chapter 11 on page 212. Alternatively, you can create a practice site for this chapter based on site template Chapter 12 Starter.stp in the practice file folder for this chapter. The practice file folder is located in the *My Documents \Microsoft Press\SharePoint Services SBS\Chapter 12* folder. See "Using the Book's CD-ROM" on page vii for instructions on how to create a practice site.

1 In the upper-right corner of the page, click **Modify Shared Page**.

2 In the Web Part Page menu, point to **Add Web Parts**, and then click **Browse**.

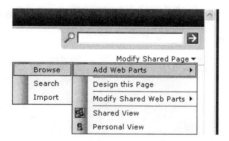

After a few moments, the Web Part Page is displayed in design mode with the Web Part tool pane's four *Web Part galleries* visible. Web Part galleries are containers where Web Parts and Web Part templates are stored. The number in the bracket to the right of each gallery states the number of Web Parts that each gallery contains. The orange box around the Team Web Site gallery indicates that you are viewing the contents of that gallery, and the Web Part List section lists those Web Parts that are held in the Team Web Site gallery. This gallery contains a Web Part for each list or document library created for this site, plus the six built-in Web Parts described earlier in this chapter.

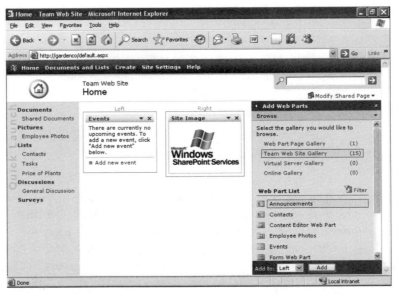

3 Move the mouse over the icon to the left of **Content Editor Web Part** so that the mouse pointer changes to a four-way arrow.

Four-way arrow pointer

4 While holding down the mouse button, drag the Content Editor Web Part to above the **Events** Web Part. As you move the Web Part, a dark blue horizontal line shows you where the **Events** Web Part will be added.

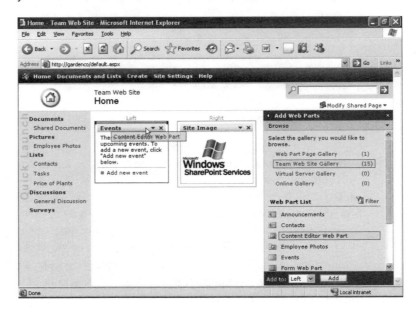

Note Using the browser, Web Parts can only be added to Web Part Page zones. Web Parts that are added to a Web Part Page zone are called *dynamic Web Parts*. Using a tool, such as FrontPage 2003, Web Parts can be added outside Web Part Page zones called *static Web Parts*.

The Web Part Page is displayed in design mode with the Content Editor Web Part placed above the Events Web Part.

5 In the Web Part List, locate the **Price of Plants** Web Part.

Tip The Web Part List section displays Web Parts in alphabetic order in groups of 10. If you cannot see the Price of Plants Web Part, it might be in the next group; click Next at the bottom of the Web Part List section to list the next group of Web Parts.

6 Repeat step 3 to add the **Price of Plants** Web Part between the **Content Editor** Web Part and the **Events** Web Part.

The Web Part Page is displayed in design mode with the Content Editor Web Part, the Price of Plants List View Web Part, and the Events List View Web Part in the Left Web Part Page zone.

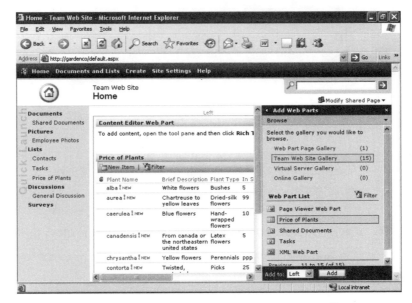

7 In the **Add Web Parts** tool pane, click **Web Part Page Gallery**.

The Add Web Parts tool pane now lists the contents of the Web Part Page gallery. This gallery holds Web Parts that were temporarily removed from a Web Part Page by using the Close option, and hence it contains only one Web Part—the Announcements List View Web Part that we removed earlier in the second exercise of this chapter.

8   At the bottom of the **Add Web Parts** tool pane, click the down arrow to the right of **Add to:** and from the drop-down list, click **Right**, and then click the **Add** button. When you use this mechanism of adding Web Parts to a Web Part Page, the Web Part is added to the top of the zone.

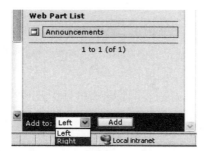

Tip   The Web Part Page gallery now contains no Web Parts because you have placed the Announcements List View Web Part back onto the Web Part Page. The Web Part Page gallery is different from the other galleries because it is a temporary storage space for Web Parts that were removed from a Web Part Page. You can compare the Web Part Page gallery to the Recycle Bin, but remember, Web Parts are only placed here if you use the Close option. If you use the Delete option, then the Web Part is permanently deleted from a Web Part Page. Web Parts placed in the other galleries act like templates. Web Parts from the other three galleries can be placed on a Web Part Page multiple times. Once the Web Part is placed on a Web Part Page, it can be uniquely customized, but the template from which the Web Part was created remains in the Web Part gallery.

9   On the **Add Web Parts** tool pane title bar, click the **Close** button.

The Add Web Parts tool pane closes and the Web page is displayed in normal mode.

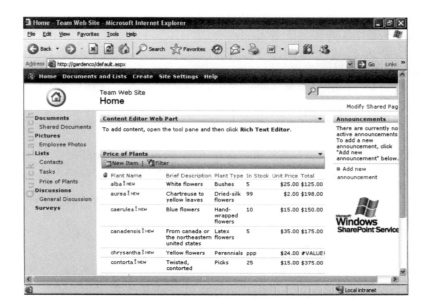

CLOSE Internet Explorer.

Tip Web Parts can be badly written, and if they are not thoroughly tested, you might find that when you add a Web Part to a Web Part Page, the page will not display. In such situations, append **?Contents=1** to the Web Part Page's URL, for example, *http://gardenco /default.aspx?contents=1*. The Web Part Maintenance Page is displayed from which you can delete the offending Web Part.

Customizing a Web Part by Using the Web Part Tool Pane

Once you have added a Web Part to the Web Part Page, you might find you have to customize it to display the content you want your Web site users to see. You might also find you have to tailor the Web Part's properties for it to take on the look and feel you require.

In this exercise, you will customize the Content Editor Web Part and a SharePoint List View Web Part.

BE SURE TO complete the second and third exercises in this chapter, "Removing a Web Part" and "Adding a Web Part from a Web Part Gallery" before you begin this exercise. Also, you must have created and populated a picture library such as the *Employee Photos* picture library created in the "Creating Picture Libraries" and "Adding Pictures" exercises in Chapter 5 on pages 92 and 99. Alternatively, you can create a practice site for this chapter based on site template Chapter 12 Starter.stp in the practice file folder for this chapter. The practice file folder is located in the *My Documents \Microsoft Press\SharePoint Services SBS\Chapter 12* folder. See "Using the Book's CD-ROM" on page vii for instructions on how to create a practice site.

OPEN a SharePoint site. The exercise will use the *http://gardenco* site, but you can use whatever site you want. If prompted, type your user name and password, and then click OK.

1 Click the down arrow on the title bar of the **Content Editor Web Part**, and then click **Modify Shared Web Part**.

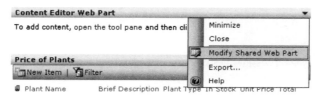

The Web page is displayed in design mode, with the Content Editor Web Part outlined in a yellow dotted line and the Content Editor Web Part tool pane visible.

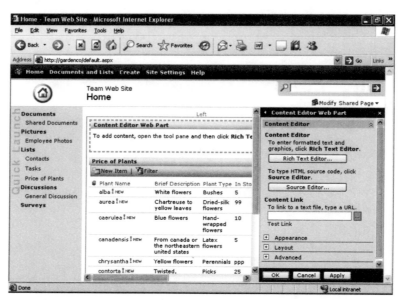

2 In the **Content Editor Web Part** tool pane, click the **Rich Text Editor** button.

The Rich Text Editor – Web Page dialog box is displayed. You can use this editor in a very similar fashion to entering text using Microsoft Word. You will be able to enter text, change styles, insert hyperlinks, insert pictures, cut, copy, paste, undo, redo, and so on. The shortcut keys you use in Word also work with this editor.

3 Click the **Help** button for more information about the Web Part.

Help

A new window is opened displaying the Rich Text Editor Button Summary topic.

4 Click the **Formatting Toolbar** link to expand the text.

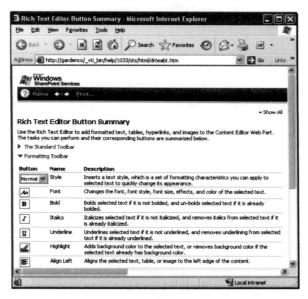

5 Close the **Rich Text Editor Button Summary – Microsoft Internet Explorer** window.

6 In the **Rich Text Editor – Web Page Dialog** box, type What can The Garden Company do for you?, and then press Enter to move the cursor to a new line.

7 Select the sentence you just typed, click the down arrow on the style drop-down list, and then click **Heading 1**.

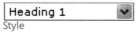
Style

8 On a new line, type We aim to provide easy-to-grow plants and have over 400 varieties of plants. We have 50 years of experience gardening and supplying high quality plants to very satisfied customers.. On a second new line, type, Who are we?, and then press Enter.

9 Format Who are we? as a **Heading 2** style, and then click the **Underline** button.

U
Underline

Insert Image

10 Place the cursor on a new line, and then click the **Insert Image** button.

The Picture dialog box is displayed.

11 In the **Picture Source** text box type the URL http://gardenco/Employee Photos /pjcov.jpg. You will need to adjust the URL for your SharePoint site location.

Important Do not refer to an image that is stored on a hard drive, such as c:/SBS_WSS/Catherinet.jpg, because, in most cases, the image will display as a broken link, and a user's browser will try to resolve the reference to the image file to the user's local hard drive, which will not contain the folder or the image. You should upload all images into picture or document libraries within the site where the Web Part Page resides, and then refer to the image by it's URL.

12 In the **Alternate Text:** text box, type Catherine Turner, from the **Alignment** drop-down list, click **Middle**, and in the **Border Thickness** text box, type 5.

13 Click **OK**.

14 On a new line beneath the picture, type Catherine Turner, Owner.

15 Select the text Catherine Turner, and then click the **Insert Hyperlink** button.

Insert Hyperlink

The Hyperlink dialog box is displayed.

16 In the **Type** drop-down list, select **mailto:**.

17 In the **URL** text box, append catherinet@gardencodom.local to mailto:.

When a user clicks on the name Catherine Turner on your Web page, their default e-mail program will open a new message for them to send an e-mail message to this person.

18 Click **OK**.

Center

19 Press ⌘+A to select all the content you have just entered, and then click the **Center** alignment button.

20 In the lower-right corner, click the **Save** button.

The Rich Text Editor – Web Page Dialog box closes and the content is displayed in the Content Editor Web Part.

Note If an Error page displays indicating that the security validation for this page has timed out, click the "Refresh page" link to try the operation again.

21 Verify that the Content Editor Web Part tool pane is open. If it is not, click the down arrow on the **Content Editor Web Part** title bar, and then click **Modify Shared Web Part**.

22 In the **Content Editor Web Part** tool pane click the expand (+) icon next to **Appearance** to expand the **Appearance** section.

23 In the **Appearance** section, in the **Title** text box, type Who are we, and then in the **Frame Style** drop-down list, click **None**.

24 Click **OK** to close the **Content Editor Web Part** tool pane.

25 On the title bar of the **Price of Plants** Web Part, click the down arrow, and then click **Modify Shared Web Part**.

The Web page is displayed in design mode with the Price of Plants List View Web Part outlined in a yellow dotted line and the Price of Plants tool pane visible.

26 In the **Price of Plants** tool pane below the **Selected View** drop-down list, click the **Edit the current view** link.

The "Price of Plants: Edit View" Web page is displayed.

27 In the **Columns** section, clear the following check boxes: **Attachments**, **In Stock**, **Unit Price**, **Total**, and **Total Cost** (if shown).

> **Tip** In this exercise you are only displaying types of plants that are *Picks*; therefore you could choose not to display the **Plant Type** column. However, when you first customize a view, it is a good practice to leave this column in place so you are able to check that the filter is configured correctly.

28 Scroll down the page until the **Filter** section is visible, select the **Show items only when the following is true** option, and then in the **Show the items when column** drop-down list, click **Plant Type**. In the first blank text box type Picks.

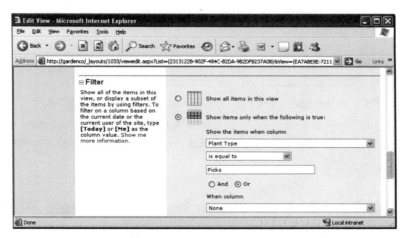

29 At the bottom of the page, click **OK**.

Your Web page is displayed. The Price of Plants tool pane is no longer visible.

30 Click the down arrow on the title bar of the **Price of Plants** Web Part, and then from the Web Part menu, click **Modify Shared Web Part**.

The Price of Plants tool pane is displayed.

31 In the **Toolbar Type** drop-down list, click **Summary Toolbar**, click the expand (+) icon for the **Appearance** section, and then in the **Title** text box, type Sale – Picks at half price.

32 Click the expand (+) icon for the **Advanced** section, and then clear the **Allow Minimize** and **Allow Close** check boxes so that a user cannot accidentally close or minimize this Web Part.

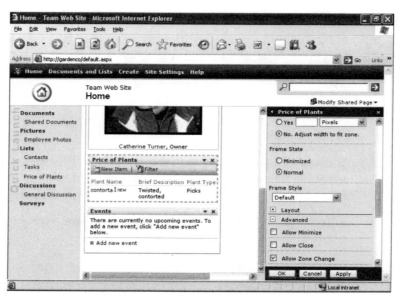

33 At the bottom of the Price of Plants tool pane, click **OK**.

34 On the title bar of the **Sales – Picks at half price** Web Part, click the down arrow and notice that the **Minimize** and **Close** options are no longer available.

CLOSE Internet Explorer.

Customizing a Home Page by Using Web Parts

As you customize your Web Part Page by adding and removing Web Parts, you might find that the Web Parts are not located where you would like them to be. In this situation it is possible to move the Web Parts around on the page to obtain the layout you require.

In this exercise you will move Web Parts on a SharePoint site's home page.

BE SURE TO complete the other exercises in this chapter before beginning this exercise.
OPEN the SharePoint site. The exercise will use the *http://gardenco* site, but you can use whatever site you want. If prompted, type your user name and password, and then click OK.

1 In the upper-right corner of the page, click **Modify Shared Page**, and from the Web Part Page menu, click **Design this Page**.

The Web Page is displayed in design mode with the zones clearly visible.

2 Move the mouse over the title bar of the **Who are we** Web Part so that the pointer changes to a four-way arrow. While holding down the mouse button, drag the Web Part to below the **Site Image** Web Part.

As you move the Web Part, a dark blue horizontal line moves from the Web Part's current location to where the Web Part will be moved.

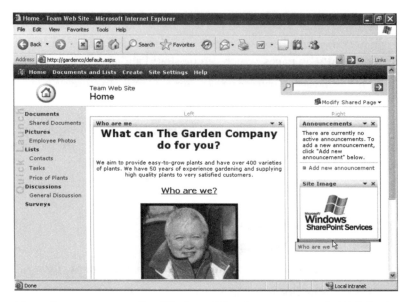

3 Move the mouse over the title bar of the **Announcements** Web Part so that the pointer changes to a four-way arrow. While holding down the mouse button, drag the Web Part to above the **Sale – Picks at half price** Web Part.

4 In the upper-right corner of the page, click **Modify Shared Page**, and then from the Web Part Page menu, click **Design this Page**. The page is no longer in Design mode.

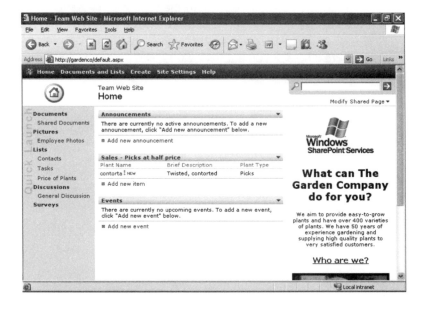

CLOSE Internet Explorer.

Creating a New Web Part Page by Using a Browser

SharePoint sites are provisioned with one or more Web Part Pages. Users can create additional Web pages, which can be stored and accessed through document libraries.

In this exercise you will create a document library to store Web Part Pages, and then create a Web Part Page.

OPEN the SharePoint site in which you would like to create Web Part Pages. The exercise will use the *http://gardenco* site, but you can use whatever site you want. If prompted, type your user name and password, and then click OK.

BE SURE TO verify that you have sufficient rights to create a document library. If in doubt, see the Appendix on page 260.

1 On the top link bar, click **Create**.

The Create Page page is displayed.

2 In the **Document Libraries** section, click **Document Library**.

The New Document Library page is displayed.

3 In the **Name** text box, type Web Part Pages

4 In the **Document Template** section in the **Document template:** drop-down list, select **Web Part Page**.

Tip You do not have to create a special document library to store your Web Part Pages. You could store them in the Shared Documents document library that is created when you create a team Web site. However, if you plan to create a number of Web Part Pages, you could place them all in their own document library. Also, by creating a document library that uses the Web Part Page document template you can create Web Part Pages by clicking the New Document button.

New Document

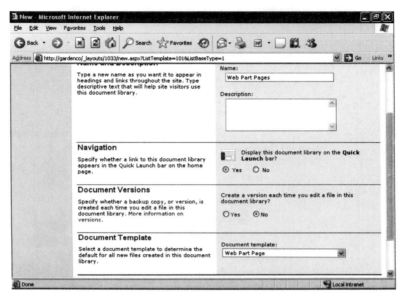

5 At the bottom of the page, click the **Create** button.

The All Documents View of the new Web Part Pages document library is displayed.

6 On the top link bar, click **Create**.

The Create Page page is displayed.

7 Scroll down the page until you can see the **Web Pages** section, and then click **Web Part Page**.

The New Web Part Page page is displayed.

8 In the **Name** text box, type Garden.

9 In the **Layout** section in the **Choose a Layout Template** list, click **Header, Left Column, Body**.

10 In the **Save Location** section in the **Document Library** drop-down list, click **Web Part Pages**.

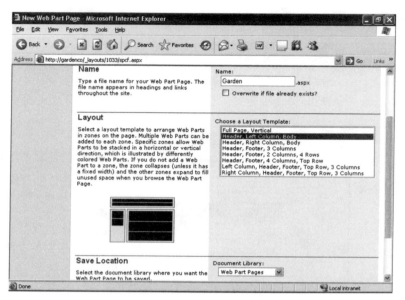

11 At the bottom of the page, click the **Create** button.

After a few moments, the new Web Part Page is displayed, which has these three Web Part Page zones: Header, Left Column, and Body. Currently the page is empty, except for the top link bar, a heading with a graphic and the Modify Shared Page link. There are no Web Parts placed within the Web Part Page zones.

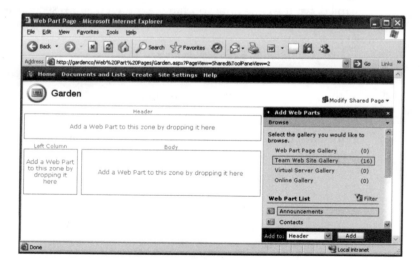

Tip   Because you created this Web Part Page within the SharePoint team site, the Team Web Site gallery contains a Web Part for each list or document library created in The Garden Company team site, plus the six built-in Web Parts described earlier in this chapter. If you completed all the exercises in this chapter, the number of Web Parts in the Team Web Site gallery should be one more than at the end of the previous exercise because you created a new document library in this exercise called Web Part Pages. You could now customize this Web Part Page using the techniques described earlier in this chapter.

Once a Web Part Page is created, you need to provide a link to the Web Part Page from your home page so the rest of your team can see it. Either make the Web Part Page document library appear on the Quick Launch bar, or if you have a links list, add a link item that points to the new Web Part Page.

CLOSE Internet Explorer.

Key Points

- Windows SharePoint Services uses a technology known as Web Part Pages, which are containers for Web Parts.

- A Web Part Page contains Web Part zones where Web Parts can be placed.

- Web Parts are reusable components that can contain any kind of Web-based content. They can display the contents of lists and libraries, as well as other content, such as the results of database queries, Web sites, Web pages, files, and folders.

- To customize a Web site you must have certain rights or be a member of the Administrator or Web Designer site groups.

- A Web Part Page can have these two views: shared view and a personal view. All users see changes made to the shared view. Changes made to the personal view are visible only to the user who altered their personal view of the Web Part Page. A user can reset their personal view back to the Shared View settings.

- Web Parts are placed in one of these four Web Part galleries: Web Part Page gallery, Team Web Site gallery, Virtual Server gallery, and Online gallery.

- The Web Part Page gallery is a temporary storage space for Web Parts that are removed from a Web page using the Close option.

- The Team Web Site gallery contains a List View Web Part for each list or library created in the team site, plus these six built-in Web Parts: Content Editor Web Part, Form Web Part, Image Web Part, Members, Page Viewer Web Part and XML Web Part.

- Using the browser, you can create additional Web Part Pages, which are stored within a document library.

Appendix

Windows SharePoint Services User Rights

In Microsoft Windows SharePoint Services, access to sites is controlled through a role-based membership system based on *site groups*. Site groups specify what rights users have on a SharePoint site. These rights determine what specific actions users can perform on the site.

The following table lists all SharePoint Services user rights, their associated permissions, and groups that include these rights by default.

Right	Permissions	Groups included by default
Add and Customize Pages	Create pages for a Web site	Web Designer, Administrator
Add Items	Add items to lists or add documents to document libraries	Contributor, Web Designer, Administrator
Add/Remove Private Web Parts	Add and remove Web Parts to personalize Web Part Pages	Contributor, Web Designer, Administrator
Apply Style Sheets	Apply a style sheet to the entire Web site	Web Designer, Administrator
Apply Themes and Borders	Apply a theme or border to an entire Web site	Web Designer, Administrator
Browse Directories	Browse the directory structure of a Web site	Contributor, Web Designer, Administrator
Cancel Check-out	Cancel the check-out action performed by another user	Web Designer, Administrator
Create Cross-Site Groups	Create or delete cross-site groups, or change membership of a cross-site group	Contributor, Web Designer, Administrator

Right	Permissions	Groups included by default
Create Subsites	Create a new subsite or workspace site, such as a Document Workspace site or Meeting Workspace site	Administrator
Delete Items	Delete list items and documents from the Web site.	Contributor, Web Designer, Administrator
Edit Items	Edit existing list items and documents in the Web site	Contributor, Web Designer, Administrator
Manage Lists	Create, edit, or delete lists and change their settings	Web Designer, Administrator
Manage List Permissions	Change permissions for a list or document library	Administrator
Manage Personal Views	Create, edit, or delete personal views on lists	Contributor, Web Designer, Administrator
Manage Site Groups	Create, delete, and edit site groups, both by changing the rights assigned to the site group and by changing which users are members of the site group	Administrator
Manage Web Site	Perform administration tasks for a particular site or subsite	Administrator
Update Personal Web Parts	Update Web Parts to display personalized information	Contributor, Web Designer, Administrator
Use Self-Service Site Creation	Use the Self-Service Site Creation tool to create a top-level Web site.	Reader, Contributor, Web Designer, Administrator
View Items	View items in lists, documents in document libraries, and Web discussion comments	Reader, Contributor, Web Designer, Administrator
View Pages	Browse pages in the Web site	Reader, Contributor, Web Designer, Administrator
View Usage Data	View reports on Web site usage	Administrator

Glossary

Address book   A collection of names, e-mail addresses, and distribution lists used to address messages.

alert   An e-mail notification of changes made to the content of a SharePoint site.

Blank Site   A SharePoint site that begins with no lists or document libraries.

Calendar   The scheduling component of Microsoft Outlook that is fully integrated with e-mail, contacts, and other Outlook features.

central template gallery   Centralized location where site templates can be stored to be available to all sites.

check in   Checking In a document is the reverse process to checking out a document. It tells SharePoint that you are done working on a document and anyone else can now check it out.

check out   Checking Out a document gives you an exclusive lock on the document. It implies that you are the one working on the document and no one else can edit the document while it is checked out to you.

Close-ended questions   Questions that have a finite set of answers from which the user chooses.

column references   Identifies a cell in the current row in a datasheet and tells a list where to look for the values or data you want to use in a formula.

columns   A SharePoint list is made up of columns or fields that define what kind of data will be collected for each list item. Document libraries also have columns or fields that define what kind of metadata will be collected to describe each document.

configuration   Section of a site definition that determines what lists, document libraries, Web Parts, and navigation will be available when a new site is created.

constant   A value that is not calculated. For example, the date 4/13/2054, the number 210, and the text "Quarterly Earnings" are all constants. Constants data types can be string, number, date, or Boolean.

contact   A person whom you wish to save information about, such as their e-mail address, home address, office address, telephone number, and fax number.

Create Subsites right   Determines whether the user has the ability to create a new site from the current site.

cross-site groups   Named collections of users, similar to Windows groups, managed in SharePoint in each site collection.

Data View Web Part   A Web Part that retrieves data from a data source in the form of XML and applies XSLT to it. Microsoft FrontPage 2003 enables you to add Data View Web Parts to a Web Part Page and has a WYSIWYG XSLT editor so you don't need to know XSLT to customize a Data View Web Part.

Datasheet view   Provides a Microsoft Excel–like environment for viewing and editing data. It displays the contents of a list or a document library in a grid of rows and columns. In Microsoft Access, this term is used for the view that displays the information in a table or query.

discussion boards   A specialized SharePoint list that enables you to create an online discussion forum. Discussion boards provide a forum on which visitors to a SharePoint site can converse about topics that interest them.

document library   A folder where a collection of files is stored and the files often use the same template. Each file in a library is associated with user-defined information that is displayed in the content listing for that library.

Document Workspace   A site that enables colleagues to work together on a particular task, document, or project. A Document Workspace can be created directly from within Microsoft Word. It provides a document library for storing the primary document and supporting files, a task list for assigning to-do items, and a Links list for resources related to the document. If the Document Workspace is created from a document in its parent site's document library, the Document Workspace can publish the document back to the source location.

Dynamic Web Parts   Web Parts placed in a Web Part Page zone.

Excel list   A block of cells that you can use to manage and analyze the data in the list independently of data outside the list.

Extensible Markup Language (XML)   A defined markup language for documents that describes document content and structure rather than appearance. An XML document has to be formatted before it can be read, and the formatting is usually accomplished by using an XSL template file.

Extensible Stylesheet Language (XSL)   A language used to create stylesheets for XML, similar to CSS (Cascading Style Sheets) that are used for HTML. XSL Transformations (XSLT) can be used to transform XML to HTML or one type of XML to another.

Flat view   A view that can be used in a Discussion Board to list replies in chronological order (the order in which they were created).

form library   A SharePoint library that enables you to use, store, and share Microsoft InfoPath forms.

Formula   An equation that performs calculations on values in a list. A formula starts with an equal sign (=).You can use a formula in a calculated column and to calculate default values for a column. A formula can also contain any or all of the following: functions, column references, operators, and constants.

function   A predefined formula that performs calculations, also known as a name procedure or routine, often used for mathematical or financial calculations. Lists do not support the RAND and NOW functions. The TODAY and ME functions are not supported in calculated columns, but are supported in the default value setting of a column.

General Discussion board   A built-in discussion board included in the default team site.

top-level site   A site that does not have a parent site.

Global Address List (GAL)   An address book provided by Microsoft Exchange Server that contains all user and distribution list e-mail addresses in your organization. The Exchange administrator creates and maintains this address book.

home page   The main page of a SharePoint Web site; it provides a navigational structure that links the site components together.

Hypertext Markup Language (HTML)   Defines the structure and layout of a Web document by using a variety of tags and attributes. Browsers are programmed to interpret HTML for display.

InfoPath form   An XML document that collects information from a user in a structured way.

InfoPath form template   A file that defines the appearance, structure, and behavior of an InfoPath form.

Internet Service Provider (ISP)   A company that provides individuals or organizations with the necessary software and information to gain access to the Internet.

Linked object   An object created in another program that maintains a connection to its source. For example, when you export a SharePoint list to an Excel spreadsheet, the Excel list in the spreadsheet is a linked object. The source in this situation is the SharePoint list.

list items   A finite collection of defined, related columns combined to create a single item in a list. Each document in a document library and its associated columns are also considered items in a list or a list item. Each list item can be created, reviewed, updated, and deleted individually.

list templates   The columns, list views, and general settings for a list used as a template to create new lists.

list view   Definition for how a list should be displayed. It has a range of options including the columns to show; the sequence from left to right to show those columns; the order in which the list items will be displayed; the filters that will be applied to the displayed list items; and any grouping, totaling, or stylization, and pagination.

List View Web Part   A built-in Web Part that can display data from various data sources including SharePoint lists, SharePoint document libraries, databases, XML files, other Web sites that return XML, and XML Web Services. A Web Part representation of content from a SharePoint list or document library.

lists   A Web site component that stores and displays information that users can add to by using their browsers. Requires a Web server that is running Windows SharePoint Services.

local machine groups   Named collections of users managed on a single computer for local use only.

Meeting request   An e-mail message inviting its recipients to a meeting.

Meeting Workspace   A SharePoint site for colleagues to collaborate around a meeting. Meeting Workspaces can be created directly from within Outlook. There are five Meeting Workspaces to choose from: Basic, Blank, Decision, Social, and Multi-page. Meeting Workspaces provide some unique out-of-the-box lists, such as Objectives, Attendees, and Agenda, tailored specifically for meetings. They use a tabbed navigational interface rather than the quick launch bar and streamline the creation of lists directly from the Web Part task pane.

metadata   Information about a document or list item used to describe a particular item to find or manipulate it easier.

named range   A group of cells in an Excel spreadsheet.

Open-ended question   Questions that give users the opportunity to answer a question in their own words, rather than just checking one of a limited list of alternatives. Open-ended questions have no definitive answer.

Operators   Specify the type of calculation that you want to perform on the elements of a formula. Lists support three different types of calculation operators: arithmetic, comparison, and text.

Outlook Profile   A group of settings that define how Outlook is set up for a particular user. For example, a profile might include access to a mailbox that resides on a Microsoft Exchange Server.

Outlook rule   A set of conditions, actions, and exceptions that process and organize messages.

Page tabs   A navigational paradigm used in Meeting Workspaces to organize Web Part Pages using a clickable row of tabs at the top of the page.

personal view   A personalized view of a SharePoint list, document library, or Web Part Page that is available only to yourself, but not for others. The personal view of a Web Part Page uses a combination of shared property values and personalized property values. You can reset a personal view back to the shared view.

Quick Launch bar   The navigation area on the home page of a SharePoint site used on team sites to organize site content by using clickable collections of links on the left of the page.

range   A block of cells in a worksheet or datasheet.

relationship   An association between common fields in two lists or tables. A relationship is maintained in SharePoint by creating a Lookup column.

Select query   A query that retrieves data matching specific criteria from one or more data sources, such as a SharePoint list or an Access table, and displays the results.

shared attachment   A document that is stored on a SharePoint site and linked to an e-mail message.

shared documents   A built-in document library included in the default team site

shared view   A view of a SharePoint list, document library, or Web Part Page that every user with the appropriate permissions on a site can see.

SharePoint Central Administration   The administrative interface that is used to manage the entire SharePoint installation.

site group   A role-based membership system that provides access control to SharePoint sites. That is, a collection of rights that determine what specific actions users can perform on the site. Each SharePoint site user belongs to at least one site group, either directly or indirectly. There are five default site groups: Guest, Reader, Contributor, Web Designer, and Administrator.

site collection   A hierarchical collection of sites headed by a top-level Web site that can have one or more subsites.

site collection site gallery   A document library in the root of the site collection that contains custom site templates.

site definitions   A set of file-based XML files that define the latent capabilities of a SharePoint site.

sites   A collection of lists and document libraries and Web pages needed to create, review, update, delete, and manage content and properties. Sites have a Web Part Page called a home page as their starting point.

site template   Similar to a configuration, a site template captures all the lists, document libraries, optionally its data, the navigation, and look and feel of a site at a point in time. This can subsequently be used to create new sites that look just like the site did when it was captured into the site template.

Static Web Parts   Web Parts placed on a Web Part Page, but not in a Web Part Page zone. A browser cannot manipulate static Web Parts, but FrontPage 2003 can.

subsite   A SharePoint site that has a parent site

survey   A specialized SharePoint list that enables you to create a Web-based questionnaire.

task pane A pane that enables you to quickly access commands related to a specific task without having to use menus and toolbars.

Team Site A SharePoint site for colleagues to work together. It is the default site when creating a new SharePoint site.

theme A named set of properties, such as fonts, colors, buttons, and backgrounds, that can be selected for altering the appearance of a site.

Threaded view In Discussion Boards, you can use the Threaded view to group comments by conversation or thread.

top-level site A site that does not have a parent site. The default, top-level site provided by a Web server or virtual server.

top link bar One of the main navigation areas of a SharePoint site, located at the top of the page, appearing on all pages within the site.

views Use metadata to display a subset or grouping of information to find information more easily.

Web folders Web folders are a feature of Microsoft Windows that enable you to open a SharePoint site like any other shared folder in Windows Explorer.

Web Part connections These connections allow Web Parts to send and receive information. Web Parts that receive data can alter their content based on the information they receive.

Web Part gallery A container for Web Parts. Web Parts are placed on a Web Part Page from a Web Part gallery.

Web Part Page A special type of Web page that contains one or more Web Parts. A Web Part Page consolidates data, such as lists and charts, and Web content, such as text and images, into a dynamic information portal built around a common task or special interest.

Web Part Page zone A container that controls the organization and format of Web Parts on a Web Part Page.

Web Part A modular unit of information that consists of a title bar, a frame, and content. Web Parts are the basic building blocks of a Web Part Page.

Windows groups An operating system method of grouping users by membership.

Windows NT groups A named collection of users, similar to Windows groups, managed in the SAM database.

workspace A specific kind of SharePoint site with additional functionality, typically with how it integrates with Microsoft Office.

XML See *Extensible Markup Language*.

XSL See *Extensible Stylesheet Language*.

XSLT See *Extensible Stylesheet Langauge*.

Index

filtering

filtering
- columns, 79
- discussion board items, 186
- lists, 79

Flat view, 263

folders
- common, 30
- creating in libraries, 99
- Web, 267

form libraries, 93, 263
form templates, InfoPath, 264
Form Web Part, 242

forms, 94
- InfoPath, 264
- libraries, creating, 22

formulas, 219, 263
frequency, of alerts, 85
FrontPage 2003, creating Web Parts with, 243
function, 264

G

galleries
- central template, 50, 262
- site collection, 50, 266
- Web Part Pages, overview, 246
- Web Parts, 243, 267

General Discussion board, 13, 17, 60, 183, 264
General settings, 115
Global Address List (GAL), 264
granting access, 36, 122
groups, 36, 260–67

H

help, 16
hierarchy, site, 2, 13, 19, 44
Home link, 14
home pages, 14, 157, 254, 264
Hypertext Markup Language (HTML), 264

I

ID column, 227
Image Web Part, 242
images, referring to hard drive, 250

importing
- contacts, 7
- data, 7
- Outlook 2003 contacts, 190
- selecting more than one list, 230
- SharePoint lists, 212

Info tab, 142
InfoPath, 5, 94, 96, 264
infrastructures, 13
internal name, 31, 62
Internet Service Provider (ISP), 264
items, list, 57

L

levels of access, granting, 36
libraries, 22, 32, 91–99
- adding new, 15
- deleting, 130
- document, 2, 92, 113, 263
- Document Workspace, 32
- form, 93, 263
- pictures, viewing, 17
- securing, 122
- specifying default templates, 115
- team sites, 13

library columns, 116
lifecycle, of Document Workspaces, 133
Likert scale, 171
linked objects, 220, 264
links, 14–17, 30
Links list and tab, 21, 142
list items, 57, 65–67, 264
- adding, 65, 215
- attaching files to, 70
- attachments, multiple, 72
- disabling attachments to, 70

- editing, 65, 215
- removing, 215
- selecting, deleting multiple, 218

list templates, 264
List View Web Part, 265
list views, 81, 264
lists, 21, 29, 57, 60–62, 265
- Access tables, importing to, 229
- adding items, 65
- adding new, 15
- columns, 73
- default list view page, 65
- deleting, 88
- Document Workspace, 32
- Excel, 263
- filtering, 79
- importing and exporting data, 7
- Links, 21, 142
- Meeting Workspaces, default, 152
- members, 142
- permissions, 35
- selecting more than one to import, 230
- shortcuts for editing, 217
- sorting, 79
- subsites, 19
- task, 2, 142
- Team Site, 32
- team sites, 13
- templates, 58
- traditional types, 32
- unique, 32, 60
- viewing, 17, 21
- views, multiple, 65

Lists link, 17
local machine groups, 265
Locale Culture ID (LCID), 30

M

Maintenance page, Web Part, displaying, 247
managing
- alerts, 85

270

About the Authors

Olga Londer

Olga Londer, MCSE/MCT, is an Infrastructure Architect at Microsoft EMEA (Europe, Middle East, and Africa). She is a winner of the British Computer Society Trainer of the Year Award, a published author, and a frequent speaker at conferences, including most recently at IT Forum, TechEd, VSLive, and DevWeek. Olga has been working with Web development and infrastructure technologies since 1992. She has co-authored several books, including *Microsoft SharePoint Products and Technologies Resource Kit* (MS Press, 2004) and *Microsoft Content Management Server 2002-A Complete Guide* (Addison Wesley, 2003). Before joining Microsoft, Olga was a Microsoft MVP (Most Valuable Professional) and worked as a Principal Technologist at QA, the United Kingdom's leading IT training company, where her responsibilities included teaching, consulting, and technical leadership for the Internet curriculum-she authored most of the company's Web infrastructure and development courses. Olga and her husband live in London, United Kingdom.

Todd C. Bleeker

With over a decade of Microsoft-centric software development in his wake, Todd C. Bleeker, Ph.D., is regarded as an innovative, resourceful, and competitive technologist and author with an intense desire to excel. Recently, Todd joined forces with Bill English to grow Mindsharp (*http://Mindsharp.com*), a high-quality training company.

Early in his career, Todd built shrewd customer service solutions for P&G; pioneered new technologies to revolutionize the transportation logistics systems for Fingerhut; shaped the disease-management tools for United Healthcare; drove the human capital procurement vision to an internationalized, commercial-grade, global solution for itiliti (now PeopleClick); and, as the CTO for IPCS, Todd managed all offshore software development operations in New Delhi, India, while actively participating in various stateside and Canadian projects.

Todd has architected many solutions for both small and large corporations. For instance, in 2003 Todd architected the software that Air Canada uses to track its roughly $30 million of annual in-flight cash sales. Todd helped the State of Minnesota webify and manage over 40,000 pages of systems documentation by using SharePoint Team Services.

Todd implemented, on behalf of Microsoft Consulting Services, a Microsoft Content Management Server Proof of Concept for the Bank of Montreal. Todd also presented on Web Services and MCMS at TechEd.

In his spare time, Todd loves to soak up whatever technology Microsoft is churning out and spend countless hours in Minnesota with his wife, Kathryn, and six "high energy" children: Landis, Lake, Lissa, Logan, Lawson, and Lexa.

Penny Coventry

Penny Coventry is a certified MCSE, MCDBA, MCSD, MSF, and MCT, together with non-Microsoft certificates such as ISEB IT Infrastructure Management and IT Project+. She focuses on the design, implementation, and development of SharePoint Technology-based solutions for Microsoft Partners in the United Kingdom and Europe. Penny has been working with SharePoint since SharePoint Portal Server 2001 and SharePoint Team Services, and co-authored the Microsoft SharePoint Products and Technologies Resource Kit. Penny received a Bachelors degree in Education (B.Ed) from Keele University and a Masters degree in Science (M.Sc) in Mathematics from The Open University, where she taught undergraduate and post-graduate courses in the Computing Faculty. Penny has more than 25 years of industry experience starting off in the mainframe environment and in 1992, she began developing and implementing solutions on the Microsoft platform.

James Edelen

James Edelen specializes in network design, deployment, and SharePoint Portal Server solutions. He co-authored *Microsoft SharePoint Products and Technologies Resource Kit*, has written numerous articles on SharePoint development and administration, and has developed several SharePoint Utilities. He is a Microsoft Certified Professional (MCP) and a Microsoft Most Valuable Professional (MVP) for SharePoint Portal Server for two consecutive years. James is currently finishing his last year at Drexel University before going back to work at Microsoft.

What do you think of this book? We want to hear from you!

Do you have a few minutes to participate in a brief online survey? Microsoft is interested in hearing your feedback about this publication so that we can continually improve our books and learning resources for you.

To participate in our survey, please visit:

www.microsoft.com/learning/booksurvey

And enter this book's ISBN, 0-7356-2075-X. As a thank-you to survey participants in the United States and Canada, each month we'll randomly select five respondents to win one of five $100 gift certificates from a leading online merchant.* At the conclusion of the survey, you can enter the drawing by providing your e-mail address, which will be used for prize notification *only*.

Thanks in advance for your input. Your opinion counts!

Sincerely,

Microsoft Learning

Learn More. Go Further.